Sustainability, Resilience, and Inclusiveness through Human-Centred Architecture and Design

EMERALD STUDIES IN SUSTAINABLE ARCHITECTURE AND DESIGN

Series Editors: Anna Visvizi and Asmaa Ibrahim

Emerald Studies in Sustainable Architecture and Design explores the critical intersection of architecture, design, and sustainability in an era defined by climate change, urbanization, and social transformation. Against the backdrop of the UN Sustainable Development Goals (SDGs), this series highlights how human-centered design can address environmental and societal challenges while fostering resilience and inclusion. While sustainability has traditionally been examined through social sciences and business disciplines, this series positions architecture and design as essential drivers of change, offering both conceptual and practical insights into how the built environment can adapt to and mitigate contemporary global pressures.

Forthcoming Volumes

AI in Modern Architecture and Design: Insights, Applications, New Openings

Design and Architecture for Sustainable, Resilient and User-Friendly Cities and Interiors

Sustainability, Resilience, and Inclusiveness through Human-Centred Architecture and Design

EDITED BY

ASMAA IBRAHIM
Effat University, Saudi Arabia

ANNA VISVIZI
Effat University, Saudi Arabia
SGH Warsaw School of Economics, Poland

MADY MOHAMED
Effat University, Saudi Arabia

AND

MOHAMMED F. M. MOHAMMED
Effat University, Saudi Arabia

United Kingdom – North America – Japan – India – Malaysia – China

Emerald Publishing Limited
Emerald Publishing, Floor 5, Northspring, 21-23 Wellington Street, Leeds LS1 4DL

First edition 2026

Editorial matter and selection © 2026 Asmaa Ibrahim, Anna Visvizi, Mady Mohamed and Mohammed F. M. Mohammed.
Individual chapters © 2026 The authors.
Published under exclusive licence by Emerald Publishing Limited.

Reprints and permissions service
Contact: www.copyright.com

No part of this book may be reproduced, stored in a retrieval system, transmitted in any form or by any means electronic, mechanical, photocopying, recording or otherwise without either the prior written permission of the publisher or a licence permitting restricted copying issued in the UK by The Copyright Licensing Agency and in the USA by The Copyright Clearance Center. Any opinions expressed in the chapters are those of the authors. Whilst Emerald makes every effort to ensure the quality and accuracy of its content, Emerald makes no representation implied or otherwise, as to the chapters' suitability and application and disclaims any warranties, express or implied, to their use.

British Library Cataloguing in Publication Data
A catalogue record for this book is available from the British Library

ISBN: 978-1-80592-882-9 (Print)
ISBN: 978-1-80592-881-2 (Online)
ISBN: 978-1-80592-883-6 (Epub)

INVESTOR IN PEOPLE

Contents

About the Editors   *ix*

About the Contributors   *xi*

Preface   *xvii*

Chapter 1   Architecture and Design in Context of Climate Change: An Introduction   *1*
Asmaa Ibrahim, Mady Mohamed, Mohammed F. M. Mohammed and Anna Visvizi

Part I: Architecture and Design for Energy Efficiency

Chapter 2   Promoting Renewable Energy Through Interior Architecture and Design: Focus on Carbon Emissions' Reduction   *15*
Habibah Mohammed Abdulaziz Almulhim and Hanan Suliman Eissa

Chapter 3   Sustainable Retrofitting: The Significance of Adapting the Already Existing Buildings   *27*
Dina Ahmed Ahmed Elmeligy and Mohammad Refaat Mohammad Abdelaal

Chapter 4   Energy Efficiency in Educational Buildings   *39*
Abobakr Al-Sakkaf, Basma Mostafa, Tarek S. Ghoniemy and Sherif Ahmed

Chapter 5   Integrating Bioengineering Principles in Interior Eco-Design for Promoting Artificial Intelligence (AI) and Sustainable Usability Responsible Functionality   *51*
Mai Ahmed Fakhrey Farahat Mousa

Chapter 6 Simulation Analysis of a Hybrid Ventilation System to Improve Internal Air Quality and Energy Performance of Buildings: A Case Study of a Residential Unit in Riyadh City, Saudi Arabia 63
Najat M.D. Al Ruwaily and Ahmed O.M.S. Mostafa

Chapter 7 Differential Pressure Effect on Air Flow Through the "Takhtabush" 83
Mady Mohamed

Part II: Architecture and Design in the Context of Heritage Protection

Chapter 8 Using Computer Applications to Measure the Efficiency of Environmental Design in Heritage Buildings 99
Reem Elhaddad

Chapter 9 Enhancing Building Climatic Performance Using AI-Assisted Facade Design: Evidence From the Literature 111
Tarek Saad Ragab, Marah Aljassem and Jury Aboanoor

Chapter 10 Investment of the Historic "Mount Uhud" to Establish Mountain Resorts, Overlooking the Prophet's Mosque in Al-Madinah 125
Nusaibah Mohammed Abdualhammed Al-shabi and Marwa Hussein Tawfik Hussein

Part III: Case Studies: An Insight Into the Day-to-Day Practice of Architecture in the Arab World

Chapter 11 Developing a Sustainable Mountain Resorts Design Framework for Aseer, Saudi Arabia 139
Haifa Al-Harbi and Mostafa Sabbagh

Chapter 12 Rethinking Home: The Influence of the Pandemic on Residential Spaces in Egypt 159
Yasmin Hesham, Hussam Salama and Ibrahim Saleh

Chapter 13   Indoor Air Quality, Mitigating CO_2 Concentration in Classrooms Using Adjacent Corridors and Atriums   *169*
Feras Balkhi, Mostafa Sabbagh and Mohannad Bayoumi

Chapter 14   Adapting Placemaking to Climate Change: Redefining the Placemaking Diagram   *181*
Tarek Saad Ragab, Ghadeer Alawi and Mady Mohamed

About the Editors

Asmaa Ibrahim, PhD, is a Professor currently serving as the Dean of the College of Architecture and Design at Effat University. She is originally a Professor of Urban Development at the Arch. Dep. Faculty of Engineering, Cairo Univ. with 18 years of academic and professional experience. She was the Hubert H. Humphrey Fellow in the SPURS program at MIT, USA (2018/2019). She was the main coordinator in the Double Master Program with Cottbus University in Germany and Alex. University. She has 14 years of experience in strategic regional and urban planning projects in UN-HABITAT, GOPP, and GIZ, with a focus on community development, gender programming, and regeneration policies in historic districts, as well as new urban expansions. She has received extensive training at the World Resource Institute in Washington, DC, and Oxfam America in Boston in 2018/2019. She has more than 20 international publications in the field of sustainable urbanism.

Anna Visvizi, PhD (dr hab.), Economist and Political Scientist, Professor at the SGH Warsaw School of Economics, and Visiting Professor at Effat University. As a seasoned editor, researcher, recognized author, and accomplished project manager, Professor Visvizi has extensive experience in academia, think-tank, and government sectors in Europe and the United States, including the OECD. Professor Visvizi's expertise covers issues pertinent to the intersection of politics, economics, and information and communication technology (ICT), which translates into her research and publications on applied aspects of ICT in such domains as smart cities, knowledge and innovation management, technology transfer, and governance. Professor Visvizi is the Editor-in-Chief of *Transforming Government: People, Process and Policy* (Emerald Publishing) as well as *Digital Policy, Regulation and Governance* (Emerald Publishing).

Mady Mohamed, PhD, is a Professor of Architecture, joined Effat University in the Fall of 2014. He received his PhD degree at Dundee School of Architecture, UK, in July/2009. He has more than 20 years of academic and practice experience. Through his private firm, Mady participated in the design and construction of several projects, and he was the sole architect and the main architectural/LEED consultant for different residential, office, medical, and educational buildings. Mady became an authorized architectural consultant by the Egyptian Syndicate for Engineering in 2013 and a LEED Green Associate by the USGBC in 2014. He has been an authorized trainer for Education for Sustainable Development ESD by the European Union/Egyptian Ministry of

Education since 2014. He is a CO-Editor of ER, IBPSA-Egypt; Editor Team Member of (EEEJ), USA; *Novelty Journals*, India; and a reviewer at (JEE), Canada. Also, he is a member of (SESG, Scotland), (IACSIT, Singapore), (GESTW, Egypt), (ISDS, Japan), and (AASCIT).

Mohammed F. M. Mohammed, PhD, is a professor of architecture and design at Effat University (previously Cairo University). He received his Master's and PhD in Architecture from Cairo University, Egypt, in 1999 and 2004, respectively. With more than 25 years of teaching experience, Dr Fekry has taught Architecture and Design at several Architecture Departments in Egypt and Saudi Arabia. Dr Mohamed's main concern now is to pass on his practical experience of design to younger generations of architects as well as to develop educational courses that reflect these concepts to the architectural students. His research interests include Architecture Theories, Design Process, Digital Modelling, Geographical Information Systems, CAAD, and Urban Conservation. He is a listed reviewer for many local, regional, and international academic journals. He is a member of the International Society for Development & Sustainability, Japan, Board of Directors; Digital Architecture Branch, Saudi Umran Society, Board of Directors, Saudi Umran Society, Jeddah Branch, and Vice-chair of the Saudi Planners Association, SPA. He has three published books, in addition to acting as an editor/co-editor for several books and proceedings.

About the Contributors

Nusaibah Mohammed Abdualhammed Al-shabi, BSc, Interior Design Department, College of Art and Design, Taibah University, Kingdom of Saudi Arabia. Research interests: urban humanization, interior design, and heritage design.

Habibah Mohammed Abdulaziz Almulhim, BSc, Interior Design Department, College of Art and Design, Taibah University, Kingdom of Saudi Arabia. Her research interests include: humanized building design, energy and carbon emission, smart design: , Energy and Carbon Emission, Smart Design.

Jury Aboanoor, Bachelor of Science in Architecture, College of Architecture & Design, Effat University.

Dina Ahmed Ahmed Elmeligy, PhD, Associate Professor, Architecture Engineering Department, Faculty of Engineering, Tanta University, Egypt. Currently: Assistant Professor in the Interior Design Department, Faculty of Art and Design, Princess Nourah Bint Abdelrahman University in Riyadh, K.S.A. Her research interests include sustainability in various directions and related to architecture and technology.

Haifa Al-Harbi, PhD candidate in Architecture, Department of Architecture and Building Science, Faculty of Architecture and Planning, King Saud University, Kingdom of Saudi Arabia. Her research interests: design for ecological and cultural sustainability, with a keen interest in the evolving relationship between people and place in contemporary urban contexts.

Marah Aljassem, Bachelor of Science in Architecture, College of Architecture & Design, Effat University.

Najat M. D. Al Ruwaily is a Master's Program Student at the Department of Architecture and Building Sciences, College of Architecture and Planning, King Saud University.

Abobakr Al-Sakkaf has an extensive background in sustainability and heritage buildings and is an expert on building energy efficiency. This work led him to his current role at Cultural Spaces Consulting Inc., where he is responsible for proposals, research, and consulting. Some of his current projects include a Holistic Framework to Evaluate the Energy Consumption of Heritage Buildings. In addition, he earned his PhD degree in Building Engineering, a Master's in

Architectural and Planning, and a B.Sc. double major in Architecture and Urban Planning. He has 10 years of experience in both academia and industry.

Ghadeer Alawi, Master of Urban Design, Effat University. Planning and Design Manager at Jeddah Historic District—Ministry of Culture.

Sherif Ahmed, an Associate Professor at the Architecture Engineering Department, Military Technical College (MTC), Cairo, Egypt. He received his PhD in Building Engineering and Sustainable Development from Concordia University, Montreal, Canada. He is the Head of the Architecture Engineering Department at MTC. He is a member of the Center of Research Excellence for Urban Environment and Sustainability Governance. He has several scientific fields of expertise and interest such as building sustainability, energy conservation in buildings, and building management. He teaches several courses for undergraduate and postgraduate students concerning building technology, green architecture, and sustainable architecture. Also, he is a Visiting Professor in the Architecture Engineering Department at Al Obour Higher Institute for Engineering and Technology (OHI). He has participated in design, executing working and workshop drawings for several mega projects in Egypt as well as supervision on the construction of these projects. He has several publications in high-impact factor and international journals related to the sustainability of buildings and energy efficiency. He has also been a reviewer for several conferences and journals.

Feras Balkhi, B.Arch in Architecture, Department of Architecture and Building Science, Faculty of Architecture and Planning, King Abdulaziz University, Kingdom of Saudi Arabia. His research interests: building design and ventilation.

Mohannad Bayoumi, PhD. in Architecture, Associate Professor, Department of Architecture, Faculty of Architecture and Planning, King Abdulaziz University. Research interests: sustainability and climatic design, building performance, and simulation.

Hanan Suliman Eissa, PhD in Architecture, Associate Professor in Department of Architecture, Faculty of Engineering, Helwan University, Egypt and Interior design Department, College of Art and Design, Taibah University, KSA. Her research interests are in employing digital and smart technologies in architectural design and applying sustainability principles to achieve quality of life and healthy, sustainable, and smart buildings.

Reem Elhaddad, PhD Assistant Professor in Architectural Engineering, Interior Design Program, Arts and Humanities college, Jazan University. Jazan 45142, Saudi Arabia. Her research interests include: Engineer, research interests: Environmental Design.

Mai Ahmed Fakhrey Farahat Mousa, PhD, Assistant Professor of Interior Architecture at the Department of Architecture, Faculty of Engineering, Horus University, Egypt, and at the Department of Architecture, College of Engineering and Information Technology, Onaizah Colleges, Qassim, Saudi Arabia.

Her research interests focus on sustainable architecture, building performance and efficiency, eco-design, bio-engineering applications in architecture, and parametric design methodologies.

Tarek S. Ghoniemy, an Assistant Professor in the Computer Engineering and Artificial Intelligence Department at the Military Technical College (MTC) in Cairo, Egypt. He received his PhD in Electrical Engineering from Concordia University, Montreal, Canada, in 2018, with a thesis focused on "Tracker-Independent Drift Detection and Correction Using Segmented Objects and Features." His research interests span a wide range of areas, including trust management in IoT systems, classification of encrypted network protocols, on-board remote sensing, and video object tracking and segmentation, medical image classification, super-resolution, and hyper-spectral image fusion.

Yasmin Hesham, BSc, Building Technology Department in German University in Cairo, is an Architect and a Teaching Assistant at the German International University (GIU). With a passion for human-centric design, Yasmin focuses on creating architectural and interior spaces that embody comfort, functionality, and a deep sense of belonging. Their research interests revolve around designing homes that truly feel like personal sanctuaries, emphasizing the harmonious blend of aesthetics and practicality. Yasmin is dedicated to exploring innovative design approaches that prioritize the well-being and experience of inhabitants.

Mohammad Refaat Mohammad Abdelaal PhD, Associate Professor, Architecture and Urban Planning Department, Faculty of Engineering, Suez Canal University, Egypt. Currently: Associate Professor, Architectural Engineering Department, College of Architectural Engineering and Digital Design, Dar Al Uloom University (DAU), Riyadh, KSA. His research interests include sustainable design in architecture and urban design.

Ahmed O. M. S. Mostafa, PhD in Architecture, Associate Professor in the Department of Architecture and Building Sciences, College of Architecture and Planning, King Saud University, Saudi Arabia. He is an active member in teaching and research in the fields of design, programming, project management, and computer applications in design and management, in addition to being a professional architect with nearly 40 years of experience in real estate, project development, predesign, and design activities; as well as PM for Design and Construction projects.

Basma Mostafa, an Assistant Professor of Computer Science and Operations Research. She earned her PhD in 2019 from the University of Montpellier, LIRMM, with a thesis titled "Optimized Monitoring for IoT Networks." Dr Mostafa currently heads the Computer Science Department and manages the cybersecurity program at the Faculty of Artificial Intelligence and Computing at Horus University. Before this role, she worked at the Faculty of Computers and Artificial Intelligence at Cairo University, where she advanced through positions as a Teaching Assistant, Lecturer Assistant, and Assistant Professor. Her expertise encompasses machine learning, simulation, optimization, and IoT. Dr Mostafa has published several papers in prestigious journals and conferences. Recognizing her contributions to science, UNESCO awarded her the For Women in Science Fellowship in 2017.

Tarek Saad Ragab is a Professor of Architecture and Urbanism at Alexandria University. He is on leave at Effat University, Jeddah, Saudi Arabia. His research interests include urban development and management and urban farming.

Mostafa Sabbagh, PhD in Architecture, Assistant Professor, Department of Architecture, Faculty of Architecture and Planning, King Abdulaziz University. Research interests: sustainability in the built environment, building performance, and indoor environment quality.

Hussam Salama, PhD in Architecture, Dean of the Architecture Department at the German International University (GIU), was a Dubai Initiative Research Fellow at Harvard University prior to joining Qatar University. Dr Hussam is also an Architect and an Urban Planner. Dr Salama earned his Bachelor's and Master's degrees in Architectural Engineering from Cairo University, a Master's of Architecture, and a PhD in Planning from the University of Southern California, Los Angeles. Dr Salama is an Assistant Professor at the National Research Centre, Egypt, where his research focuses on urban development in the Middle East during the era of Globalization. Dr Salama's recent research project at Harvard University, "Dubai: A Narrative of Places Shaped for Global Flows," looks at how Dubai has been aggressively developed in order to attract global flows, rather than being transformed in response to the gradual and natural growth of those flows.

Ibrahim Saleh, PhD in Architecture, is currently an Assistant Professor at Effat University—College of Architecture and Design—Architecture Department—KSA. He was previously an Assistant Professor at the Architecture and Urban Design Department at the GUC since September 2015, and he was a Teaching Assistant at the department from 2012 to 2015. He was also a Teaching Assistant at Cairo University Department of Architecture Credit Hour System (CHS) and at A.A.S.T. (Arab Academy for Science, Technology and Maritime Transport) Department of Architecture between 2010 and 2012. Ibrahim graduated from the Architecture Department, Faculty of Engineering, Cairo University in 2010 with an honor rank (10th). His graduation project was awarded the Architecture Department's Best Environmental Graduation Project prize, and he continued his Master's studies at Cairo University in 2011 doing the Pre-Master courses in Environmental Control and Energy Efficiency In Buildings (ranked first) and finished his Master thesis "SCHOOL DESIGN THROUGH PARTICIPATION—with Reference to Children in Primary Education," at Cairo University, under the supervision of Prof. Dr Ahmed Reda Abdin in January 2015.

Marwa Hussein Tawfik Hussein, Assistant Professor, Department of Interior Design, Faculty of Applied Arts, Helwan University, EGYPT—Faculty of Art and Design, Tibah University, Kingdom of Saudi Arabia. Her research interests revolve around integrating traditional interior design and heritage furniture with modern technology, aiming to preserve cultural essence while enhancing functionality, sustainability, and harmony in contemporary spaces.

Preface

Climate change and its implications, pressures on social cohesion, and a pervasive feeling of uncertainty, present urgent and complex challenges to contemporary society, including political systems and economy. While no panacea exist, this book emerges from the conviction that human-centered architecture and design, supported by hybrid, technology-based and heritage-driven tools and approaches may contribute to mitigating some of these pressures. Guided by the principles of the United Nations 2030 Sustainable Development Agenda, and especially informed by Sustainable Development Goals 7, 9, and 11, this book invites architects, designers, scholars, and policymakers to rethink the built environment as a critical space for sustainable transformation.

Today's sustainability discourse, though rich and expansive, has grown increasingly fragmented, often focusing either on narrow technical aspects or theoretical treatments of space, or becoming overly superficial, thus leaving the questions of "what to do?" and "how to do it?" under-explored. This book seeks to reorient that discourse toward an integrated, interdisciplinary approach, i.e. one that reconnects architecture and design with questions pertaining to ensuring energy efficiency, protecting and preserving cultural heritage, facilitating community resilience, and enhancing social inclusion. In this sense, this book and its content make a case for architects and designers centrality in the broader discussion on sustainability.

Drawing on diverse perspectives, with particular attention to the Arab world, a region acutely experiencing the effects of climate change, this book offers a multifaceted view of modern architecture and design, where tradition and heritage seamlessly blend with modern technology, including artificial intelligence, machine learning, augmented reality, virtual reality, and others. The key message that this book emulates is that dialogue and respect for our common heritage and tradition may inspire scalable, context-sensitive solutions. Ultimately, and so is the intent of its editors; this book hopes to foster a culture of collaboration, innovation, and inclusion, essential for building a sustainable future.

The editors of this book would like to express their gratitude to all contributing authors for their hard work and patience that they presented throughout the lengthy review process. Notably, initial versions of chapters included in this volume have been presented at the 2nd International Architecture and Design Conference, 2023, titled Man and Place 2: Reinventing the ARCHIDES through Humanization and Emerging Technologies. New Creative and Investment

Perspectives, hosted by the Effat University. Special "thank you" goes to reviewers who collaborated closely with the editors in view of making the best of the initial drafts of all chapters. Gratitude is expressed to the publisher, Emerald Publishing, and the entire team, for their support and professionalism. Last, but not least, sincere appreciation is expressed to the President of the Effat University, Dr Haifa Jamal Al-Lail, for her guidance. Gratitude is extended also to the Provost of the Effat University, Dr Chuman Mervat, for her continuous encouragement and support.

The Editors
Asmaa Ibrahim,
Anna Visvizi,
Mady Mohamed,
Mohammed F. M. Mohammed

Chapter 1

Architecture and Design in Context of Climate Change: An Introduction

Asmaa Ibrahim[a], Mady Mohamed[a], Mohammed F. M. Mohammed[a] and Anna Visvizi[a,b]

[a]Effat University, Saudi Arabia
[b]SGH Warsaw School of Economics, Poland

Abstract

Considering the complex and multifaceted implications of climate change and the growing recognition of the need to take action to mitigate them, this book explores how human-centered architecture and design may do so. Rooted in the framework of the UN 2030 Sustainable Development Goals (SDGs), particularly SDG 7, 9, and 11, this book investigates the potential of architecture and design to foster energy efficiency, heritage preservation, and community development. Emphasizing the importance of collaborative action across domains, the book underscores how the built environment directly impacts environmental and societal well-being. It argues that the voices of architects and designers—interpreting challenges through a human-centered lens—are essential in the broader sustainability dialogue. Drawing on examples and expertise from the Arab world, where the effects of climate change are especially visible, the book highlights how local insights can inform global strategies. Through an inclusive and culturally attuned perspective, the book advocates for renewed dialogue, innovation, and design practices that align with both tradition and emerging technological possibilities to contribute to the global effort of navigating climate change.

Keywords: Sustainable Development Goals (SDGs); architecture; design; the Arab world; inclusive communities; sustainability; energy efficiency

---

Sustainability, Resilience, and Inclusiveness through Human-Centred Architecture and Design, 1–11
Copyright © 2026 Asmaa Ibrahim, Mady Mohamed, Mohammed F. M. Mohammed and Anna Visvizi
Published under exclusive licence by Emerald Publishing Limited
doi:10.1108/978-1-80592-881-220261001

1. Introduction

In a context defined by growing concerns as to how to handle the implications of climate change and challenges to social contracts all over the world (Heffron & De Fontenelle, 2023; Neave, 2006; Shafik, 2021), this book guides the reader through the ways in which human-centered architecture and design may alleviate some of these concerns. The onset of the UN 2030 Sustainable Development Agenda triggered research on sustainability, with the latter becoming one of the buzzwords of today (Shao, 2024; Visvizi, 2022). Initially, the connection between sustainability and architecture has been a part of this research (Balen Zamora et al., 2021; Horry et al., 2022). Nevertheless, at some point, it seems, research exploring the world through the sustainability, architecture, and design lens has lost its focus. In other words, today it is highly fragmented, addressing highly specific, e.g. technical topics, or dwelling on the literature aspects of space development, etc. (Nasir et al., 2018; Teferi & Newman, 2017). Arguably, a clearly delineated research agenda is in order if the potential inherent in architecture and design in relation to climate change and its implications for our societies is to be utilized. This book does it by looking explicitly at the question of how architecture and design may contribute to more efficient energy use and heritage protection while also supporting the growth and development of sustainable, resilient, and inclusive communities (Baldi & Botti, 2024). In this sense, the content of chapters comprising this book speaks to several of the UN SDGs, that is, SDG 7: Ensure access to affordable, reliable, sustainable and modern energy for all; SDG 9: Build resilient infrastructure, promote inclusive, and sustainable industrialization, and foster innovation; and SDG 11: Make cities and human settlements inclusive, safe, resilient, and sustainable.

This book derives from the understanding that, amidst challenges our societies face today, including pressures on sustainability, climate change, and social exclusion, to mention just a few, only a concerted action in all domains of human activity can alleviate the so-defined pressures. Notably, the potential architecture and design have in adding to the common effort of addressing the implications of climate change, inequality, exclusion, etc. frequently remained under-recognized (Reckien et al., 2017). And yet, who would disagree that the way our cities, buildings, public spaces, and products are designed has a direct impact on the environment, including natural resources and their efficient use, for example, energy sources, and on the society, including inclusion and empowerment (Giorgi, 2022; Zallio & Clarkson, 2021). Indeed, this book is rooted in the conviction that the debate on sustainability, resilience, and inclusiveness has to include voices and insights specific to the community of architects and designers, whereby the interpretive lens of the debate should be the human-being (Greek: ἄνθρωπος) (Ramírez-Gordillo et al., 2024).

The content of the book is interdisciplinary, if not multidisciplinary, because to address the complex set of questions defining the objective of the book, a variety of insights originating from such fields as architecture, design, urban studies, and others need to be employed. In other words, the discussion in this book builds bridges across disciplines to navigate complex challenges that mar today's societies around the globe. While climate change and its implications seem to pose an insurmountable challenge, this book suggests that ways of alleviating it exist. To this end, advances in technology as well as insights drawn from culture, tradition, and heritage may be very useful. To reap the promise they offer, however, it is necessary that a culture of dialogue is nurtured among experts, professionals, educators, and students. While this book presents a view dominated by insights from the Arab world, in several ways and in several instances acutely challenged by changing weather and temperature patterns, it highlights that the experience and expertise that this region exhibits may be of great value in several locations around the world. We simply need to listen to each other. The argument in this chapter is structured as follows: The next section elaborates on the book's objectives. Then, the book's structure and content are introduced. Conclusions follow.

2. The Book's Objectives

The objective of this book is to examine in which ways, i.e. through which mechanisms and to what end, human-centered architecture and design may contribute to the overarching imperatives of sustainability, as framed by the Sustainable Development Goals (SDGs) and the corresponding United Nations (UN) Agenda 2030 for Sustainable Development. The chapters included in this book address the question of how architecture and design can foster energy efficiency and thus contribute to the net-zero imperative. The sustainability argument notwithstanding, the question of how to reconcile climate change and societal considerations, including public spending, and the imperative of heritage preservation and protection, is also addressed in respective chapters. Well-founded and empirically grounded insights are of primary value in this context. Thus, this book elaborates on case studies as well.

In more detail, the chapters included in this book explore the evolving role of architecture and design in addressing the pressing environmental and societal challenges of today. Central to this exploration is the commitment to sustainability, energy efficiency, and the integration of emerging technologies within the built environment. To this end, this book investigates how renewable energy solutions can be effectively incorporated into interior architecture, reducing carbon emissions and advancing the development of zero-energy buildings. A significant focus of the discussion in this book is placed on sustainable retrofitting, emphasizing how aging structures can be revitalized through innovative strategies that leverage design alterations with cutting-edge tools, such as artificial intelligence (AI), virtual reality (VR), and augmented reality (AR). This book also delves into the integration of bioengineering in interior eco-design, proposing responsible, AI-assisted solutions for future-ready living spaces. Health and wellness are addressed through a detailed examination of Indoor Air Quality (IAQ), ventilation systems. In this context the Sick Building Syndrome (SBS) is brought into the discussion to showcase how hybrid systems and simulation tools can optimize energy performance while promoting occupant well-being.

From a different angle, this book also considers culture, heritage, and tradition to make a case that passive cooling strategies and low-energy design techniques may form a part of the solution to living conditions in hot arid climates. By analyzing elements such as courtyards and *takhtabush*, the book advocates for a reinvention of vernacular approaches that prioritize thermal comfort and cultural continuity. In the same manner, the chapters included in the book outline how passive techniques and hybrid ICT-enhanced tools may support energy-saving interventions in historic buildings, ensuring both functionality and conservation. By offering a detailed insight into real-life case studies, this book seeks to contribute to the debate on alleviating the implications of climate change and ensuring our societies' well-being.

3. The Book's Structure and Issues Addressed

The book has been divided into three parts and 14 chapters dealing with diverse aspects of the triple challenge pertaining to sustainability, resilience, and inclusiveness as seen through the lens of advances in both conceptual approaches and current practice in architecture and design. Part 1 (Chapters 2–7), titled Architecture and Design for Energy Efficiency, focuses on ways in which modern architecture addresses the challenge of energy scarcity, the rising cost of energy, and the need to navigate environmental and societal challenges resulting from CO_2 emissions. Part 2 (Chapters 8–10), titled Architecture and Design in the Context of Heritage Protection, navigates the question of how modern architecture and design may ease the tension between the imperative of heritage stewardship, urban development, and sustainability. Part 3 (Chapters 11–14), titled Case Studies: An Insight into the Day-to-Day Practice of Architecture in the Arab World, offers a captivating journey into best practices and challenges of today's architecture and design in selected locations in the Arab peninsula.

Part 1 of this book opens with Chapter 2, titled Promoting Renewable Energy Through Interior Architecture and Design: Focus on Carbon Emissions' Reduction, authored by *Habibah Mohammed Abdulaziz Almulhim and Hanan Suliman Eissa. As the authors argue,* environmental challenges, frequently driven by consumerist lifestyles, necessitate solutions to mitigate risks and promote sustainable economic development. Reducing carbon emissions and preserving global energy reserves have become critical priorities. With buildings and construction being the most energy-intensive sector globally, it is imperative that ways to minimize energy consumption in buildings are sought. This chapter advocates for designing highly efficient indoor spaces and establishing research centers to accelerate the transition toward zero-carbon buildings. It highlights strategies for creating sustainable energy-saving and energy-producing models that support economic growth without depleting environmental resources. The chapter presents a design aimed at reducing electricity consumption, cutting carbon emissions, and achieving energy efficiency in buildings. Additionally, it explores the role of buildings in energy generation, transforming them into energy producers. A descriptive, analytical, and qualitative approach was employed, including expert interviews, to analyze interior architecture's relationship with renewable energy. The findings suggest that understanding the design of existing buildings can pave the way for creating sustainable and energy-efficient structures.

Chapter 3, titled Sustainable Retrofitting: The Significance of Adapting the Already Existing Buildings, by Dina Ahmed Ahmed Elmeligy, Mohammad Refaat Mohammad Abdelaal Tanta explores the question of ways of adapting the already existing buildings to the challenges and demands of sustainability. Notably, the built environment is critical in attaining sustainability today, when this objective is vital. This chapter explores the essential role of anticipating the built environment, specifically focusing on adapting existing buildings. Here, the built environment, sometimes thought of as merely the background to our everyday existence, is examined in light of its potential for transformation. The chapter emphasizes the significance of two fundamental elements: visionary and dynamic features of the built environments. When these components are in harmony, it is anticipated that the existing buildings will undergo substantial renovations to meet the sustainability standards necessary for their enhancement. A noteworthy outcome of this chapter is the promotion of tools for anticipatory engagement with the built environment, mainly through utilizing VR and virtual environments (VE). By adopting these technologies, we can facilitate sustainable enhancements to existing buildings. This chapter not only aims to raise awareness of the anticipatory aspect of the built environment but also examines various retrofitting scenarios that underscore this principle. Utilizing Virtual Singapore (VSG) as a case study emphasizes the chapter proposal related to the closed loop. Furthermore, this chapter forecasts potential research trajectories in pursuing sustainability through anticipatory improvements in the built environment.

Chapter 4, authored by Abobakr Al-Sakkaf, Basma Mostafa, Tarek S. Ghoniemy, and Sherif Ahmed, focuses explicitly on promoting and ensuring energy efficiency in educational buildings. The construction sector, whether households, commercial, educational, or industrial, is expected to promote energy sustainability. However, buildings are the primary consumers of energy, especially electricity. Energy overconsumption results in greenhouse gas emissions, depletion of natural resources, and high financial costs. Hence, monitoring, controlling, and managing energy are the key goals of building management that opt to achieve energy efficiency and cost-effective operation and maintenance, which are the main objectives of sustainable development goals. Educational buildings are significant in their function and require more energy to operate and maintain, especially for lighting, achieving suitable thermal comfort, and using reliable IT systems and other equipment. The reliability and flexibility offered by wireless technologies have been the driving force toward the vision of the Internet of Things (IoT). They have contributed to attracting growing interest in the market. This work presents an energy-efficient IoT solution to monitor the energy consumption model by deploying a Building Management

System (BMS). Integrating multiple battery-operated sensors into the building allows critical data to be dynamically provided in real time to improve overall building efficiency. Introducing the IoT in managing energy in educational facilities can be more cost-effective and convenient than traditional building BMSs.

Chapter 5, by Mai Ahmed Fakhrey Farahat Mousa, is titled Integrating Bioengineering Principles in Interior Eco-Design for Promoting AI and Sustainable Usability Responsible Functionality. This chapter explores the integration of bioengineering principles in interior eco-design to enhance AI and promote sustainable, responsible functionality. It examines how biomimicry, biophilic design, and other bioengineering concepts improve occupant well-being and reduce environmental impact. Through a literature review and case studies, the chapter identifies the benefits and challenges of incorporating bioengineering in interior design and proposes a framework for its integration. Findings suggest that bioengineering enhances AI performance and fosters sustainability in interior spaces. This chapter contributes to the emerging field of eco-design, offering insights for designers, architects, and engineers to create intelligent, dynamic, and environmentally responsible interiors. By understanding human sensory interactions with the environment, designers can adopt a biomimetic approach that aligns with natural systems. Human sensory systems have evolved to respond positively to natural environments, promoting health, comfort, and productivity. Designing interiors that replicate these sensory experiences supports well-being while minimizing environmental impact. Furthermore, natural systems exhibit inherent sustainability, resilience, and efficiency. Integrating these principles into interior architecture allows for the creation of adaptable, low-impact spaces that function harmoniously with both AI technologies and ecological systems.

Chapter 6, titled Simulation Analysis of a Hybrid Ventilation System to Improve Internal Air Quality and Energy Performance of Buildings: A Case Study of a Residential Unit in Riyadh City, Saudi Arabia, is authored by Najat M.D. Al Ruwaily and Ahmed O.M.S. Mostafa. The authors make a case that improving IAQ is one of the most, if not the most, essential factors in addressing the so-called SBS and achieving the health and well-being of the inhabitants. Note, the latter may spend up to 90% of their time therein. inside the built environment in which people spend about 90% of their time. Good ventilation is one of the important factors in improving IAQ, and it has been handled by many researchers. In spite of the emerging smart mechanical ventilation systems said to have the power to achieve thermal comfort for internal spaces using minimum energy, it has been reported that the energy consumption of the housing sector is still high, and the IAQ is not up to the healthy levels. This represents the problem and incentive of this chapter, which aims, through a descriptive and experimental methodology, to overcome the challenge of achieving the balance between energy efficiency and healthy IAQ. Results showed that a proposed hybrid ventilation system, natural and mechanical, could achieve the thermal comfort levels of internal spaces while enhancing both the IAQ and the building energy performance. The importance of this chapter emerges from the dual effect of its results related to achieving both sustainability and human well-being.

Chapter 7, authored by Mady Mohamed and titled Differential Pressure Effect on Air Flow Through the "Takhtabush" explores how traditional, historically consolidated architectural design practices are of value in the context of contemporary environmental challenges. As the author argues, since ancient times, people sought to adapt buildings to harsh climate conditions in the hot-dry zone by reducing heat impacts. They used to open their houses onto a private internal open space that was visually and acoustically separated from the outside, called Sahn, "The courtyard." The courtyard helps maintain cooled indoor temperatures by employing the stack effect phenomenon. Clean, oxygen-rich air for breathing is human life's most pressing environmental requirement. The Takhtabush, "A covered outdoor sitting area at ground level," was introduced to the traditional courtyard to ensure the airflow. It is located between the courtyard and the back garden, opening completely onto the courtyard and through a Mashrabiya onto the back garden, which ensures a steady flow of air by convection. Since the back garden is bigger and has more sunlight, it will heat up faster than the courtyard. The sun's radiation will make air movement and create cool airflow in the Takhtabush, leading to the courtyard. However, the orientation of the building is also a big matter when using Takhtabush. Knowing the good wind and the sunlight orientation will surely affect the way it works. This chapter aims to investigate the effectiveness of the size of the backyard and its exposure to solar radiation on the thermal performance of the courtyard on the urban scale. The expected results confirm quantitatively and qualitatively the importance of employing the Takhtabush with the exposed-to-sun backyard to enhance the thermal performance of the open courtyard.

Part 2 of the book, where the focus of the conversation moves to heritage protection and preservation, starts with Chapter 8, titled Using Computer Applications to Measure the Efficiency of Environmental Design in Heritage Buildings, and authored by Reem Elhaddad. Here, the spotlight is directed at the Al Dosariyah Castle, a heritage building located in the Saudi Jazan Province. The castle is perched atop a mountain with a view of the Red Sea. By exploring the case of the Al Dosariyah Castle, the objective of this chapter is to investigate the efficiency of the environmental design of heritage buildings. The castle in question was designed with very thick walls and an internal courtyard, which protects it from high outdoor temperatures and facilitates natural ventilation. The building rooms have been selected to represent two different scenarios. The scenarios are concerned with the level of protection from sunlight and saving natural ventilation that influences the value of thermal comfort in indoor spaces. A design builder simulation was conducted to investigate the thermal comfort of indoor spaces throughout the whole year to determine the highest and lowest quantities with and without these passive techniques. The findings of the research motivate old self-used building methods, which have positive effects on improving thermal comfort and reducing total energy consumption.

Chapter 9, by Tarek Saad Ragab, Marah Aljassem, and Jury Aboanoor, and titled Enhancing Building Climatic Performance Using AI-Assisted Facade

Design: Evidence From Literature, delves into the corpus of research concerning the employment of AI in the realm of building design, particularly focusing on the myriad AI methodologies applicable for optimizing building facades to enhance climatic performance. The primary objective is to identify pivotal factors influencing IAQ and assess the feasibility and relevance of AI implementation to ameliorate these factors. Notwithstanding the recent emphasis on optimizing architectural configurations, there exists a notable dearth of scholarly inquiry in this domain. This chapter endeavors to augment the understanding of how AI can be leveraged to enhance building facade design and promote the sustainability of built environments. The methodology entails a thorough examination of extant literature pertaining to the utilization of AI during the prebuilding design phase, with a particular emphasis on the optimization of facade components and materials. Furthermore, the chapter scrutinizes case studies and practical applications of AI in facade design, illustrating its potential to enhance environmental performance and foster innovative design solutions; however, given the nascent nature of this field.

Chapter 10, titled Investment of the Historic "Mount Uhud" to Establish Mountain Resorts, Overlooking the Prophet's Mosque in Al-Madinah, is authored by Nusaibah Mohammed Abdulhammed Al-shabi and Marwa Hussein Tawfik Hussein. Against the backdrop of the imperatives entailed in the KSA Vision 2030, especially in view of promoting KSA as a tourism destination, this chapter delves into the case of Mount Uhud, a site of religious and historical significance to Muslims. Over the past years, over 30 licenses have been issued to establish accommodation facilities in the Aseer region alone. However, none of the projects has been completed so far. Sustainable Tourism Development in Aseer should integrate environmental sensitivity and community consideration and aim to save natural resources. Additionally, the natural mountainous landscape of Aseer can be an ideal location to construct sustainable resorts that can revive the tourism industry. Given the lack of sustainable resorts in Aseer, this chapter offers insights into developing a sustainable mountain resort design framework. A qualitative approach involving the analysis of five case studies from different countries was used to identify the principles of the proposed design framework. The framework was categorized as follows: landscape integration, sustainable construction, water and energy efficiency, and local community engagement. The framework offers stakeholders and architects essential guidance for designing sustainable resorts in the mountainous area of Aseer.

Part 3 of the book opens with Chapter 11, authored by Haifa Al-Harbi and Mostafa Sabbagh. This chapter, similarly as the previous one, sheds light on developments in the Saudi Aseer region. The focus of the discussion in this chapter is the question of sustainable tourism development. By employing a qualitative approach involving the analysis of five case studies from different countries, the authors of this chapter propose a framework geared toward facilitating sustainable tourism development. In this context, a case is made for landscape integration, sustainable construction, water and energy efficiency, and local community engagement.

Chapter 12, titled Rethinking Home: The Influence of Pandemic on Residential Spaces in Egypt, is authored by Yasmine Hesham, Hussam Salama, and Ibrahim Saleh. The authors restate that the COVID-19 pandemic altered a number of facets of our daily life, including residential space design. The case of Egypt is, in this context, of particular interest because a sizable section of the population lives in urban areas with little access to outside public spaces. The chapter explores how the COVID-19 pandemic affected Egypt's residential areas with the goal of identifying design approaches that might improve inhabitants' quality of life and well-being. To do so, the authors adopted a quantitative and qualitative approach to research, including a literature review, and an online survey, including local respondents. The findings presented in the chapter suggest that the pandemic changed how people use their homes, placing a greater emphasis on leisure time, online learning, and remote work. The chapter also highlights the importance of having access to outdoor spaces, natural light, and ventilation in order to raise the standard of living spaces. In projecting future trends, the chapter anticipates a paradigm shift toward eco-conscious and technologically integrated architecture. Green roofs, sustainable materials, and energy-efficient designs emerge as essential elements, promoting environmental sustainability and reducing the ecological footprint of residential spaces. Moreover, integrating smart home technologies, augmented reality interfaces, and advanced security systems envisions a futuristic living experience, where architecture seamlessly interfaces with digital innovations to enhance comfort, convenience, and safety. Based on these findings, the chapter proposes design strategies that can be applied to new and existing residential spaces in Egypt to enhance their functionality and improve residents' quality of life.

Chapter 13, titled Indoor Air Quality: Mitigating CO_2 Concentration in Classrooms Using Adjacent Corridors and Atriums, and authored by Feras Balkhi, Mostafa Sabbagh, and Mohannad Bayoumi, adds a further empirical component to Chapter 4's discussion on educational buildings. Specifically, this chapter studies the classroom's IAQ during the preparatory (freshmen) year at Jeddah. An existing and in-use building was used as a case study. The variables affecting IAQ were measured and analyzed by installing sensors to measure and record these variables in this classroom. After that, research was done to determine the optimal range of these variables and compare them to check whether these results were within the acceptable range of each variable. The results show that it is important to propose improvement measures to reduce CO_2 concentration and ensure thermal comfort. Occupants need to realize that the quality of the indoor environment is important for their health, comfort, and efficiency.

Chapter 14, by Tarek Ragab, Ghadeer Alawi, and Mady Mohamed, is titled Adapting Placemaking to Climate Change: Redefining the Placemaking Diagram. The chapter explores the issue of managing the implications of climate change in urban systems, including heightened temperatures, the emergence of urban heat islands, and the increased frequency of temperature disparity waves. As these developments have a profound impact on people's thermal comfort in public spaces, this chapter proposes a set of design guidelines to mitigate these developments. To this end, the place diagram instrument is employed to assess both present and future developments in public spaces.

4. Conclusions and Take-Aways

The content of the book will be of great value to scholars and practitioners. Several reasons contribute to that. Sustainability has turned into an opaque concept, and thus it is necessary to talk about it, to explain it, and to showcase how it is relevant to all of us. This book does it. From a different vantage point, sustainability, resilience, and inclusiveness form a powerful nexus, yet it is a rare case that readers, including researchers, students, and practitioners, get a clear answer to the question "how it works?" in the domains of architecture and design. This book does it. Finally, by identifying and discussing the implications, best practices, and lessons that can be drawn from the case studies included in this book, it will have great practical value for all those involved in teaching, researching, and planning relating to architecture, design, and sustainability. Last but not least, the case studies included in this book will be of great interest to scholars, as well as instructors and students, interested in respective fields. However, it is the content of the entire book, and so also the thrust of the argument that weaves throughout the chapters, that will give the reader a holistic insight and understanding of the challenges ahead and ways of facing them effectively.

References

Baldi, G., & Botti, A. (2024). The use of technology enhancing tourist engagement at an archaeological site: A cross-cultural analysis. In A. Visvizi, O. Troisi, & V. Corvello (Eds.), *Research and innovation forum 2023. RIIFORUM 2023. Springer proceedings in complexity*. Springer. https://doi.org/1007/978-3-031-44721-1_43

Ballen Zamora, S. A., Medina Campos, L., & Ortega Morales, J. A. (2021). Sustainable architecture and construction. In W. Leal Filho, A. M. Azul, L. Brandli, A. Lange Salvia, & T. Wall (Eds.), *Industry, innovation and infrastructure. Encyclopedia of the UN sustainable development goals*. Springer. https://doi.org/1007/978-3-319-95873-6_120

Giorgi, E. (2022). How technology devices can help or harm vulnerable communities in technocene. Issues for designers, architects, and policy makers. In E. Giorgi, T. Cattaneo, A. M. Flores Herrera, & V. d. S. Aceves Tarango (Eds.), *Design for vulnerable communities. The urban book series*. Springer. https://doi.org/1007/978-3-030-96866-3_2

Heffron, R. J., & De Fontenelle, L. (2023). Implementing energy justice through a new social contract. *Journal of Energy and Natural Resources Law, 41*(2), 141–155. https://doi.org/1080/02646811.2023.2186626

Horry, R., Booth, C. A., Mahamadu, A. (2022) Environmental management systems in the architectural, engineering and construction sectors: A roadmap to aid the delivery of the sustainable development goals. *Environment, Development and Sustainability 24*, 10585–10615. https://doi.org/1007/s10668-021-01874-3

Nasir, M., Khan, H. A., Zaffar, N. A., Vasquez, J. C., & Guerrero, J. M. (2018). Scalable solar dc micrigrids: On the path to revolutionizing the electrification architecture of developing communities. *IEEE Electrification Magazine, 6*(4), 63–72. https://doi.org/1109/MELE.2018.2871297

Neave, G. (2006). Redefining the social contract. *Higher Education Policy, 19*, 269–286. https://doi.org/1057/palgrave.hep.8300130

Ramírez-Gordillo, T., Mora, H., Maciá-Lillo, A., Amador, S., & Gil, D. (2024). Human-centric solutions and AI in the smart city context: The Industry 5.0 perspective. In A. Visvizi, O. Troisi, & V. Corvello (Eds.), *Research and innovation forum 2023. RIIFORUM 2023. Springer proceedings in complexity*. Springer. https://doi.org/1007/978-3-031-44721-1_16

Reckien, D., Creutzig, F., Fernandez, B., Lwasa, S., Tovar-Restrepo, M., Mcevoy, D., & Satterthwaite, D. (2017). Climate change, equity and the sustainable development goals: An urban perspective. *Environment and Urbanization, 29*(1), 159–182. https://doi.org/1177/0956247816677778. (Original work published 2017).

Shafik, M. (2021). *What we owe each other: A new social contract for a better society*. Princeton University Press. https://doi.org/1515/9780691220277

Shao, G. (2024). Aligning buzzword trends of sustainability with true sustainable development. *The International Journal of Sustainable Development and World Ecology, 31*(8), 1145–1146. https://doi.org/1080/13504509.2024.2412821

Teferi, Z. A., & Newman, P. (2017). Slum regeneration and sustainability: Applying the extended metabolism model and the SDGs. *Sustainability, 9*, 2273. https://doi.org/3390/su9122273

Visvizi, A. (2022). Artificial intelligence (AI) and sustainable development goals (SDGs): Exploring the impact of AI on politics and society. *Sustainability, 14*, 1730. https://doi.org/3390/su14031730

Visvizi, A. & Perez del Hoyo, R. (Eds.). (2021). *Smart cities and the UN SDGs*. Elsevier. https://www.elsevier.com/books/smart-cities-and-the-un-sdgs/visvizi/978-0-323-85151-0

Zallio, M., & Clarkson, P. J. (2021). Inclusion, diversity, equity and accessibility in the built environment: A study of architectural design practice. *Building and Environment, 206*, 108352. https://doi.org/1016/j.buildenv.2021.108352

Part I

Architecture and Design for Energy Efficiency

Chapter 2

Promoting Renewable Energy Through Interior Architecture and Design: Focus on Carbon Emissions' Reduction

Habibah Mohammed Abdulaziz Almulhim and Hanan Suliman Eissa

Helwan University, Egypt

Abstract

Environmental challenges, frequently driven by consumerist lifestyles, necessitate solutions to mitigate risks and promote sustainable economic development. Reducing carbon emissions and preserving global energy reserves have become critical priorities. With buildings and construction being the most energy-intensive sector globally, it is imperative that ways to minimize energy consumption in buildings are sought. This chapter advocates for designing highly efficient indoor spaces and establishing research centers to accelerate the transition toward zero-carbon buildings. It highlights strategies for creating sustainable energy-saving and energy-producing models that support economic growth without depleting environmental resources. This chapter presents a design aimed at reducing electricity consumption, cutting carbon emissions, and achieving energy efficiency in buildings. Additionally, it explores the role of buildings in energy generation, transforming them into energy producers. A descriptive, analytical, and qualitative approach was employed, including expert interviews, to analyze interior architecture's relationship with renewable energy. The findings suggest that understanding the design of existing buildings can pave the way for creating sustainable and energy-efficient structures.

Keywords: Renewable energy; carbon emissions; interior architecture; design alterations; zero-energy buildings; sustainability

1. Introduction

One of the biggest challenges our society faces today is related to the environment. That is, the consumer lifestyle has destroyed the environment around us, which has provoked within us the search for ways to ward off the risks flowing from these problems and the search for solutions that achieve sustainable economic development, in light of the international solidarity toward achieving zero carbon neutrality and confronting the global energy shortage. The Saudi Arabia's Vision 2030 aims to optimize the Kingdom's share of renewable energy production, balance the mix of domestic energy sources, and meet the Kingdom's commitments to reduce carbon dioxide (CO_2) emissions. Since the building sector has the largest share of energy consumption, it was necessary to highlight ways to invest in renewable energy through architecture and research on alternative means to achieve the highest energy efficiency and in pursuit of achieving the goals of the Kingdom's Vision 2030, which prompted us to ask about the role of interior designers and architects in achieving energy efficiency in different architectural facilities and how to invest in renewable energy technologies in buildings to reduce greenhouse emissions causing damage to the environmental envelope. The chapter is determined by time limits (2023) and spatial limits (Saudi Arabia).

This chapter is based on the theoretical framework, which includes the concept of renewable energy and its relationship to interior architecture, and the applied framework, which includes interview questions for architects, interior designers, and renewable energy specialists and the analysis of their answers, in addition to designing a three-dimensional proposal (3D) for a research center project specialized in renewable energy studies for zero-energy buildings. This research was based on the use of the descriptive analytical approach, as the problem related to energy sources, and the qualitative approach was studied through research interviews to explore the opinions of experts in the fields of architecture, interior design, and renewable energy, and analyzing and organizing the results in line with SWOT.

It can be said that the engine of growth and development is energy, as it is the main element for all sectors of the economy and the companion of human life. There is an urgent need for advanced research and development to enhance and accelerate the pace of innovations in the field of renewable energy technologies in the architectural facility, so the research submitted a proposal to establish a research center that contributes to accelerating the transition toward zero-carbon buildings, saving and producing energy, and expanding the boundaries of innovation through global cooperation. Previous studies have discussed the environmental impact resulting from the use of design alterations in buildings to reduce carbon emissions and reduce electrical energy consumption, as global trends toward achieving zero carbon neutrality have begun in recent years due to the negative impact of emissions on environmental resources and thus on the health of individuals. Because buildings account for 42% of energy consumption, where the resulting emissions amounted to 32%, which is the most dangerous type of Emissions. Consequently, intensifying efforts to reduce energy consumption and application of renewable energy technologies (Mekhlafi & Rabouh, 2022; M. Mohamed, 2019).

The results of earlier studies have shown that the use of design alterations that achieve thermal comfort in spaces, such as thermal insulation treatments for roofs and walls, reduces energy waste. Multiple studies indicate that about two-thirds (~66%) of residential electricity in Saudi Arabia is used for space cooling, highlighting the value of robust thermal insulation in the building envelope and in HVAC components (e.g., ducts and air-handling units) to cut cooling (and any incidental heating) loads and avoid wasted electric power (Hamed, 2023). Additionally, it is possible to employ technologies based on thermal energy resulting from geothermal pumps, where hot water is supplied to buildings through pumps that carry heat from one place to another (Mekhlafi & Rabouh, 2022). Thermal energy is distinguished from other renewable energy sources by being available 24 hours a day, seven days a week, while other energy sources, such as solar and wind power, are available in about one-third (1/3) of geo-thermal energy (Aalhashem et al., 2022).

In general, the literature indicates the need to use as many design alterations as possible, whether for cooling and heating or the use of light colors and heat treatment in painting facades, in addition to the use of energy-saving lamps such as LEDs (Hamed, 2023). In addition, continuous awareness in social media about the importance of saving energy. As well as rooting the concepts of sustainable development and environmental treatments for architecture and interior design students to establish good environmental treatments in buildings (Hamed, 2023).

However, there has been little interest in investing in renewable energy in architecture to generate it. Most of these studies have used the quantitative and descriptive analytical approach to study the role of architecture in reducing carbon emissions through design alterations and the employment of renewable energy technologies, while this chapter seeks to use the qualitative approach in the manner of objective analysis of interviews with specialists and experts in architecture and renewable energy. Accordingly, the objective of this chapter is to address the following questions:

RQ1. What is the role of the interior designer and architect in achieving energy efficiency for buildings?
RQ2. How can renewable energy technologies be invested in buildings to reduce greenhouse emissions that harm the environmental envelope?
RQ3. How effective are design treatments in reducing carbon emissions and achieving energy efficiency?

2. Literature Review

There are many concepts for renewable energy, but in general, it is defined as energy that is derived from nature's inexhaustible sources. According to the definition of the International Energy Agency (IES) renewable energy is energy formed by natural energy sources, such as sunlight and wind. These sources of energy are renewed naturally at a higher rate than their consumption (Suleiman, 2022). It can be said that energy that results from abundant natural resources is not inexhaustible but regenerative and is not a threat to the environment; rather, it is sustainable and clean energy (Bakery, 2023). Due to the increasing demand for electricity driven by changes in standards of living and population growth, demand for electricity will increase exponentially over the next decade. Hence, the importance of investing in renewable energy is evident through its link in three influential axes: the environmental dimension, the human dimension, and the economic dimension. In terms of environmental importance, renewable energy has a prominent role in addressing environmental challenges, as the diversity of its sources allows for the availability of energy, which reduces dependence on traditional energy sources such as oil, gas, and coal. This in turn reduces carbon emissions and greenhouse gases. In addition, it will contribute to the reduction of negative impact on climate (Almabrouk & Abulifa, 2023). From the point of view of the economic dimension, renewable energy achieves a vital value because of its role in diversifying sources of national income and strengthening the local economy by investing in sustainable energy projects and reducing countries' dependence on fossil fuel imports, which achieves energy independence for countries (Almabrouk & Abulifa, 2023; Bakery, 2023).

Renewable energy sources are diverse and are available around the world. Each type of energy has a characteristic that distinguishes it from the others. In addition, there are characteristics that they all share, such as renewability and sustainability. Although renewable energy sources have disadvantages, all renewable energy sources are vulnerable to weather variability and changing weather conditions (Almabrouk & Abulifa, 2023). Considering that the buildings sector is the most consuming sector of electrical power globally, the operation of residential buildings has the highest consumption rate (ca. 21%) than any other sector of real estate and construction, e.g. nonresidential buildings (ca. 9%) and building construction (ca. 4%). The reason being, its significant reliance on electricity for indoor environments, using lighting and ventilation, in addition to devices that raise quality of life in general. Alternative means that contribute to reducing this problem and even striving toward a healthier and emission-free life by investing in renewable energy are worth a try. Below, we present the most prominent Design methods and techniques based on renewable energy, which in turn will contribute to reducing energy consumption in buildings and even generating energy and shifting towards zero-energy buildings.

Photovoltaic concrete is an effective alternative in the construction of buildings that generate renewable energy, as it combines a system of channel concrete panels with a thin, lightweight solar layer, called Helia film. This means that it is possible to build using ready-made concrete panels for buildings without the need to install solar panels on roofs; through the use of this compact technology, it can be said that all the walls of the building will take the role of solar panels, which means that every square meter of the building is a power generator. The benefit of this technology is not limited to concrete only; it can be combined with glass, which already exists, and in operating buildings, by replacing ordinary building windows with photovoltaic windows.

The use of this technology shows double effectiveness, especially in commercial, administrative, or educational buildings with glass windows, as the film used in glass converts light energy into electrical energy as well as reducing ultraviolet and infrared rays, which will achieve good thermal insulation of the building, and thus will not need to waste more energy for cooling and heating (Muteri et al., 2020). This does not pose a concern about glass losing its transparency and its light transmittance, as it is traditional glass coated with paint that contains amorphous silicon, making it light sensitive and highly efficient, even if it is cloudy (Muteri et al., 2020). Lighting costs come second highest after cooling, heating, and ventilation (HVAC) costs. Therefore, it is more likely to use sunlight inside the voids. One of those means are solar pipes, which collect sunlight using a set of internal repercussions to give a consistent amount of lighting throughout the day. Sun pipes are one of the simplest solar pipe models that allow light in interior spaces vertically in existing buildings and even in the lower parts of buildings (Gneady et al., 2022).

Considering that the costs of cooling and heating occupy the first place in energy consumption, it is worth paying attention to and seeking alternatives for thermal insulation treatments to keep spaces cold in summer and warm in winter. Insufficient insulation and heat leakage are the main causes of energy loss in most buildings, and it has been proven globally that good thermal insulation of buildings—whether residential or otherwise—reduces energy consumption at a rate between 30% and 40% (Mekhlafi & Rabouh, 2022). Thermal insulation can be achieved by insulating walls and ceilings or using insulating glass, and the design is compatible with the environmental and climatic conditions surrounding the building and solar energy variables. In addition, it controls the movement of air inside the building by studying its location in general and the location of the internal air vents in particular and studying its orientation and prominent elements that facilitate the control of heat, which leads to raising the efficiency of the thermal performance of the building, so it no longer needs to compensate and equalize the heat using electricity-consuming devices.

The best solution to these problems is to start from the root causes. Electricity is often consumed in buildings in operation to achieve thermal, audio, or light comfort, so it is necessary to employ ideal design alterations intelligently and according to the type of space (administrative, residential, and educational). For example, the use of self-treatments such as insulation materials (foam polyurethane, foam cement, rock wool, vegetable cork, and hollow walls). In addition, employing lighting treatments is part of the light energy produced by lighting units is converted into thermal energy, so the so-called heat emission occurs, which in turn will affect the degree of ventilation and temperature of the vacuum, so it is necessary to choose the optimal lighting devices and integrate the use between natural and artificial lighting, taking care to study the distances accurately between lighting devices to use the least possible number of lighting devices.

In addition, the use of sensors that measure factors such as temperature and air quality is an ideal solution. To reach the minimum energy consumed, the sensors sense the presence of users inside the space and turn off the lighting and air conditioning if the space is empty of its users. Additionally, energy consumption can be reduced by 30% through taking advantage of the geothermal energy technologies that are inherent in the ground and are not affected by the weather, which means that they can supply electricity continuously throughout the year (Aalhashem et al., 2022).

Regarding power generation, voltaic cells have an indispensable role in reaching zero-energy buildings, and types of them have evolved to become an integrated part with most parts of the building's façade instead of being confined to roofs. For example, the integrated photovoltaic system (BIPV) is characterized by its ability to support the design ideas of buildings with flexible and modern designs, which makes them of a functional and aesthetic dimension in a sustainable manner that enhances environmental performance, and its performance is not limited to power generation but also work as sound and heat insulators. When designing the surrounding environment, the general site and the trees it contains should be taken into consideration and studied, as they affect the productivity of voltaic cells. Additionally, mechanical maintenance and design should be taken into consideration, which in turn will affect the quality of energy efficiency in the building (Peronto, 2022).

3. Methods and Materials

In collecting data and information, the researchers used a form as the main tool for collecting information. It was designed using research literature and adapted to the research goal, and it included two main samples: renewable energy experts and interior architecture experts. Four Arab experts were interviewed individually in several regions of Saudi Arabia. Interviews were not limited to a specific geographical scope; therefore, the interviews were conducted online using Microsoft Teams, and the selection criteria included more than a decade of scientific experience in the field of scientific research in general and the field of renewable energy and architecture in particular. Accordingly, an open-ended question form was designed for each field separately, and it is worth noting that participation in the forms was anonymous to preserve confidentiality and that the results of the interviews will be used for scientific research purposes only.

The researchers targeted experts and specialists in both the fields of renewable energy and interior architecture to explore the role of the interior designer and architect in achieving sustainability by saving and generating energy through the architectural elements and processors available to contribute to reducing carbon emissions and reducing energy consumption.

The researchers divided the interview questions into three main axes that included the following points. General demographic information about the interviewees, for example, educational level, nationality, field of expertise, and number of years of experience, was collected first. Then more specific questions were addressed to the Architecture Experts, focusing on defining a sustainable building, optimizing building design and orientation for energy efficiency, integrating renewable energy sources in Saudi architecture, enhancing energy efficiency through interior design, leveraging renewable energy research, reducing carbon emissions in construction, and utilizing sewage networks, particularly greywater, to improve building sustainability. The third group was addressed to the Renewable Energy Experts Questionnaire, focusing on the future of renewable energy in Saudi Arabia, the potential to reduce oil dependence through renewables, the influence of architecture on renewable energy production, and the most viable renewable sources for integration into construction and interior design. The interviews were recorded with the consent of the participants; subsequently, the interviews were transcribed in view of the analysis of the results.

4. Findings

The results of interviews conducted with architecture experts can be summarized as follows:

With regard to Q.1: What do you think is a simplified description of a sustainable building?, the interviewees agreed that sustainable buildings contribute to reducing electricity consumption, participant P.1 Said that a sustainable building is any building capable of producing or saving energy, whether during the design process, the construction process, or during the period of use of the building, taking into account the preservation of environmental resources and reducing excessive and unstudied consumption, as the participant P.2 added, saying that a sustainable building is a beautiful comfortable shelter that does not cause damage to the land and tends to use materials that can be recycled after the end of life of the building.

With regard to Q.2, that is, how can the design of the building and its interior spaces contribute to the generation of, or reduce the consumption of, electricity? The participants pointed out that buildings have an active role in reducing electricity consumption through means and design standards. P.1 However, reducing electricity consumption is a consequence or reaction associated with the use of renewable energy alternatives. He added, for example, the movement of people on sidewalks can generate energy using cutting-edge technologies that are currently available. Participant P.2 added that this can be achieved in the long term, which is the thermal insulation of the building and the effective role that insulators achieve in reducing vacuum temperature leakage, whether by using certain materials or adding some materials to cement mixtures to achieve thermal insulation in general. Sun breakers also have a role that cannot be ignored in reducing the consumption of refrigerants by vacuum occupants. He also pointed out the active role of windows in saving and generating energy, as some windows consist of two layers of glass interspersed with a space full of air, so this space constitutes an insulation that prevents heat from entering the building, and at the same time the glass panel outside the building can absorb solar energy and convert it into energy as mentioned earlier in the theoretical framework, glass windows can be used with Heliatek technology.

As regards Q.3, that is, how can the orientation of the building and its architectural openings contribute effectively to generating and saving energy? The experts agreed that directing the building and its openings is one of the most important studies that the architect or designer cannot overlook because of its active role in achieving the sustainability of the building. P1 Environmental control is interested in studying the orientation, openings, and ventilation of the building based on its current location, and many architects believe that studying the location of the building and studying its internal spaces and activities within each space is important in terms of psychological and social comfort. In terms of psychological comfort, nature must have an impact on the health and improvement of the mood of the building's residents or visitors, and this is done by adding green elements and water bodies, such as trees, fountains, or waterfalls, and the green elements must contribute to air renewal, which in turn improves the ventilation of the space. Alas, in terms of saving energy consumption, talking about environmental architecture, and returning to traditional architecture, there were no architects at that time, but "builders," and if we take, for example, the southern region in the Kingdom of Saudi Arabia, specifically the Al-Baha region, its buildings were previously based on the use of local building materials and local construction methods as well. We conclude from this that a large percentage of energy consumption of the architectural sector lies in two things: one is the transfer of building materials from one area to another, and the other is the means of construction itself.

From a different angle that calls for reflection, the same respondent added that in comparison, which is Riyadh, it is noticeable that in the difference between the two regions, the buildings in Riyadh and Al-Baha have the same openings, which are narrow and do not allow the passage of the sun due to climatic conditions, and although the residents of the Al-Baha region are more in need of sunlight to heat the internal spaces, but building materials achieved their role as an insulator, so the building was satisfied with its ability to retain internal heat and not discharge it during the day. There is no doubt that the social lifestyle plays a role, as most social activities in the past were conducted under the sun, such as herding and agriculture. Participant P.2 added that energy saving through solar energy is remarkably available in the Kingdom of Saudi Arabia, but it is limited to specific buildings, such as commercial and administrative buildings, pointing to the extent to which residential buildings lack energy investment through solar panels due to their size compared to the sizes of other facilities. For example, the space in which family meetings abound is directed toward the desired winds and so on.

With regard to Q.4., that is considering that renewables are abundant in Saudi Arabia, what do you think are the top four sources that can be invested in and employed through interior design and architectural elements? The participants agreed that the most prominent wealth that can be invested in renewable energy is the sun and the light and thermal energy resulting from it. Participant P.1 believes that we can invest in wind, solar, and water energy, but it is believed that the sun is the only source that can be invested in the architecture sector through solar panels. Confirming his statement, participant P.2 also added that the most prominent energies available in the Kingdom of Saudi Arabia are wind, solar, and hydro energy, but he believes that oil is one of the most important energies that we have and is indispensable.

As regards Q.5., that is, how does interior design contribute to raising the energy efficiency of the building? Participant P.2 believes that through simple and enhanced design for sustainability, high efficiency in energy management can be achieved. For example, allocating balconies or outdoor yards in the building that include trees that provide shade in addition to some water bodies in the yards or open areas in the workplaces achieves thermal comfort for the place and thus motivates the residents of the building to sit in these places away from excessive consumption inside the house due to lighting and air conditioning. Participant P.2 added that insulators have a prominent role in reducing energy consumption. One of the efforts of the Kingdom of Saudi Arabia is that it stipulated in the Saudi Building Code the use of insulators to conserve energy. Additionally, he added that the lack of types of insulators may be an obstacle, and this prompts us to search for simple solutions for insulation in terms of innovation and development of raw materials with their chemical and physical properties.

In reply to Q.6., that is, as an interior designer or architect, how do you think renewable energy research centers in the architectural sector can add to designers and architects, Participant P.2 pointed out that the most important need for designers and architects interested in scientific research is to provide places and scientific research laboratories that help research groups conduct research in a continuous manner that achieves the knowledge of each individual on the results of the other and his findings, even if these groups are in different places, and as an effective suggestion can use modern technologies such as (hologram). Participant P.1 said that he sees it as an opportunity that can be used in the research and development of energy-generating or energy-saving materials that are environmentally friendly.

In reply to Q.7., that is, how can we generate or save energy in both the construction phase (construction operation and maintenance) and the post-construction phase (demolition of the building)? Participant P.1 stated that during the construction phase, the architect and designer should visit the project site and see the surrounding buildings so as not to be negatively affected by what is around them and added that 60–70% of the sunlight and heat entering can be reduced. At the construction stage, it is advisable to choose the right building materials. After construction, using modern methods, treatments can be applied in such a way that they can be disassembled and reinstalled elsewhere in case the building is removed for some reason. Participant P.2 said that energy can be saved by using waste from buildings either during or after construction by converting waste into renewable energy through private centers.

As for Q.8., how can we reduce or control carbon emissions from building materials and the construction sector? Participant P.1 said that buildings cause carbon emissions not in the building itself but in power plants; for example, lighting a bulb inside your room in Riyadh causes air pollution in Yanbu (the area that includes power plants), as oil is burned there to generate the electrical energy you use, citing this he asked the question of the number of lights and appliances that consumes electricity without the need of the occupants of the space, and based on what he said, he stressed the need to use lights and air conditioners that work by sensing the movement of the inhabitants of the space, thus saving electrical energy and thus reducing carbon emissions. Participant P.2 added that to achieve the principle of simplicity, it is possible to dispense with some spaces inside buildings; for example, in residential buildings, it is possible to invest in living rooms more than bedrooms, and thus this will reduce the seating of individuals alone in different spaces, where each consumes some amount of electricity in lighting, air conditioning, and charging electrical appliances. Therefore, it is necessary to address some societal behaviors that may affect energy consumption in some way.

Finally, in response to Q.9., how can the development of the sewage network contribute to raising the energy efficiency of buildings, especially the greywater generated by the building? The experts agreed on the importance of greywater reuse. P.1 However, providing well-studied paths by the engineer and interior designer at the planning stage will help to link the internal garden or the building garden with gray water pipes, adding that many people are ignorant of natural resources, as desalinated water is used to irrigate plants even though it does not produce fruit, and although gray water contains nutrients for the plant. Participant P.2 added that it can be developed by returning it to treatment plants so that it returns to its source, and then it can be used somewhere, such as for irrigating trees in public areas or for using it in toilets, washing yards, and cars.

The results of the interviews conducted with renewable energy experts can be summarized as follows.

In regard to Q.1, how do you see the future of renewable energy in Saudi Arabia?, the participating experts stated that the Kingdom of Saudi Arabia has significant efforts to provide a prosperous future through investment in renewable energy, and participant P.3 stated that according to the Vision 2030 program, the aim is to have 50% of electricity based on renewable energy, especially wind and solar thermal energy. Participant P.4, with Vision 2030 and the determination of the Ministry of Energy, renewable energy participation will be effective in the supply of electricity under the 5050 plans.

As regards Q.2, in the future, relying on renewables, do you think we can reduce reliance on oil by 50%–70%? To what extent does the building and architecture sector influence the production of renewable energy? Participant P.3 mentioned that oil enters many industries other than electricity production and transportation, and therefore it is completely indispensable. Engineering codes and legislative requirements tend to make buildings achieve energy efficiency in general and rely on a secondary source such as renewable energy. Participant P.4 added that the pursuit of renewable energy investment in the building sector will reduce the carbon footprint, but the presence of oil is inevitable, as it is related to the wheel of a circus or a closed circuit; for example, polymer is one of the oil derivatives, which is used in the manufacture of wind turbines. P.4 said. It can be used as transparent glass solar panels for power generation elements. As they are transparent, we conclude that the architect or designer can employ them aesthetically in the elements of the building, such as the façade or the surrounding environment.

In reply to Q.3, renewables are abundant in Saudi Arabia, what do you think are the most prominent sources that can be exploited in the construction and interior design sector? Participant P.4 mentioned that wind energy can be invested in by placing wind turbines on the facades of commercial buildings, for example, and added that for this purpose special turbines are used, which are low-sound turbines that do not cause disturbance. As it is horizontal rather than vertical, he also added that solar energy, whether photovoltaic or thermal energy produced by the sun, is the dominant energy. Participant P.3 The underground potential energy (thermal energy) is generously available in Medina, specifically (Harrat), as it is close to the surface of the earth, some of which can be reached by digging only three meters.

5. Discussion and Conclusion

Design for energy efficiency by optimizing the use of design processors will contribute to reducing carbon emissions. The study and understanding of the mechanisms of design alterations used in old buildings and projecting them on modern architecture with contemporary concepts will contribute to enhancing and accelerating the pace of innovations for functional treatments to reach zero-energy buildings and result in an economic impact. The use of different forms of solar panels achieves the utmost results. The interior designer and architect can design buildings in an energy-efficient manner while maintaining the esthetic and philosophy of the design. Design alterations related to thermal insulation are one of the most important treatments to achieve energy efficiency, as most of the energy wasted in buildings is for thermal comfort. If wind turbines are used to generate energy, it is necessary to consider the good sound insulation of the building, especially buildings that must achieve auditory comfort, such as educational, residential, and health buildings. Prior to the construction process, it should be ensured that special areas are designed with design standards that ensure the results of technologies are used for renewable energy; for example, when using solar heaters, they must be established outside the building, away from shade or elements that can block sunlight. On the other hand, transformers that convert wind energy into electrical energy must be away from any heat source because heat disrupts the functions of semiconductor systems.

To address the growing need for sustainable development and energy efficiency, several key initiatives and recommendations have been identified. Establishing a training center dedicated to the installation and maintenance of renewable energy generators is essential, as these systems require ongoing upkeep. This initiative will not only ensure the optimal operation of renewable energy systems but also create significant job opportunities. Interdisciplinary collaboration is also crucial. Including joint courses for architecture, design, and electrical engineering students in academic curricula will foster a deeper understanding of renewable energy applications in construction and building. Additionally, scientific research and innovation should focus on the development of local raw materials in the Kingdom of Saudi Arabia, aiming to create advanced insulating materials and materials capable of absorbing carbon emissions. Implementing minimum standards for energy consumption as a prerequisite for building construction is also recommended to ensure sustainability. The use of energy-efficient technologies, such as solar and energy-saving lamps, is strongly encouraged. Finally, achieving energy efficiency in buildings requires conducting energy audits, ensuring thermal comfort, and adopting practices like carbon offset purchases. These measures collectively aim to reduce carbon emissions and promote environmental sustainability.

For more information and a deeper understanding of the topic, readers are encouraged to refer to the author's extended work available at the following link: [https://drive.google.com/file/d/1TGi4C9POPXad1jUev7OrgXIpopw0n4yh/view?usp=sharing]. This additional resource includes illustrative images that demonstrate the final output and provide further visual clarification of the results.

References

Aalhashem, N. A., Naser, Z. A., Al-Sharify, T. A., Al-Sharify, Z. T., Al-Sharify, M. T., Al-Hamd, R. K. S., & Onyeaka, H. (2022, November). Environmental impact of using geothermal clean energy (heating and cooling systems) in economic sustainable modern buildings architecture design in Iraq: A review. In *AIP Conference Proceedings* (Vol. 2660, No. 1, p. 020119). AIP Publishing LLC.

Almabrouk, A., & Abulifa, S. A. (2023). The technology of renewable energy and its role in achieving sustainable development. *International Journal of Electrical Engineering and Sustainability*, 2, 1–9.

Bakery, D. A. A. B. A. (2023). Orientation towards investment in renewable energy. *The Arab Journal of Islamic and Sharia Studies*, 331–378.

Gneady, A., Taha, A., & Ahmed, M. (2022). Methods of retrofit office buildings' envelopes in Egypt to integrate photovoltaic cells and its effect on energy production. *Journal of Engineering Sciences*, 50(6), 337–357.

Hamed, M. S. Abd El (2023). Design treatments in the interior architecture of zero-energy buildings (Study on housing in Upper Egypt). *Journal of Architecture, Arts and Humanities*, 8(9), 110–128.

Mekhlafi, M., & Rabouh, H. (2022). *Stimulating the efficient use of energy in buildings using renewable energy as a tool to achieve sustainable development*. Kasdi Merbah Ouargla University.

Mohamed, M. (2019). Saving energy through using green rating system for building commissioning. *Energy Procedia* (Special Issue on Emerging and Renewable Energy: Generation and Automation), 162, 369–378. https://doi.org/10.1016/j.egypro.2019.04.038

Muteri, V., Cellura, M., Curto, D., Franzitta, V., Longo, S., Mistretta, M., & Parisi, M. L. (2020). Review on life cycle assessment of solar photovoltaic panels. *Energies*, 13(1), 252. https://doi.org/10.3390/en13010252

Peronto, J. (2022). Federation of Korean industries headquarters. *Thornton Tomasetti*. [Online]. https://www.thorntontomasetti.com/project/federation-korean-industries-headquarters

Suleiman, P. P. (2022). The economics of renewable energy and its relationship to sustainability. *Journal of Economics*, 6(11), 144–172.

Chapter 3

Sustainable Retrofitting: The Significance of Adapting the Already Existing Buildings

Dina Ahmed Ahmed Elmeligy[a,b] and Mohammad Refaat Mohammad Abdelaal[c,d]

[a]Tanta University, Egypt
[b]Princess Nourah bint Abdulrahman University, Riyadh, K.S.A
[c]Suez Canal University, Egypt
[d]Dar Al Uloom university Riyadh, K.S.A

Abstract

The built environment is critical in attaining sustainability today, when this objective is vital. This chapter explores the essential role of anticipating the built environment, specifically focusing on adapting existing buildings. Here, the built environment, sometimes thought of as merely the background to our everyday existence, is examined in light of its potential for transformation. The chapter emphasizes the significance of two fundamental elements: visionary and dynamic features of the built environments. When these components are in harmony, it is anticipated that the existing buildings will undergo substantial renovations to meet the sustainability standards necessary for their enhancement.

A noteworthy outcome of this chapter is the promotion of tools for anticipatory engagement with the built environment, mainly through utilizing virtual reality (VR) and virtual environments (VE). By adopting these technologies, we can facilitate sustainable enhancements to existing buildings. This chapter not only aims to raise awareness of the anticipatory aspect of the built environment but also examines various retrofitting scenarios that underscore this principle. Utilizing Virtual Singapore (VSG) as a case study emphasizes the chapter proposal related to the closed loop. Furthermore, this chapter forecasts potential research trajectories in pursuing sustainability through anticipatory improvements in the built environment.

Sustainability, Resilience, and Inclusiveness through Human-Centred Architecture and Design, 27–37
Copyright © 2026 Dina Ahmed Ahmed Elmeligy and Mohammad Refaat Mohammad Abdelaal
Published under exclusive licence by Emerald Publishing Limited
doi:10.1108/978-1-80592-881-220261003

Keywords: Sustainable retrofitting; retrofitting buildings; envisioning; artificial intelligence; virtual reality; augmented reality and built environment

1. Introduction

The proactive strategy of anticipating building retrofits is essential to our built environment's robust and sustainable growth. Furthermore, it is a calculated reaction to the demands of a constantly evolving urban landscape, as this proactive strategy has increased occupant safety and comfort, decreased environmental impact, and improved energy efficiency. As a result, to meet the problems brought on by aging infrastructure and changing sustainability goals, this process calls for a thorough examination of motivations, tactics, and creative solutions. With the aid of technology, especially artificial intelligence (AI), virtual reality (VR), and augmented reality (AR), the fields of architecture and building design can witness a massive transformation. In some manner, it has also been accomplished in the case study of this chapter (Virtual Singapore).

Thus, combining artificial intelligence (AI), VR, and AR has ushered in a new era of innovation in planning, architecture, and building design. Because of these technologies, professionals can now conceptualize, produce, and engage with urban and architectural projects in ways never possible before, creating more efficient, sustainable, and user-centered designs. In this realm, this chapter explores the practice of the integration of AI, VR, AR, and sustainable building retrofitting, focusing on the significance of this integration in envisioning and realizing a more sustainable, resilient, and environmentally responsible built environment to achieve the visionary and dynamic aspects of built environments. It also tries to explore various retrofitting scenarios that underscore this principle. In this view, the key research question (RQ) is:

> *RQ1.* Can predicting the built environment to achieve sustainability for retrofitting existing structures be merged with AI-VR/AR-AI "Scenario as Closed Loop Development"?

To address this question, this chapter employs a mixed-methods approach to explore the integration of AI, VR, and AR for achieving sustainability. A comprehensive literature review and theoretical study will establish the theoretical framework, while the Virtual Singapore case study will illustrate practical applications. Discussion and conclusions will follow.

2. Literature Review

Buildings' retrofitting is a crucial procedure briefly reviewed in this literature, along with the history of sustainability and building retrofitting to improve existing structures' sustainability, usability, and resilience, in addition to the earlier advancements and phases of AI, VR, and AR integration in building retrofitting. As illustrated in Fig. 3.1 the retrofitting process can be roughly split

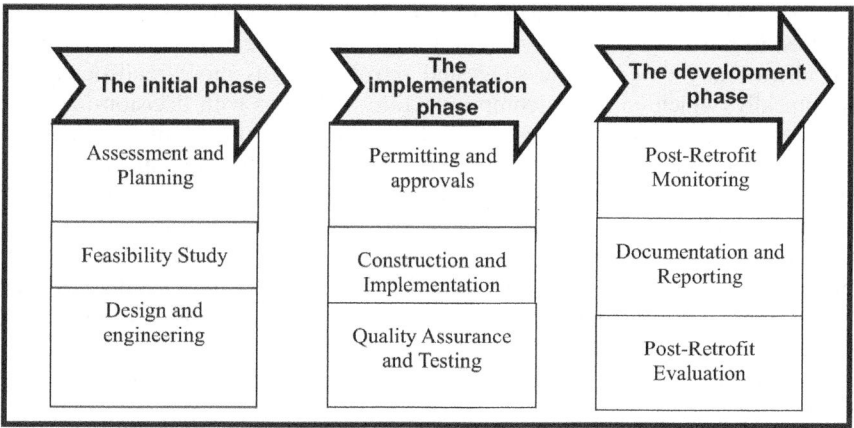

Fig. 3.1. The Stages of Building Retrofitting to Achieve Sustainability. *Source:* Authors.

into multiple stages, each with a specific function in reaching the intended result and sustainability (Ali et al., 2018).

Fig. 3.1 displays a flowchart illustrating the three phases of the retrofitting process for retrofitting, including the initial phase, the implementation phase, and the development phase. The phases are visually connected by large arrows pointing right, symbolizing a sequential process from the initial phase to the development phase.

Retrofitting is a procedure of altering already existing machinery, systems, or structures to boost energy efficiency, increase performance, or attain all of these (Jensen, 2023). Retrofitting of buildings denotes incorporating new components or materials to boost the structural integrity or energy efficiency of a given building. In the past, energy efficiency of many existing buildings has been overlooked; today, many of them require energy retrofitting and renovation (Chen et al., 2022) (Alsaid et al., 2023). Energy retrofitting techniques could improve and preserve comfortable indoor settings while drastically reducing greenhouse gas emissions and world energy consumption (Jensen, 2023; Ma'bdeh et al., 2023; Pan et al., 2023). Second, on the evolution and phases of applying AI and VR/AR in building retrofitting. The fields of building retrofitting and AI, VR, and AR have advanced significantly, improving the efficacy and efficiency of the retrofit process.

Architects and designers began investigating the usage of VR in their work by the 1990s. VR technology allows professionals to develop and interact with 3D virtual models of areas and buildings. Using VR for client presentations and design visualization, architecture companies were among the early adopters.

The advent of VR and AR technology in the late 20th and early 21st centuries gave engineers and architects new tools for visualizing and planning retrofit projects. With the development of VR and AR technology, stakeholders involved in retrofitting projects can now enjoy immersive experiences. Architects and clients may now see the suggested retrofit designs more realistically and dynamically, which enhances communication and helps with decision-making.

On the other hand, imitating human labor gave rise to the "intelligent agent" in the 1990s. As sensing and actuation hardware grew more affordable and dependable, designing systems powered by real-world data became possible. As computing power and storage capacity increased, statistical approaches were developed to extract answers from the massive volume of data collected by the Internet. By the late 1990s, AI-related statistical learning techniques were responsible for the decreased uncertainty in decision-making. Fuzzy logic, an AI idea that was successfully utilized in many areas of life, from the operation of high-speed trains to the functioning of washing machines, was introduced during this era (Pan et al., 2023).

Therefore, AI has gained widespread use in several domains, such as environmental monitoring, disease prediction, and pollution prediction. For example, research on using AI to reduce air pollution has grown recently (Ali et al., 2018).

In summary, rapid technological advancements significantly impact the potential uses of AI, VR, and AR in society. The potential benefits of AI, VR, and AR are astounding and well worth the work required to limit the risks and explore the possibilities despite the acknowledged fact that fear and mistrust in AI systems have also developed in response to the perceived hazards of losing control (IEA, 2008; Dai et al., 2023). This is what motivates all of the inventions and research in this area.

The process of retrofitting the already existing buildings offers significant opportunities for reducing global energy consumption and greenhouse gas emissions. This is regarded as one of the primary methods for attaining sustainability in the built environment at a relatively low cost with a high adoption rate. Meanwhile, building retrofit optimization aims to maximize energy performance within a given set of operational restrictions by identifying, putting into practice, and utilizing the most affordable retrofit technologies. This is done while preserving acceptable indoor thermal comfort and satisfactory factory service levels. When addressing the nature of a building retrofit problem, the following factors need to be adequately considered in the two aspects listed below, that is, visionary retrofitting and dynamic retrofitting.

Visionary retrofitting of buildings entails applying creative and progressive ideas to improve energy efficiency, sustainability, and general usability. Thus, considering the physical environment, the financial advantages of innovative urban planning, and how such creative planning can raise property values and advance sustainability (Farzaneh et al., 2021; Hegazi et al., 2021), some ways that retrofitting construction could take advantage of the visionary component include smart building systems, energy efficiency upgrades, and adaptive reuse of resources, for example, water, as well as green roof and wall solutions.

The dynamic aspects of a building's retrofitting reflect a responsive and continuous process that incorporates changes in technology, the environment, the economy, and society. Effective retrofitting solutions must be flexible, adaptable, and forward-oriented to meet the changing possibilities and challenges in the built environment. This dynamic perspective is, therefore, essential for building robust, sustainable, and future-ready retrofitted structures. They recognized the value of flexibility in the face of changing environmental circumstances. So, numerous factors influence the performance of building retrofit programs. The main components that significantly influence buildings' retrofits include client resources and expectations, policies and regulations, retrofit technology, information relevant to the building, human variables, and other uncertain aspects (Ma, 2021).

Retrofitting existing buildings has many challenges and opportunities. The main challenge encountered is many uncertainties, such as climate change, service change, human behavior change, and government policy change, all of which are directly related to dynamic aspects and affect the selection of retrofit technologies and hence the success of a retrofit project (Ma, 2021). Therefore, visionary and dynamic retrofit projects may require a blend of engineering ingenuity, digital technology integration, sustainability principles, and architectural know-how. A multidisciplinary team must be included, and adaptability, occupant well-being, and long-term sustainability must all be considered for implementation to be effective (Chen, 2012).

According to Vilches, Garcia-Martinez, and Sanchez-Montanes, they are retrofitting to enhance older buildings mainly to improve structural integrity, energy efficiency, and sustainability (Dai et al., 2023). Retrofitting involves adding new components or materials to existing buildings, a critical step given the often-neglected energy efficiency of older structures. The goal is to extend a building's lifespan, minimize environmental impact, and improve occupant comfort.

The retrofitting process consists of six steps (Jensen, 2023; Pan et al., 2023). It begins with defining the problem by identifying the core issues of the building's condition, followed by collecting information through energy audits and the implementation of energy-efficient technologies. The next step involves brainstorming and analyzing potential solutions, such as improving water consumption. Once viable strategies are identified, a solution is developed by incorporating Internet of Things (IoT) devices and building management systems for efficient monitoring and control. Feedback is then gathered to track retrofitting progress and promote sustainable practices among tenants. Finally, the process is refined and improved through continuous monitoring and assessment to ensure ongoing enhancements.

Integrating AI, VR, and AR in retrofitting existing buildings presents transformative scenarios. AI can analyze vast amounts of data to optimize retrofit strategies, forecast energy needs, and identify efficiency improvements, leading to more intelligent and cost-effective renovations. VR offers immersive previsualization, enabling architects and engineers to explore and test retrofitting designs in a virtual environment, enhancing planning accuracy and creativity. AR brings an interactive dimension to the retrofitting process, overlaying digital information on physical spaces to guide construction, provide real-time data insights, and facilitate seamless team collaboration. This integration streamlines the retrofitting process and significantly enhances the potential for sustainable and innovative building solutions.

The retrofitting of existing structures could be enhanced by AI by increasing the building's overall performance, comfort, and efficiency (Farzaneh et al., 2021). To gather and interpret data, AI in building retrofitting necessitates the integration of multiple sensors, IoT devices, and data analytics systems. With this data-driven approach, building owners and operators may make more informed decisions to enhance their current structures' comfort, sustainability, and efficiency. Therefore, Wang claimed that the structure, behavior, capabilities, function, and principles could be used to describe AI, which can be the activity devoted to making machines intelligent that form, according to Nilsson's definition, the quality that enables an entity to function appropriately and with foresight in its environment (Farzaneh et al., 2021). The relationship between AI applications and the retrofitting of existing structures can be understood through various applications. AI can analyze past and present energy usage to forecast future consumption trends and recommend energy-efficient retrofit techniques (IEA, 2008). One of the most promising uses of AI in urban energy systems is the rise of smart buildings, which help protect the environment, reduce operational costs, and conserve energy (Mariano-Hernández et al., 2021; Raza & Khosravi, 2015). AI also enables proactive maintenance by analyzing sensor data and historical maintenance records to predict system failures. Additionally, AI enhances occupant interaction through smart thermostats that learn user preferences, optimize HVAC systems, and improve indoor air quality (Dai, 2021). In lighting, AI optimizes energy use by adjusting brightness based on occupancy, time of day, and natural light levels while also predicting component failures for preventive maintenance. Security is another crucial area, as AI can process sensor data to detect fire hazards or security threats by analyzing surveillance feeds. AI also improves space utilization by adapting workplaces to different team sizes and changing needs. Lastly, AI-driven demand response strategies help organizations enhance energy efficiency, reduce costs, and create a more resilient and sustainable energy infrastructure (Hasik et al., 2019).

Due to the unique tools and applications they offer design, planning, and visualization, VR and AR can potentially be significant in retrofitting existing buildings.

Integrating the first step of AI (Artificial Intelligence) with VR/AR (Virtual Reality/Augmented Reality) in existing building retrofitting was an emerging trend with potential applications and benefits. So, the efficiency, sustainability, and overall tenant experience of retrofitting existing buildings can be improved by utilizing AI, VR, AR, and IoT technologies, as demonstrated by these examples.

AI and VR/AR retrofitting of existing buildings ensures that the upgrade satisfies sustainability and building efficiency goals while streamlining the process and improving communication and safety. Better results will eventually result from giving stakeholders a deeper comprehension of the project. In the first scenario, "AI applications in existing buildings retrofitting," AI applications can be retrofitted into existing buildings to improve their usefulness and efficiency. This also lowers operating costs and environmental effects while improving tenants' quality of life.

In the second scenario, "(VR/AR) applications in existing buildings retrofitting," become familiar with their new environment, (VR/AR) aids building users in adjusting to the modifications made to the retrofitted building. VR and AR help in the process of simplification, enhance communication, and decrease design errors. VR/AR helps users adapt to retrofitting building changes by familiarizing them with the new environment. (VR/AR) helps streamline the process, improve communication, and reduce design errors.

The third scenario is "AI-(VR/AR) integrated applications in existing buildings retrofitting." This integration improves sustainability, control, efficiency, and communication while providing a comprehensive approach to design, construction, and management. It also increases user engagement and communication. It emphasizes how AI's powers and VR's immersive visuals complement each other. Therefore, this integration offers a holistic design, construction, and management approach, enhancing efficiency, control, and sustainability while improving communication and user engagement. It underscores the synergy between AI's capabilities and VR's immersive visualizations.

However, in all three scenarios, there are some weaknesses in the last two steps of the design process, including feedback collection and design improvement. According to the common practice, developers still depend on the "traditional feedback collection methods."

In contrast to all three previous scenarios, an AI-(VR/AR)-AI integrated scenario will optimize retrofit projects by integrating data-driven decision-making, immersive visualization, and real-time engagement. The smooth exchange of information and feedback between AI and VR/AR platforms is demonstrated in this scenario, which guarantees the effectiveness, sustainability, safety, and occupant-friendliness of retrofit projects.

3. Case Study (Virtual Singapore)

Undoubtedly, the notion of smart cities is not a novel one. But what's new, or at least different from earlier, is how quickly the idea of smart cities appears to be evolving. The primary impediment to change rate of progress is the lack of information and awareness of the potential benefits of efficient data utilization. There is also a lack of knowledge about what can be accomplished when data-sharing techniques are wholly embraced. So, a 3D representation of Singapore that is integrated, detailed, and rich in semantics—a "digital twin" of sorts—will be part of the collaborative platform VSG. It is being developed to promote greater cooperation in creating tools and apps that address new and complex urban concerns and facilitate data sharing among the public, business, and research communities (Crawford, 2018).

Therefore, the VSG platform is a digital twin of the city-state of Singapore. It lets users create complex tools and applications for test-bedding ideas and services across several industries. Planning, decision-making, and research on technologies that could address complex and new problems facing the nation are also aided by it (Crawford, 2018). The second most densely inhabited country in the world, a land-scarce city-state, Singapore has experienced significant vertical development over the years due to a lack of horizontal space. As a result, an increasing number of people live in high-rises, and underground space is used for utilities, freeing up valuable surface land for more livable uses like housing and recreation. Due to the overlapping of ground-level data with subsurface and aerial spaces, conventional 2D town planning maps are no longer sufficient to accurately map and depict the complex environment caused by vertical development. A 3D digital model was created by gathering the entire nation's high-resolution 3D map data to overcome the limitations of 2D maps (Crawford, 2018). This clarifies AI-(VR/AR)-AI integrated in the existing buildings retrofitting scenario to ensure its application in this case study (VSG) as follows:

(1) *Define* the problem using an AI application by studying all the problems on a large scale and in different domains. For example, in traffic management, the problem is economic losses and environmental pollution caused by traffic congestion and inefficiencies in transportation networks. As well as another example of Infrastructure Maintenance: The platform of VSG facilitates the upkeep and administration of metropolitan infrastructure. For example, it may forecast utility maintenance requirements based on usage trends and model how infrastructure upgrades will affect traffic flow.

(2) *Collect* Information by using AI applications, especially for Geospatial Data and Mapping, to gather geospatial data on land usage, vegetation, urban development, and environmental changes, and employ satellite and aerial imagery in VSG. Environmental monitoring is also done by environmental sensors, which use water and air quality sensors to monitor environmental factors, including pollution levels and water quality. Additionally, AI is used in environmental analysis, which evaluates the effects of urban activity on the environment, finds sources of pollution, and analyzes environmental data (Mariano-Hernández et al., 2021).

(3) *Brainstorm* and analysis by using AI applications: through using AI-powered brainstorming by Generative AI Models (like GPT-4) that serve as Ideation and Creativity Tools to support brainstorming sessions and offer recommendations, fresh concepts, and imaginative solutions for sustainability, retrofitting, and urban planning projects. Additionally, AI-powered idea mapping tools can be used to generate idea trees and mind maps from stakeholder input, which aid in organizing and visualizing brainstorming sessions. Besides Virtual Collaboration Spaces: Provide AI-powered online forums for stakeholders to share ideas in real time. AI-powered chatbots may be included in these platforms to help with conversation and to deliver pertinent information. Lastly, crowdsourced innovation uses AI to evaluate feedback from experts, companies, and citizens gathered through online surveys and platforms to find creative solutions and ideas (Abdulrahman Yarali, 2021; Mariano-Hernández et al., 2021).

(4) *Develop* a solution by using AR and VR applications: With the use of digital twin technology, technical and physical assets can be virtually simulated and maintained while remaining unchanged, whereas VSG uses AR and VR technology to improve user experience and interaction. Particularly for immersive visualization, VR enables stakeholders to "walk through" and experience planned urban development realistically. This is in addition to "Augmented Insights," which helps planners and developers make decisions by superimposing real-time data and analytics on the physical world (Yarali, 2021).

(5) *Feedback* collection by using AI applications, such as AI-driven content delivery, based on tenant preferences and behavior patterns, and using AI to provide individualized training and tips. Also, online discussion boards have been provided where building managers and tenants may interact, exchange stories, and ask questions while working together on sustainability projects. These forums can be moderated by AI, which can also highlight critical debates to create cooperative platforms inside VSG where interested parties can exchange information about sustainability and retrofitting, as well as best practices and success stories. The most important example is the AI-driven Feedback Loop, which has constant monitoring. AI is used to monitor tenant behavior and building performance continuously. This makes it possible to evaluate and modify retrofitting tactics continuously (Yarali, 2021).

(6) *Improve* the design by using AI applications: The Digital Twin system must use techniques like artificial AI, machine learning, and neural networks to continuously learn and adapt its mode of operation based on inputs and updates. Digital twins and other technologies, like the IoT, have made data integration and cyber-physical interaction more advantageous (Yarali, 2021).

This case study has many benefits, like improved planning. Using a virtual environment, urban planners may see how new developments affect the area and make better decisions. Before implementing land use or transportation network changes, planners might model several urban scenarios to evaluate their potential effects, called "scenario testing." It has also been used in disaster, emergency response, sustainability, and environmental management.

Thus, the VSG project is an innovative endeavor that uses cutting-edge 3D modeling and data integration to produce an interactive, highly detailed digital twin of the entire city-state. To simulate and evaluate complex urban dynamics, this digital representation includes the physical characteristics of infrastructure and buildings and incorporates data from other sources.

VSG is a prime example of how technology may promote sustainable urban development and enhance the quality of life. It also acts as a reproducible model for other cities looking to include AI, VR, and AR technology. Singapore is establishing a standard for future smart cities by showcasing the capabilities of a digital twin. VSG is an innovative example of how cities may use state-of-the-art technology to create efficient and sustainable urban settings. Built to combine AI with VR and AR technology for urban planning and management, it is a three-dimensional digital twin of the city-state. This large-scale project offers a forward-looking perspective on how digital technologies can transform our engagement with the built world. So, this case study demonstrates the revolutionary potential of combining AI and VR/AR in urban innovation, opening the door to a more resilient and sustainable global community.

4. Discussion and Conclusions

Integrating AI, VR, and AR into the retrofitting of existing buildings is revolutionizing the field, offering innovative and efficient solutions. AI algorithms analyze building data, predict energy consumption patterns, and optimize retrofitting strategies. This results in more precise and cost-effective interventions. VR technology creates immersive simulations, allowing architects and engineers to visualize and experiment with retrofitting changes before implementation. This aids in identifying potential issues and exploring creative solutions without physical constraints. AR, on the other hand, assists on-site applications by overlaying digital information in the real world, which can guide construction work, provide real-time data, and enhance collaboration among different teams. Together, these technologies improve the accuracy and efficiency of retrofitting projects and pave the way for smarter, more sustainable building management and a more interactive and informed approach to building renovation.

Furthermore, AI applications are critical because they may boost productivity, enable data-driven decision-making, and improve user experiences. Therefore, an AI-(VR/AR)-AI closed-loop development scenario for existing building retrofitting can represent a forward-thinking approach that harnesses the power of data, visualization, and user engagement to create sustainable, efficient, and user-friendly building environments.

Ultimately, the chosen case study provides a solid illustration of a research hypothesis, which is the VSG project serving as an example of how digital twin technology might transform urban planning and management. Its many advantages in the areas of planning, disaster relief, sustainability, community involvement, economic growth, and education highlight its significance as a critical instrument for building a more intelligent, resilient, and livable city to confirm the effectiveness of the closed-loop AI-(VR/AR)-AI-integrated retrofitting scenario for existing buildings.

References

Ali, U., Shamsi, M. H., Hoare, C., Mangina, E., & O'Donnell, J. (2018). An intelligent knowledge-based energy retrofits recommendation system for residential building at an urban scale. *Building Performance Modeling Conference, SimBuild Conference, 8*, 84–91.

Alsaid, A. M., Hegazi, Y. S., Shalaby, H. A., & Mohamed, M. A. (2023). Methodology to improve energy efficiency of heritage buildings using HBIM-Sabil Qaitbay: A case study from Egypt. *Civil Engineering and Architecture, 11*(1), 425–449. https://doi.org/10.13189/cea.2023.110134

Chen, G., Cheng, L., & Li, F. (2022). Integrating sustainability and users' demands in the retrofit of a university campus in China. *Sustainability, 14*(16), 10414. https://doi.org/10.3390/su141610414

Crawford, J. (2018). Enhancing virtual Singapore with BIM data. *SIG International*. https://www.gim-international.com/content/article/enhancing-virtual-singapore-with-bim-data

Dai, X., Shang, W., Liu, J., Xue, M., & Wang, C. (2023). Achieving better indoor air quality with IoT systems for future buildings: Opportunities and challenges. *Science of The Total Environment, 895*, 164858. https://doi.org/10.1016/j.scitotenv.2023.164858

Farzaneh, H., Malehmirchegini, L., Bejan, A., Afolabi, T., Mulumba, A., & Daka, P. P. (2021). Artificial intelligence evolution in smart buildings for energy efficiency. *Applied Sciences, 11*(2), 763. https://doi.org/10.3390/app11020763

Hasik, V., Escott, E., Bates, R., Carlisle, S., Faircloth, B., & Bilec, M. M. (2019). Comparative whole building life cycle assessment of renovation and new construction. *Building and Environment, 161*, 106218. https://doi.org/10.1016/j.buildenv.2019.106218

Hegazi, Y. S., Shalaby, H. A., & Mohamed, M. A. A. (2021). Adaptive reuse decisions for historic buildings in relation to energy efficiency and thermal comfort—Cairo Citadel, a case study from Egypt. *Sustainability, 13*(19). https://doi.org/10.3390/su131910531

IEA. (2008). *World Energy Outlook 2008*. International Energy Agency. https://www.iea.org/reports/world-energy-outlook-2008

Jensen, L. (2023). *Human-centered sustainability in architectural practice*. Routledge.

Ma'bdeh, S. N., Ghani, Y. A., Obeidat, L., & Aloshan, M. (2023). Affordability assessment of passive retrofitting measures for residential buildings using life cycle assessment. *Heliyon, 9*(2), e13574. https://doi.org/10.1016/j.heliyon.2023.e13574

Mariano-Hernández, D., Hernández-Callejo, L., Zorita-Lamadrid, A., Duque-Pérez, O., & Santos García, F. (2021). A review of strategies for building energy management systems: Model predictive control, demand side management, optimization, and fault detection & diagnosis. *Journal of Building Engineering, 39*, 101692. https://doi.org/10.1016/j.jobe.2020.101692

Pan, Y., Zhu, M., Lv, Y., Yang, Y., Liang, Y., Yin, R., Yang, Y., Jia, X., Wang, X., Zeng, F., Huang, S., Hou, D., Xu, L., Yin, R., & Yuan, X. (2023). Building energy simulation and its application for building performance optimization: A review of methods, tools, and case studies. *Advances in Applied Energy, 10*, 100135. https://doi.org/10.1016/j.adapen.2023.100135

Raza, M. Q., & Khosravi, A. (2015). A review on artificial intelligence-based load demand forecasting techniques for smart grid and buildings. *Renewable and Sustainable Energy Reviews, 50*, 1352–1372. https://doi.org/10.1016/j.rser.2015.04.065

Yarali, A. (2021). *Intelligent connectivity: AI, IoT, and 5G*. Wiley-IEEE Press.

Chapter 4

Energy Efficiency in Educational Buildings

Abobakr Al-Sakkaf[a,b], Basma Mostafa[c,d], Tarek S. Ghoniemy[e] and Sherif Ahmed[e]

[a]Concordia University, Montreal, Canada
[b]College of Engineering & Petroleum, Hadhramout, Yemen
[c]Faculty of Computers & Artificial Intelligence, Cairo University, Egypt
[d]Faculty of Artificial Intelligence & Computing, Horus University, Egypt
[e]Concordia University, Canada

Abstract

The construction sector, whether households, commercial, educational, or industrial, is expected to promote energy sustainability. However, buildings are the primary consumers of energy, especially electricity. Energy overconsumption results in greenhouse gas emissions, depletion of natural resources, and high financial costs. Hence, monitoring, controlling, and managing energy are the key goals of building management that opt to achieve energy efficiency and cost-effective operation and maintenance, which are the main objectives of sustainable development goals. Educational buildings are significant in their function and require more energy to operate and maintain, especially for lighting, achieving suitable thermal comfort, and using reliable IT systems and other equipment. The reliability and flexibility offered by wireless technologies have been the driving force toward the vision of the Internet of Things (IoT). They have contributed to attracting growing interest in the market. This work presents an energy-efficient IoT solution to monitor the energy consumption model by deploying a Building Management System (BMS). Integrating multiple battery-operated sensors into the building allows critical data to be dynamically provided in real time to improve overall building efficiency. Introducing the IoT in managing energy in educational facilities can be more cost-effective and convenient than traditional building BMSs.

Keywords: Energy efficiency; IoT; buildings' sustainability; building management system; educational buildings

1. Introduction

The escalating demand for energy and increasing concerns about environmental sustainability have prompted the requirement for energy-efficient solutions, particularly in high-consumption sectors such as buildings (Himer et al., 2023; Oliveira & Pimenta, 2023). Approximately 40% of the total energy in the world is consumed by buildings (Jain et al., 2017; Lizana et al., 2017; Loukaidou et al., 2017), which contributes to one-third of global greenhouse gas emissions (Huang et al., 2017; Mytafides et al., 2017); about 20% of this percentage could have been saved if we started using energy more efficiently. Confronting such a problem will affect both the environment and our society (Mischos et al., 2023).

Within the building sector, educational buildings represent a considerable percentage of nonresidential buildings. (Birol, 2013; IEA, 2023) and are considered the central energy-consuming sector. With complex operational schedules, varied occupancy patterns, and several factors influencing electricity consumption, educational buildings present a challenging landscape for energy management. Moreover, the academic community is vital in terms of its impact on our future, as the students of today represent the citizens of tomorrow, and they should acquire the technological and scientific skills that enable them to overcome future challenges and climate change impacts.

Extensive research has been dedicated to building energy management systems (BEMS), which monitor and control energy consumption in building equipment. Building poorly managed and controlled equipment can prevent a significant amount of energy from being wasted. Researchers have recently investigated using Internet of Things (IoT) in BEMS to maximize energy efficiency by minimizing losses and environmental impact, which leads to sustainable energy development in buildings (Deng et al., 2014). Smart buildings enable remote operation and automatic power management with low electricity consumption (Zafar et al., 2020). Without using sensors to acquire environmental information, the building management system has limited intelligence to adapt autonomously to the dynamic variation in the situation (Marinakis et al., 2013). However, we must cope with power consumption and data transmission issues to adopt IoT in a real environment. Therefore, it is necessary to understand which technologies can be applied to deliver data on time. Monitoring energy consumption in real time, changing the energy wastage behavior of occupants, and using automation with incorporated energy savings scenarios are ways to decrease the global energy footprint.

The objective of this chapter is to develop an IoT-based energy management system to monitor the energy efficiency of educational buildings. The proposed model targets efficient monitoring to achieve efficiency and low-cost energy management per square meter area of an academic building, improve energy efficiency in classrooms and lecture rooms, and reduce energy consumption costs campus-wide. The paper starts by exploring previous work in BEMS, and the role of IoT in energy is presented next. The proposed model requirements and objectives follow this. The model architecture is presented next, followed by a detailed description of the chapter methodology and the challenges faced. Evaluation and discussion are described, followed by the conclusion.

2. Literature Review

Traditional works related to BEMS are based on simulations and data set testing. However, using smart meters, EMS can monitor and provide real-time monitoring of home energy consumption (Mataloto et al., 2019), as well as online access to devices' status, thus allowing remote control of devices by customers. Guoqiang et al. (2013) developed a smart IoT gateway for signal transmitters, in which all smart meters are linked with a gateway to deliver the signals conveniently without extra computers. Jara et al. (2013) proposed a Zigbee protocol for realizing high-speed data exchange in a real-time controlling and monitoring system to increase electricity efficiency.

Ma et al. (2015) developed an energy-saving system to control distributed electricity appliances remotely in a low-cost approach. Jaradat et al. (2015) proposed a statistical table solution by collecting information from environment sensors, used appliances, and user behavior based on the uncontrolled and imprecise behavior of the buildings' occupants in managing electricity consumption. After analyzing these data, a behavior planning model was structured to formulate automatic energy-saving decisions.

Other studies applied scheduling approaches to optimize energy consumption, as presented in Lee et al. (2017). The lack of standardized protocols and regulations was the main challenge in considering intelligent DC-powered homes as a suitable replacement to alternate current (AC) power systems. Challenges could be overcome with IoT, which will provide an integrated platform for DC-powered technologies with inefficient energy distribution. IEA (2013) and Birol (2013) suggest a cost modeling framework for an energy management model that utilizes optimization to decrease consumer energy expenses. Another study found that a home energy management system can reduce electricity consumption by 15%, potentially with acceptable discomfort (Dittawit & Aagesen, 2014). To optimize the results, Loukaidou et al. (2017) conducted several studies on electricity savings to determine which feedback an energy management system should have. Their verdict was that real-time feedback systems are the most effective, rather than estimated or periodical feedback reports.

IoT has emerged as a pivotal technology in managing energy efficiency (Himer et al., 2023). IoT can interconnect a grid of devices and sensors, enabling real-time monitoring and data collection and facilitating immediate adjustments to energy consumption patterns. Smart lighting, intelligent HVAC systems, and automated energy meters are examples of IoT successfully being adopted in educational buildings to optimize energy usage (Hasan et al., 2021). In this context, a project called Green Awareness in Action (GAIA) aims to develop an IoT platform that aims to increase awareness about energy consumption and sustainability relying on real-world sensor data gathered from school buildings, which enables students and teachers to interact with the displayed energy data by changing their behavior of energy consumption, which will lead to achieving energy efficiency (MacNaughton et al., 2013). While IoT provides connectivity and data collection infrastructure, the real computational power in making sense of these data comes from Artificial Intelligence (AI) and Deep Learning algorithms (Kim et al., 2023). AI algorithms can process and analyze data from different energy-consuming sectors within an educational building, providing actionable insights into optimizing energy usage. Deep Learning techniques, a subset of machine learning, can analyze complex datasets and patterns, enabling more accurate predictions of energy needs and potential savings (Mischos et al., 2023).

Building equipment that is poorly managed and controlled can cause a significant amount of energy to be wasted, which can be monitored and controlled by building energy management systems (BEMS). Researchers have recently investigated using IoT in BEMS to maximize energy efficiency by minimizing losses and environmental impact, which leads to sustainable energy development in buildings (Deng et al., 2014). The escalating demand for energy and increasing concerns about environmental sustainability have prompted the need for energy-efficient solutions, particularly in high-consumption sectors such as educational buildings and institutional environments. With complex operational schedules, varied occupancy patterns, and several factors influencing electricity consumption, such environments present a challenging landscape for energy management (Himer et al., 2023; Oliveira & Pimenta, 2023). The introduction of advanced technologies such as IoT, AI, Deep Learning, and Embedded Systems has radically transformed the approach to energy efficiency in these settings (Valencia-Arias et al., 2023).

Embedded Systems serve as the operational core of most IoT devices, executing the control algorithms that drive energy-saving actions (Frutuoso et al., 2023). These systems have evolved to become increasingly energy-efficient, contributing to overall energy savings (Abolhassani Khajeh et al., 2022). Integrating low-power, high-performance embedded microcontrollers and processors in IoT devices ensures minimal energy consumption by the monitoring and control systems. The real power in enhancing energy efficiency comes from the synergistic combination of IoT, AI, and Embedded Systems (Abolhassani Khajeh et al., 2022). IoT provides the hardware framework, AI and Deep Learning offer the analytical capabilities, and Embedded Systems contribute to efficient onboard processing. This integrated system enables real-time adjustments and predictive controls, thereby optimizing energy consumption proactively (Saba et al., 2022).

The amalgamation of IoT, AI, Deep Learning, and Embedded Systems offers a comprehensive and potent solution for energy management in educational buildings. While significant progress has been made, ongoing research and development are essential to overcome existing challenges and to adapt to the ever-changing landscape of energy needs and technological advancements. The available systems are designed and intended exclusively for a predefined number of cases and systems without expansion and interoperability with other applications due to the lack of semantics. The differentiation and heterogeneity of the offered solutions at both hardware and software levels diverge from the basic principles of the IoT, which require a standard unified model for maximum functionality to be ensured.

Chifu et al. (2021) propose a deep learning-based approach for forecasting energy consumption in public buildings using Long Short-Term Memory Networks. The authors tested their method on a data set from the National Archives of the United Kingdom and used Mean Absolute Error and Mean Absolute Percentage Error as evaluation metrics. The proposed approach shows promising results and can be used to optimize energy consumption in public buildings, contributing to the sustainability of the IoT ecosystem. The respected authors must explicitly tackle the possibility of applying the proposed method to other types of buildings. However, the proposed approach is based on past energy consumption measurements, and hence, it could be used for different kinds of buildings with similar data available.

Essa et al. (2023) provide a comprehensive overview of the potential of IoT to improve energy consumption in public buildings and identify four key areas where IoT can be used to enhance sustainability: energy efficiency, air quality, occupant comfort, and water conservation. The paper argues that IoT has the potential to reduce energy consumption by up to 30%, improve air quality by up to 50%, and increase occupant comfort by up to 20%.

Elsisi et al. (2021) propose a deep learning-based approach that combines Industry 4.0 and the IoT to optimize energy management in smart buildings. The authors suggest using the YOLOv3 algorithm for people recognition and propose a new structure for controlling air conditioner operation based on IoT. Energy consumption can be reduced by automatically adjusting the air conditioner operation based on the number of detected persons in a specific area. The paper emphasizes the importance of remote management of controllable devices and highlights the potential for applying the proposed approach to other devices to decrease energy loss and cost. The experimental results demonstrate the accuracy of the deep learning-based recognition algorithm in detecting the number of persons, and the status of the air conditioners can be monitored through the IoT platform's dashboard. Overall, this paper presents a promising tool for implementing Industry 4.0 in smart energy systems and improving energy efficiency in buildings.

This chapter focuses on creating an Energy Management System for educational buildings using the IoT. The objective is to enhance energy efficiency and establish a cost-effective system per square meter. The model specifically targets classrooms and lecture halls, aiming to minimize energy usage costs across the entire campus while ensuring optimal energy efficiency. The following part addresses the challenges associated with IoT for BEMS in educational buildings and the model's requirements and objectives in response to those challenges.

Integrating IoT in BEMS, particularly educational buildings, presents several challenges that need careful consideration. First, the complexity and diversity of educational buildings, which can range from historic structures to modern facilities, pose a significant challenge to the standardization and compatibility of

IoT solutions. Moreover, ensuring a robust and secure network infrastructure is crucial, as IoT devices generate and transfer large volumes of data that must be transmitted securely to prevent breaches. This is particularly sensitive in educational environments where student and staff privacy is paramount. Another major challenge is the scalability and interoperability of IoT systems. IoT solutions must be able to integrate seamlessly with existing management systems and protocols, ensuring smooth operation and data exchange across various platforms and devices. Furthermore, the maintenance and reliability of IoT systems are critical concerns. Continuous monitoring and periodic updates are essential to ensure systems' smooth operation, which can be resource-intensive. Finally, the success of IoT systems in efficiently managing energy depends on the active participation of building occupants, such as students and faculty.

The IoT network topology is often unstable due to resource constraints, node mobility, unreliable connectivity, and the transient link connections between nodes (Jara & Ladid, 2013). These challenges are why monitoring the ongoing management phase of the IoT device's life cycle is one of the most critical drivers of the value of IoT. Remote monitoring capabilities are mandatory nowadays; device status must be monitored to support proper management actions. Monitoring is the ability to employ a device's data to make decisions regarding its performance. In general, network monitoring mechanisms aim to detect and localize network faults. The system should provide the appropriate tools for overseeing the network state, availability, and connectivity between nodes. The necessary corrective measures can be taken by mapping symptoms of detected problems to possible root causes. Focusing on mission-critical IoT network services, the main problem is guaranteeing network reliability, nodes' availability, and robust connectivity. The proposed monitoring mechanism aims to observe network traffic to verify the availability of the critical set of nodes; thus, the transmission of mission-critical-related information can be guaranteed. Node failures can be used to model failures of physical nodes and links (Ma et al., 2015). IoT networks are of enormous scale, consisting of potentially hundreds of thousands of nodes. Naturally, it is required that monitors be embedded (placed) in the correct locations to guarantee complete monitoring coverage. Given the constrained resources of LLNs, the monitoring cost must be reduced. This energy consumption differs from the energy dedicated to the thing's primary function. Therefore, the number of monitors to be placed must be minimized while satisfying the coverage condition.

3. Materials and Methods

Data collection is a main aspect of BEMS. Sensors, submeters, and smart meters are incorporated to collect real-time data to assess building energy performance. Data analytics can be utilized to provide further insights for energy-efficient management. Various types of data are collected, such as active and proactive maintenance schedules of equipment, meter data, billing information, and costs of energy consumption of different building equipment.

IoT devices collect and transmit sensitive data, which can be vulnerable to cyber-attacks and breaches. Accordingly, a high level of security should be assured, as this management system stores a large amount of information and employs numerous keys and passwords. Hence, privacy, consistent and uncorrupted data tracking and recording, integrity, and collection and exchange without missing data are the security requirements for this type of application. Using the internet may make this information and data susceptible to cyber-attacks, as the software and smart devices can be used for artificial control and monitoring of BEMS functions such as switching on/off air conditioners, dishwashers, televisions, lights, fans, PCs, and alarming operators.

Interoperability issues: IoT devices may use different communication protocols, making integration into a unified system complex.

Power consumption: IoT devices require power to operate, and their continuous use can lead to high energy consumption and associated costs.

Calibration and maintenance: IoT sensors must be calibrated and maintained regularly to ensure accurate and reliable data collection. 4-Cost: IoT systems' initial investment and ongoing maintenance costs can be high, which may limit their adoption in some settings. The costs of IoT-based BEMS include energy costs, operating costs, costs of the energy storage system's materials, smart appliances, building construction or renovation costs, technological costs, and maintenance costs.

Reliability: Reliable IT-BEMS can ensure the achievement of sustainable development goals. Inaccurate information and decisions may lead to irrecoverable damages. Therefore, the power supply must be stable and reliable (Jaradat et al., 2015). 6-Scalability: Since most of the devices utilized in IoT are energy-constrained and have limited memory, the real-time energy consumption monitoring data should be routed efficiently; reliability and scalability in the network should be accounted for. Otherwise, sent data packets will not reach the destination efficiently; given that data passes through many hops, new devices can be added to the network unpredictably.

Adding new devices to the system while maintaining stability is called scalability. A nonscalable system cannot be expanded in the future, which contradicts consumers' expectations from the system, as consumers intend to obtain new services every time.

Addressing such challenges requires further research and development in areas such as data security, standardization of communication protocols, energy-efficient design, and cost-effective solutions. Consequently, the EMS must be energy-efficient. We will use scheduled energy monitoring to distribute and balance the monitoring role between the sensors to prolong network longevity. Moreover, interoperability should be maintained to integrate existing (and future) IoT services.

4. Proposed Model

Considering the specific requirements of mission-critical IoT networks, our goals and contributions are highlighted in the following. These goals are achieved through a methodology that comprises four phases, which will be illustrated in detail in the Methodology Section. The four phases are (1) literature review, (2) development of an IoT-based management model, (3) ensuring scalability, reliability, and interoperability of the management system, and (4) validating the model.

Optimal monitor coverage. Monitors are placed in specific locations to guarantee full monitoring coverage. We propose the optimal placement of monitors to cover a mission-critical IoT network. By formulating a binary integer program, we provide an exact solution to the defined IoT minimum monitoring placement problem.

Scheduled monitoring. To prolong network longevity, the monitoring role should be distributed and balanced among the entire set of nodes. In a given period, if a node is not assigned to monitoring or has another role, it can turn into a sleeping mode. However, multiple state transitions consume extra energy (Ma et al., 2009). The proposed formulation considers the presence of sleeping nodes by duty-cycling the monitoring while minimizing the monitoring state transitions and always respecting the monitoring coverage requirement, regardless of the lack of current network activity.

Interoperable monitoring. To realize the integration with already-existing (and future) IoT services, it is detrimental that monitoring prepositions are entirely interoperable with the standardized IoT protocol suite. Interoperability is challenging mainly because IoT solutions are often tailored to specific scenario requirements without focusing on horizontal integration with other IoT services or reusability. To overcome that challenge, the proposed monitoring mechanism is embedded within RPL, the standardized routing protocol for LLNs, and works in tandem with 6LoWPAN.

Energy-efficient communication. The 6LoWPAN Border Router (6BR) has unconstrained resources and a global view of the network state, enabling it to perform powerful analysis of the monitoring data and further corrective measures. Through multi-hop communication, the gathered data can be forwarded from monitors to the 6BR, then to a Network Operations Center (NOC), where sophisticated data analysis and mining can be performed. However, energy can be lost in the communication between monitors and the 6BR, so finding the shortest path regarding the number of hops to the 6BR is necessary. In our proposed model, monitors are optimally placed, and the energy consumed in relaying the data to the 6BR is minimized.

In a nutshell, the objective of the mathematical model is to minimize the amount of energy consumed in (1) passively monitoring the set of critical nodes, (2) communication of the monitoring data to a central entity (6LoWPAN Border Router), and (3) transition between monitoring active/sleep states. Experimentation is designed using network instances of different topologies. Results demonstrate the effectiveness of the proposed model in realizing full monitoring coverage with minimum energy consumption and communication overhead while balancing the monitoring role between nodes. Fig. 4.1 illustrates a schematic of an educational building adopted with the system interconnection for all

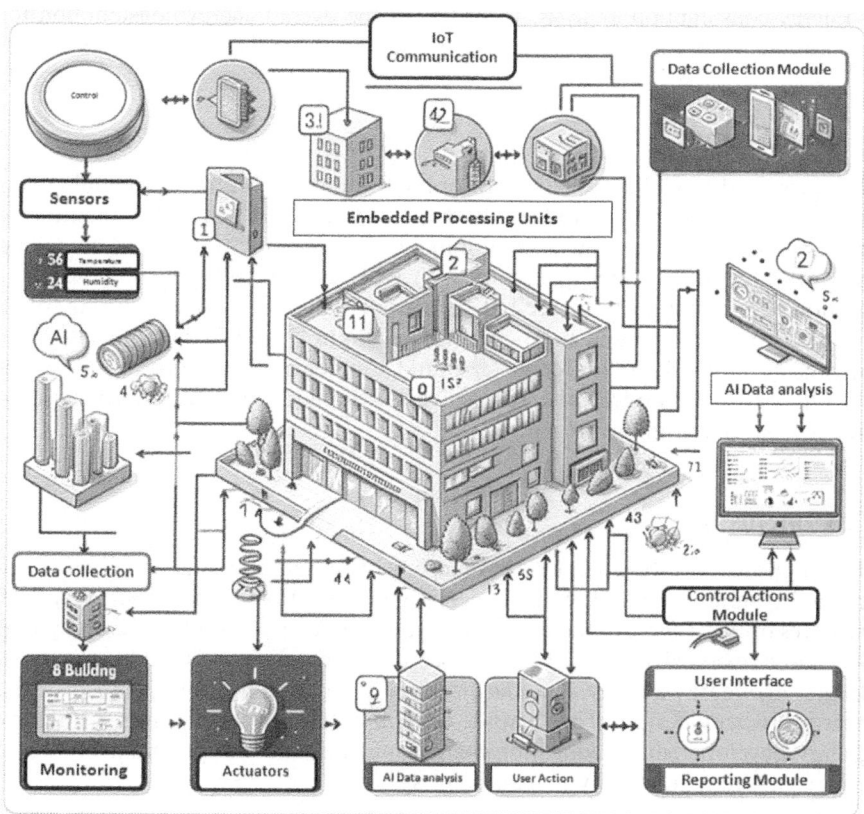

Fig. 4.1. Proposed Model Architecture. *Source:* By Authors.

system components, such as power stations, wireless access points, and embedded systems for data collection.

Inputs: 1-Network topology: Information about the physical layout of the IoT network, including the locations and types of nodes. 2-Energy consumption rates: Estimates of the energy consumption for nodes' active monitoring, communication, and sleep states. 3-Critical node locations: Identification of the nodes that require mandatory monitoring. 4-Communication protocol parameters: Specifications of the communication protocol used within the network (e.g., 6LoWPAN).

Outputs: 1-Optimal monitor placement: Locations for sensors to provide complete coverage of critical nodes with minimal energy consumption. 2-Scheduling plan: Assignment of monitoring roles to nodes in different time periods, balancing the load and minimizing sleep-wake transitions. 3-Routing paths: Optimal hop-by-hop paths for data transmission from monitors to the 6LoWPAN Border Router.

4-Energy consumption analysis: Estimates of the overall energy consumption for monitoring, communication, and state transitions under the proposed model.

5. Discussion

The proposed model achieves: 1- an optimal monitor placement for full coverage, ensuring no critical node goes unmonitored. 2- A scheduled monitoring balances the load among nodes and minimizes sleep-wake transitions, extending network lifespan. 3- Interoperability with RPL and 6LoWPAN promotes integration with existing and future IoT systems. 4- The shortest path routing to the 6BR minimizes communication energy consumption, and 5- The model can be applied to networks of different sizes and topologies. By balancing the monitoring load, the model enhances network reliability and prevents individual nodes from becoming overloaded.

6. Conclusion

The proposed IoT-based Energy Management System presents an effective solution for monitoring and managing energy in educational buildings. The model achieves optimal energy efficiency and cost-effective operation by leveraging IoT, AI, and embedded systems. Future research directions include addressing challenges like data security, standardization of communication protocols, and energy-efficient design. The chapter contributes to understanding sustainable energy development in educational environments and the potential of IoT in enhancing building energy management systems.

References

Abolhassani Khajeh, S., Saberikamarposhti, M., & Rahmani, A. M. (2022). Real-time scheduling in IoT applications: A systematic review. *Sensors, 23*(1), 232. https://doi.org/10.3390/s23010232

Birol, F. (2013). The changing energy map: Drivers and implications. *The APPEA Journal, 53*(3). https://doi.org/10.1071/AJ12118

Chifu, V. R., Pop, C. B., Chifu, E. St., & Barleanu, H. (2021). Deep learning for forecasting the energy consumption in public buildings. In *20th RoEduNet IEEE conference: Networking in education and research (RoEduNet)* (pp. 1–6). https://doi.org/10.1109/RoEduNet54112.2021.9638281

Deng, S., Wang, R., & Dai, Y. (2014). How to evaluate performance of net zero energy building–A literature research. *Energy, 71*, 1–16.

Dittawit, K., & Aagesen, F. (2014). Home energy management system for electricity cost savings and comfort preservation. In *2015 IEEE international conference on consumer electronics-Berlin (ICCE-Berlin)* (pp. 1–6). https://doi.org/10.1109/ICCE-Berlin.2014.7034267

Elsisi, M., Tran, M.-Q., Mahmoud, K., Lehtonen, M., & Darwish, M. M. F. (2021). Deep learning-based Industry 4.0 and internet of things towards effective energy management for smart buildings. *Sensors, 21*(4), 1038. https://doi.org/10.3390/s21041038

Essa, M. E.-S. M., El-shafeey, A. M., Omar, A. H., Fathi, A. E., El Maref, A. S. A., Lotfy, J. V. W., & El-Sayed, M. S. (2023). Reliable integration of neural network and internet of things for forecasting, controlling, and monitoring of experimental building management system. *Sustainability, 15*(3), 2168. https://doi.org/10.3390/su15032168

Frutuoso, M. I., Neto, H. C., Véstias, M. P., & Duarte, R. P. (2023). Energy-efficient and real-time wearable for wellbeing-monitoring IoT system based on SoC-FPGA. *Algorithms, 16*(3), 141. https://doi.org/10.3390/a16030141

Guoqiang, S., Yanming, C., Chao, Z., & Yanxu, Z. (2013). Design and implementation of a smart IoT gateway. In *2013 IEEE international conference on green computing and communications and IEEE internet of things and IEEE cyber, physical and social computing* (pp. 720–723). https://doi.org/10.1109/GreenCom-iThings-CPSCom.2013.130

Hasan, M. K., Ahmed, M. M., Pandey, B., Gohel, H., Islam, S., & Khalid, I. F. (2021). Internet of things-based smart electricity monitoring and control system using usage data. *Wireless Communications and Mobile Computing*, 1–16. https://doi.org/10.1155/2021/6544649

Himer, S. E., Ouaissa, M., Ouaissa, M., Krichen, M., Alswailim, M., & Almutiq, M. (2023). Energy consumption monitoring system based on IoT for residential rooftops. *Computation, 11*(4). https://doi.org/10.3390/computation11040078

Huang, Z., Lu, Y., Wei, M., & Liu, J. (2017). Performance analysis of optimal designed hybrid energy systems for grid-connected nearly/net zero energy buildings. *Energy, 141*, 1795–1809.

International Energy Agency (IEA). (2013). *World Energy Outlook 2013*. OECD Publishing.

Jain, M., Hoppe, T., & Bressers, H. (2017). Analyzing sectoral niche formation: The case of net-zero energy buildings in India. *Environmental Innovation and Societal Transitions, 25*, 47–63. https://doi.org/10.1016/j.eist.2016.11.004. https://research.utwente.nl/en/publications/analyzing-sectoral-niche-formation-the-case-of-net-zero-energy-bu?utm_source=chatgpt.com

Jara, A. J., Ladid, L., & Gómez-Skarmeta, A. F. (2013). The internet of everything through IPv6: An analysis of challenges, solutions and opportunities. *Journal of Wireless Mobile Networks, Ubiquitous Computing, and Dependable Applications, 4*(3), 97–118.

Jaradat, M., Jarrah, M., Bousselham, A., Jararweh, Y., & Al-Ayyoub, M. (2015). The internet of energy: Smart sensor networks and big data management for smart grid. *Procedia Computer Science, 56*, 592–597.

Kim, K., Jang, S.-J., Park, J., Lee, E., & Lee, S.-S. (2023). Lightweight and energy-efficient deep learning accelerator for real-time object detection on edge devices. *Sensors, 23*(3). https://doi.org/10.3390/s23031185

Lee, T., Jeon, S., Kang, D., Park, L. W., & Park, S. (2017). Design and implementation of intelligent HVAC system based on IoT and big data platform. In *IEEE international conference on consumer electronics (ICCE)* (pp. 398–399). https://doi.org/10.1109/ICCE.2017.7889369

Lizana, J., Chacartegui, R., Barrios-Padura, A., & Valverde, J. M. (2017). Advances in thermal energy storage materials and their applications towards zero energy buildings: A critical review. *Applied Energy, 203*, 219–239.

Loukaidou, K., Michopoulos, A., & Zachariadis, T. (2017). Nearly-zero energy buildings: Cost-optimal analysis of building envelope characteristics. *Procedia Environmental Sciences, 38*, 20–27. https://doi.org/10.1016/j.proenv.2017.03.069

Ma, J., Lou, W., Wu, Y., Li, X.-Y., & Chen, G. (2009). Energy efficient TDMA sleep scheduling in wireless sensor networks. *IEEE INFOCOM*, 630–638.

Ma, L., He, T., Swami, A., Towsley, D., & Leung, K. K. (2015). On optimal monitor placement for localizing node failures via network tomography. *Performance Evaluation, 91*, 16–37.

MacNaughton, J., Moyo, D., Tanaka, N., & Nasser, A. (2013). *World energy trilemma 2013: Time to get real – The case for sustainable energy investment. Executive summary*. World Energy Council.

Marinakis, V., Karakosta, C., Doukas, H., Androulaki, S., & Psarras, J. (2013). A building automation and control tool for remote and real-time monitoring of energy consumption. *Sustainable Cities and Society, 6*, 11–15.

Mataloto, B., Ferreira, J. C., & Cruz, N. (2019). LoBEMS—IoT for building and energy management systems. *Electronics, 8*(7), 763. https://doi.org/10.3390/electronics8070763

Mischos, S., Dalagdi, E., & Vrakas, D. (2023). Intelligent energy management systems: A review. *Artificial Intelligence Review, 56*(10), 11635–11674. https://doi.org/10.1007/s10462-023-10441-3

Mytafides, C. K., Bikas, D., Mardiris, V., & Tsikaloudaki, A. (2017). Energy performance and environmental impact assessment of residential buildings in different climatic zones. *Energy and Buildings, 154*, 293–306.

Oliveira, A. C., & Pimenta, J. M. (2023). Towards net-zero buildings: Integrating smart technologies and passive design in sustainable architecture. *Journal of Building Engineering, 67*, 105835.

Saba, T., Rehman, A., Kolivand, H., & Sharif, M. (2022). Smart buildings and energy optimization: Integration of IoT and artificial intelligence for sustainable management. *Sustainable Energy Technologies and Assessments, 53*, 102581.

Valencia-Arias, A., García-Pineda, V., González-Ruiz, J. D., Medina-Valderrama, C. J., & Bao García, R. (2023). Machine-learning applications in energy efficiency: A bibliometric approach and research agenda. *Designs, 7*(3), 71. https://doi.org/10.3390/designs7030071

Chapter 5

Integrating Bioengineering Principles in Interior Eco-Design for Promoting Artificial Intelligence (AI) and Sustainable Usability Responsible Functionality

Mai Ahmed Fakhrey Farahat Mousa

Horus University, Egypt and College of Engineering and Information Technology, Onaizah Colleges, Qassim, Saudi Arabia

Abstract

This chapter explores the integration of bioengineering principles in interior eco-design to enhance artificial intelligence (AI) and promote sustainable, responsible functionality. It examines how biomimicry, biophilic design, and other bioengineering concepts improve occupant well-being and reduce environmental impact.

Through a literature review and case studies, the chapter identifies the benefits and challenges of incorporating bioengineering in interior design and proposes a framework for its integration. Findings suggest that bioengineering enhances AI performance and fosters sustainability in interior spaces. This chapter contributes to the emerging field of eco-design, offering insights for designers, architects, and engineers to create intelligent, dynamic, and environmentally responsible interiors.

By understanding human sensory interactions with the environment, designers can adopt a biomimetic approach that aligns with natural systems. Human sensory systems have evolved to respond positively to natural environments, promoting health, comfort, and productivity. Designing interiors that replicate these sensory experiences supports well-being while minimizing environmental impact.

Furthermore, natural systems exhibit inherent sustainability, resilience, and efficiency. Integrating these principles into interior architecture allows for the creation of adaptable, low-impact spaces that function harmoniously with both AI technologies and ecological systems.

Keywords: Bioengineering; artificial intelligence; genetic algorithm; responsible functionality; interior eco-design

1. Introduction

Bioengineering is a discipline that applies engineering principles of design and analysis to biological systems and biomedical technologies. Also is the application of biology principles and engineering tools to make usable and tangible products and designs. A method that uses biotechnology in architecture and interior design combines natural patterns and processes with technology (Chayaamor-Heil & Vitalis, 2021) to create sustainable, aesthetically pleasing, and environmentally friendly designs. Biomimicry, a study of natural patterns, aims to incorporate natural systems into design, resulting in more sustainable and aesthetically pleasing spaces. This paper explores the benefits of biomimicry in architecture and interior design, emphasizing the need to integrate evolutionary theory and simulation-based optimization methods for climate change reduction. Capsule building system–The debtor system–A group of genetic algorithmic techniques that are used to optimize architectural designs over time. Bio-architecture focuses on creating sustainable, adaptable structures using renewable materials (Goel et al., 2014) reducing environmental impact and indoor pollution, promoting prosperity, and using locally accessible, untreated, recyclable materials. Fig. 5.1 outlines the main argument of the chapter.

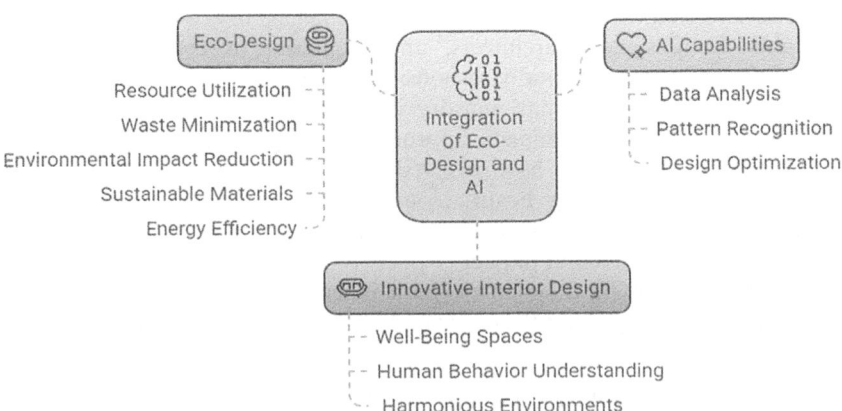

Fig. 5.1. Outline of the Main Argument. *Source:* Analysis by the author.

The natural world, inspired by Leonardo da Vinci's 15th-century bird imitation, has significantly influenced human fields like medicine, engineering, and sustainable design, particularly through bioengineered materials that can self-heal, adapt, and regenerate in response to environmental changes. Evolutionary architecture, a philosophy based on studying nature's processes, living organisms, structures, and materials, focuses on designing spaces that are mobile, responsive, interactive, and flexible, redefining design and construction. Capsule architecture follows a multi-unit building system governed by a dynamic network, where prefabricated units are designed to meet maintenance requirements. Similarly, modular architecture employs a scalable and reusable building system, consisting of a network of units that can be combined to form a complete structure, utilizing natural principles to identify adaptive strategies. Taking a biomimetic approach to architecture and interior design, this study explores the impact of technological advancements on the educational system, particularly in evolutionary architecture trends like biomimicry, adaptive architecture, and generative design, with an emphasis on form and technology. The capsule construction system is based on creating a modular and customizable structure, specifically incorporating the capsule construction system, the debtor system, and the system of genetic algorithms.

This chapter aims to develop an AI-driven model that optimizes eco-design principles for interior spaces. By integrating bioengineering concepts such as biomimicry and biophilic design, the model will focus on maximizing resource efficiency and enhancing human well-being. It will analyze environmental data, material properties, and user preferences to create intelligent and adaptive interior environments. Through a comprehensive evaluation, the study seeks to assess the model's effectiveness in generating sustainable and harmonious spaces, ultimately fostering a stronger connection between humans and nature.

This chapter investigates how bioengineering principles can be effectively integrated into interior eco-design to enhance AI system performance and promote sustainable functionality. It explores the key benefits and challenges associated with implementing biomimetic and biophilic design and aims to develop a framework that optimizes their integration for improved occupant well-being and environmental impact reduction. Additionally, the study examines how AI-driven biomimetic approaches contribute to creating dynamic and sensory-rich interior spaces that replicate natural experiences, supporting both human health and productivity.

This chapter focuses on ecologically sustainable and biomimetic solutions in architecture, particularly their application in AI-enhanced interior eco-design. It examines the role of bio-based materials and AI-driven optimization in reducing energy consumption and carbon footprints while promoting adaptable and resource-efficient spaces. The research highlights the potential of emerging materials, such as bio-composites, in producing free-form geometries and sustainable building elements with low environmental impact. By bridging architecture, engineering, and digital technology, this study aims to establish an innovative approach to designing interior spaces that align with sustainability and human-centric design principles.

The sections of the research start with a literature review and then delve into the methodology and the application to end up with the results, discussion of findings, and recommendations.

2. Literature Review

The study of biological mimicry involves various disciplines, including biology, physics, chemistry, and materials science, to understand biological functions, structures, and principles of nature. This understanding can lead to designs inspired by or derived from living nature, often referred to as "bio-inspiration" or "dynamic design" (Goel et al., 2014). "Nature" has evolved over 3.8 billion years, using low-cost materials for high-performance features. Biological materials are organized at molecular, nanoscale, and macroscopic scales, with complex nanostructures forming functional elements. Designers, materials scientists, and chemists create commercial materials and devices inspired by nature and natural materials.

Biology inspires engineering developments, with biomimicry and bio-technology being key concepts (Goel et al., 2014). Biomimicry involves resembling nature's models and systems to solve complex human problems, while biotechnology uses scientific principles to manipulate living organisms for improved products.

Table 5.1 elaborates that biomimicry, as a field of study, has significantly contributed to the development of renewable energy sources and sustainable building materials by drawing inspiration from nature.

Bioengineering is a new discipline that integrates bio-inspired design into art and architecture, focusing on multiscale solutions to global human problems (Nguyen & Reiter, 2017). It involves a clear approach to design, material selection, principal extraction, and coherence of parts (Chayaamor-Heil & Vitalis, 2021). This interdisciplinary approach develops living materials like bio-concrete and self-healing facades, resulting in sustainable structures.

Genetic algorithms are a computational technique used in architecture to solve complex functional and formal problems, serving as a design tool within the architectural evolutionary system to enhance building performance and its

Table 5.1. Biomimicry, a Field of Study, Has Significantly Contributed to the Development of Renewable Energy Sources and Sustainable Building Materials by Drawing Inspiration From Nature.

Biomimicry	
Bio-inspired design	All these means: Innovation inspired by NATURE
Biomimetic	
Bio-design	

interaction with the surrounding environment (Zari, 2007). Genetics and bio-digital architecture encompass various concepts, including metaphysics and computation, theories of emergence, the fundamentals of genetics, the emergent character of life, eco-manipulation, genetic versus generative approaches, digital tools and organic forms, new bio- and digital techniques, and genetic and bio-digital architectural design.

Information systems in architecture integrate digital tools and organic forms, utilizing technologies such as generative software, parametric-association software, scripting, production tools, and CAD-CAM machining, all of which are essential for project development and advancing design methodologies.

Research on integrating biology in architecture aims to enhance sustainability and reduce waste. Genetic algorithms can expand virtual preliminary studies, and projects like X Phylum and The Recursive Library suggest intelligent network systems for architecture. The project focuses on the post-human era and challenges traditional notions of physical space. By incorporating bionic information and recursive generation, the library can serve as a platform for immersive virtual experiences, blurring the boundaries between the real and digital worlds.

The integration of biological and digital technologies in architecture enhances building performance and functionality (Callegari et al., 2013). This interdisciplinary approach develops living materials like bio-concrete and self-healing facades, incorporating genetic, cyber-digital, and environmental-ecological approaches, resulting in sustainable structures that meet societal needs.

The development of living organisms is a simulation of environmental systems in nature and how to benefit from them in the field of architecture (Callegari et al., 2013). Growth has its own natural laws that make it independent of the will of living beings, and the origin of man in the theory of evolution is that all creatures reproduce from each other over the years because of natural evolution (Goel et al., 2014). Genetics is the science that studies inherited traits and the resulting diversity in living organisms. Art and architecture throughout history have looked to nature for inspiration, as we will see in examples later. However, it's important to note that these forays into neighborhood-inspired design haven't gone far enough. Even these examples fail to take full advantage of what science has to offer.

The table provides an overview of the significant developments in the morphological mass of internal spaces. These advancements have resulted in the creation of geometrically complex spaces that offer a dual sense of pleasure to their users. By examining Table 5.2, we can gain insights into the evolution and transformation of these internal spaces over time (Ripley & Bhushan, 2016).

Notable examples of designs inspired by nature demonstrate the potential of biomimetic materials across various fields. The discovery that hippopotamus sweat contains red and orange pigments with antiseptic qualities and UV protection suggests applications in biomedicine, consumer health products, art, and architecture, despite the mechanisms not being fully understood (Nguyen & Reiter, 2017). Biomimetic research enables the development of optimal designs that leverage evolutionary advancements and promote sustainable resource use,

Table 5.2. Flexibility in the Internal Space Is Achieved by Dealing With Parametric Techniques and Modeling Programs at Various Stages of Design.

The Morphological Mass of Internal Spaces	
Design flexibility as a primary driver of formal flexibility	• The principle of flexibility is the basis of the numerical parametric design, which is achieved in the parametric interior space either structurally by creating design elements that achieve flexibility or in a formative way by dealing well with the design foundations. • The study explores the integration of biological and digital technologies in architecture, focusing on sustainable and innovative designs, utilizing living materials like bio-concrete and self-healing facades.
From expression of design philosophy	• Design philosophy guides designers, focusing on functionality, aesthetics, user experience, and sustainability. It encourages innovation, creativity, and problem-solving to enhance usability and address user needs. • Parametric design techniques have significantly influenced interior design, transformed creativity, and created innovative spaces with rich formations, leading to a shift in design philosophy. • Designers emphasized topological space, a heterogeneous inner space based on Euclidean geometry, creating a curious, interesting emptiness with illusory limits, offering a unique spatial experience.

shaping green science and technology through biologically inspired materials and surfaces. Architecture, fundamentally a practice rather than just a product, integrates interdisciplinary themes to create innovative and evolving fields of study.

3. Methodology

The methodology of this study relied on a qualitative approach to collect information on historical roots of biomimicry and theoretical underpinnings of various levels and design approaches of biomimicry, analyzes and interprets data by looking at how eco-solutions can be used to achieve sustainability in architecture, and uses correlational analysis to assess the strength of the relationship between biomimicry and sustainability (López et al., 2017).

Biomimetic architecture (Zari, 2007) is a cross-disciplinary approach that combines biology and architecture. Architect Göran Pohl and biologist Werner Nachtigall use biological principles as inspiration for architectural solutions. However, finding and applying these principles is challenging, as they need to be abstracted within an interdisciplinary analogy. This process involves three steps: research, abstraction, and implementation.

Engineering applications of hydrophobic surfaces present numerous opportunities across various fields. These surfaces help prevent corrosion in steel components, ensure fabrics and clothing remain dry in rainy conditions, and provide flexibility in controlling microfluidic devices. They also hold potential for new innovations, leading to energy-efficient and sustainable products that are nontoxic and environmentally friendly. Additionally, hydrophobic materials have significant military applications and contribute to advancements in 3D printing, further expanding their impact on modern engineering and technology.

A digital representation of physical or hybrid space in real-time plays a crucial role in various aspects of architecture and construction. From an operational perspective, the Internet of Things (IoT) captures and stores building data for analyzing trends, occupier behaviors, and overall performance. In construction, a highly dynamic environment with numerous assets and phases, real-time monitoring enhances safety, optimizes progress, and anticipates potential issues. Integrating IoT into a 3D environment contextualizes data, improving decision-making and efficiency. While most current applications focus on static environments, integrating digital twins into dynamic construction sites offers additional benefits, such as enhanced safety, quality monitoring, optimized asset and material usage, and waste reduction.

A digital representation of physical or hybrid logical space, architecture, or cities in near real time is shaping the future through AI-driven insights, bio-algorithms, and automation. Future advancements in cyber-thinking and automation will enhance spatial intelligence, optimizing urban and architectural environments. Concepts like digital quintuplets, patterns of data behavior, in-house AI engines, and data warehouses will contribute to a more adaptive and efficient built environment. These technologies will improve human-level performance by integrating AI-driven analysis, enhancing decision-making, and fostering innovation in architecture and urban planning.

4. Case Study Analysis

Through the foregoing, biomimicry is often described as a tool to increase the sustainability of human-designed products, materials, and the built environment. Supposedly, biomimicry methods are applied to implement sustainability in architecture, where eco-solutions are considered to achieve this result more effectively. Therefore, analyzing the following case studies will further clarify the three-dimensional relationship between biomimicry, ecological design solutions, and sustainability.

The lily stem, a lightweight and efficient structure, is not a massive concrete column but an internal Voronoi structure, demonstrating the efficiency of natural design. As humans learn from nature (Ozcam, 2017), we can create structures and systems that mimic the sustainability found in the natural world. The architectural design incorporates natural elements like the Moringa oleifera as a "tree of life" to create a harmonious connection between the structure and the environment. Estevez's innovative approach blurs the lines between biology and architecture, creating a visually stunning design. The south elevation of the ramps features wide arches and a Moringa oleifera as a "tree of life."

Biomaterials, including matter, surfaces, and artificial tissues (Zari, 2007), have been utilized since ancient times and can be derived from nature or synthesized through innovative bioengineering. They play a crucial role in regenerative medicine and tissue engineering, enabling the creation of new organs and replacements (Ozcam, 2017). These materials must be highly resistant to environmental conditions such as heat, pressure, and humidity, possess low friction coefficients for joint applications, and exhibit multifunctionality. Additionally, biomaterials should function under ambient temperature conditions and have the ability to self-heal and adapt to their surroundings. The integration of bio-design principles with systematic bioengineering is essential for developing independent biomaterials. Engineers focus on designing and producing these materials, while scientists emphasize sustainability and adaptation (López et al., 2017). Various raw materials can be used in biomaterial development, including extracellular matrix (ECM); biopolymers such as collagen, alginate, and chitosan; sensitive polymers like polyglycolic acid and polylactic acid; hydrogels such as polyvinyl alcohol; and ceramic materials like calcium phosphate and hydroxyapatite.

Influx Studio has designed Tree Pods, inspired by the Dragon Tree, a unique tree with a large canopy that provides shading and supports solar panels for an air cleaning system (Rian & Sassone, 2014). These tree pods are not designed to replace natural trees but act as small air-cleaning infrastructures, increasing CO_2 absorption (Zari, 2007). The tree pods have a canopy surface that provides shadow and hosts solar panels for energy harvesting. The canopy's branching structure ends with bulbs that multiply contact points between air and CO_2, serving as filters.

Artificial intelligence (AI) has the potential to completely transform society by utilizing computer algorithms capable of performing intricate and interpretative tasks quickly, efficiently, and intelligently. Since these tasks can be quantified, computers can assist in various fields, including geometry, efficient use of space, building material calculations, wind pattern analysis, load-bearing assessments, and foot traffic predictions. When faced with design challenges, AI can generate solutions autonomously, often requiring minimal human intervention. In bio-digital architecture, natural software consists of living elements that undergo automated growth through genetic research, creating self-sustaining spaces and materials. By converting living cells into building materials, genetic design fosters 100% sustainability and eco-friendly construction without manual labor, as structures grow independently. On the other hand, artificial software integrates cybernetic and robotic design, enabling self-construction and adaptive growth. This approach enhances mass production capabilities, reduces construction costs through digital DNA, and promotes architectural flexibility.

Mathias Bengtsson created the cellular chair in 2011, inspired by the natural processes of self-organization. The chair, made of lightweight epoxy, mimics the regeneration of bone tissue, resulting in a lightweight yet sturdy chair. The cellular structure allows for flexibility, strength, and visual appeal. Bengtsson's design showcases the potential of biomimicry in creating functional and aesthetically pleasing objects inspired by nature's efficient and elegant processes.

Biomimicry, a concept based on organisms (Ozcam, 2017), aims to create a built environment that mimics natural processes and functions like an ecosystem. However, it doesn't guarantee sustainability at the material or detail level. Buildings should replicate natural processes and function like an ecosystem during their formation, usage, and eventual demise. To make an architectural project more sustainable (Nguyen & Reiter, 2017), broad ecosystem principles should be used throughout the design process.

5. Results and Discussion of Findings

Interior eco-design, guided by biomimicry principles, allows designers to create sustainable and efficient spaces that mimic the natural world. AI enhances this process by analyzing data and identifying patterns that inform design decisions. By integrating ecological and biological functions, designers can develop spaces that are not only aesthetically pleasing but also sustainable and functional, fostering a more harmonious relationship between humans and nature. Bioengineering, as a multidisciplinary field combining biology and engineering, plays a crucial role in developing new design technologies, sustainable production methods, and renewable energy sources. Bioengineers collaborate with experts across various disciplines to innovate and push scientific and technological boundaries. The integration of AI and interior eco-design represents a transformative trend in sustainable architecture, enabling the creation of environmentally friendly, smart, and efficient spaces. Prioritizing sustainable usability and responsible functionality, user-centric design principles are merged with ethical and innovative practices to reduce environmental impact. Through this approach, digital solutions are developed not only to meet user needs but also to contribute positively to the built environment and the world at large, demonstrating the potential of bioengineering and AI in revolutionizing interior design.

6. Conclusion

Eco-design is a design method that aims to create ecologically friendly and sustainable structures and environments. It entails researching the natural environment and comprehending biological processes to inform the design process. Designers create environments that are practical, sustainable, and environmentally friendly by incorporating ecological and biological processes into their designs. Integrating ecological and biological concepts enables designers to optimize resource utilization, reduce waste, and lessen environmental impact. Eco-design includes the use of renewable, recyclable, or biodegradable materials, as well as the design of places that promote energy efficiency and natural lighting and ventilation.

AI plays a crucial role in advancing eco-design by leveraging data analysis and pattern recognition capabilities. (AI) systems can process vast amounts of data related to environmental factors, material properties, energy consumption, and user preferences to identify patterns and optimize design solutions. This can lead to more efficient and innovative design outcomes that align with sustainability goals. In the context of interior design, AI can revolutionize the way spaces are designed by providing insights into how to create environments that promote well-being, productivity, and connectivity with nature. By utilizing (AI) technologies, designers can better understand human behavior, preferences, and interactions with the built environment, leading to the creation of harmonious spaces that enhance the quality of life. Ultimately, the integration of eco-design principles and artificial intelligence has the potential to not only drive innovation in interior design but also foster a more sustainable and symbiotic relationship between humans and nature.

Biomimicry, as a multidisciplinary approach integrating electronics, biology, chemistry, physics, design, and engineering, leverages advanced technology to study and emulate nature's creative functions and processes. By learning from nature and extracting its fundamental principles and characteristics, designers can apply these insights to solve specific design challenges. The core objective of biomimicry is to achieve sustainability by fostering environmentally responsible design solutions. Future architects and designers must focus on developing bio-inspired design adaptations that emulate nature's best ideas, ensuring that all futuristic buildings are inherently sustainable and aligned with ecological principles.

References

Callegari, C., Bortolaso, C., Piva, A., & Sgarbossa, F. (2013). A methodology for project management and design in construction. *Procedia - Social and Behavioral Sciences, 74*, 46–55. https://doi.org/10.1016/j.sbspro.2013.03.014

Chayaamor-Heil, N., & Vitalis, L. (2021) Biology and architecture: An ongoing hybridization of scientific knowledge and design practice by six architectural offices in France. *Frontiers of Architectural Research, 10*(2), 240–262. https://doi.org/10.1016/j.foar.2020.10.002. Ouci+1ResearchGate+1

Goel, A. K., Vattam, S., Wiltgen, B., & Helms, M. (2014). Information-processing theories of biologically inspired design. In A. K. Goel, D. A. McAdams, & R. B. Stone (Eds.), *Biologically inspired design: Computational methods and tools* (pp. 127–152). Springer.

López, M., Rubio, R., Martín, S., & Croxford, B. (2017). How plants inspire façades. From plants to architecture: Biomimetic principles for the development of adaptive architectural envelopes. *Renewable and Sustainable Energy Reviews, 67,* 692–703.

Nguyen, A. T., & Reiter, S. (2017). Bioclimates in architecture: An evolutionary perspective. *International Journal of Design & Nature and Ecodynamics, 12*(1), 16–29.

Ozcam, I. (2017). Relation between contemporary furniture and technology. *Press Academia Procedia, 4*(1), 300–305.

Rian, I. M., & Sassone, M. (2014). Tree-inspired dendriform and fractal-like branching structures in architecture: A brief historical overview. *Frontiers of Architectural Research, 3*(3), 298–323.

Ripley, R. L., & Bhushan, B. (2016). Bioarchitecture: Bioinspired art and architecture—A perspective. *Philosophical Transactions of the Royal Society A: Mathematical, Physical and Engineering Sciences, 374*(2073), 20160192. https://doi.org/10.1098/rsta.2016.0192

Zari, M. P. (2007). Biomimetic approaches to architectural design for increased sustainability. *The SB07 NZ Sustainable Building Conference.* https://www.evolo.us/artificial-trees-clean-bostons-air-treepods-initiative-influx-studio/. Accessed on November 21, 2023.

Chapter 6

Simulation Analysis of a Hybrid Ventilation System to Improve Internal Air Quality and Energy Performance of Buildings: A Case Study of a Residential Unit in Riyadh City, Saudi Arabia

Najat M.D. Al Ruwaily and Ahmed O.M.S. Mostafa

King Saud University, Saudi Arabia

Abstract

Improving Indoor Air Quality (IAQ) is one of the most, if not the most, essential factors in defeating sick building syndrome (SBS) and achieving the health and well-being of occupants inside the built environment, in which people spend about 90% of their time. Good ventilation is one of the important factors in improving IAQ, and it has been handled by many researchers. In spite of the emerging smart mechanical ventilation systems said to have the power to achieve thermal comfort for internal spaces using minimum energy, it has been reported that the energy consumption of the housing sector is still high, and the IAQ is not up to the healthy levels. This represents the problem and incentive of this chapter, which aims, through a descriptive and experimental methodology, to overcome the challenge of achieving the balance between energy efficiency and healthy IAQ. Results showed that a proposed hybrid ventilation system, natural and mechanical, could achieve the thermal comfort levels of internal spaces while enhancing both the IAQ and the building energy performance. The importance of this chapter emerges from the dual effect of its results related to achieving both sustainability and human well-being.

Sustainability, Resilience, and Inclusiveness through Human-Centred
Architecture and Design, 63–82
Copyright © 2026 Najat M.D. Al Ruwaily and Ahmed O.M.S. Mostafa
Published under exclusive licence by Emerald Publishing Limited
doi:10.1108/978-1-80592-881-220261006

Keywords: Indoor Air Quality (IAQ); sick building syndrome (SBS); ventilation; hybrid ventilation; energy performance; simulation

1. Introduction

Though the building sector is derived from the idea to develop and improve the quality of human life, it is also a source of negative impacts and risks related to users' health, energy, and climate change. Building users are affected by a syndrome called "Sick Building" (SBS), where they often feel unwell and unhealthy without there being a clear medical cause. The building sector is also considered one of the sectors sharing in the global energy crisis. In addition, its effect on climate change is clear due to the nature of its relationship with energy consumption (Mohamed, M. 2019).

SBS describes poor Indoor Air Quality (IAQ) in a building. This causes illnesses to anyone inside the building. This syndrome is caused due to many reasons related to gaseous effects, such as chemicals from cleaning supplies, second-hand smoke, molds, Radon gas emitted from building materials, molds, bacteria, pollen, and other biological pollutants. With the fact that people stay more than 90% of their times inside buildings, the symptoms of this syndrome is more likely to happen, such as headache, cough, fever, skin rash, muscle aches, and sore throat.

Indoor Air Quality (IAQ) has been considered a multidisciplinary phenomenon that is difficult to be defined due to its varying factors, and for this reason. In addition, this topic is broad, and it is not easy to define what is considered good IAQ. However, one general definition of the IAQ was announced by the Unites States Environmental Protection Agency (EPA) as air that is free of harmful concentrations of pollutants and that 80% of its occupants are satisfied with its quality (Türk, 2022). In addition, the EPA has defined three main elements of good IAQ: adequate ventilation, control of air contaminants, and maintaining appropriate thermal comfort (Bas, 2004) ANSI/ASHRAE Standards 62.1 and 62.2 are the recognized standards for ventilation system design and acceptable IAQ. Expanded and revised for 2022, both standards specify minimum ventilation rates and other measures in order to minimize adverse health effects for occupants (ASHRAE, 2022). Sick building users' symptoms may include respiratory problems, including coughs, chest tightness, and shortness of breath; dry, itchy, or irritated eyes, nose, and throat fatigue, headaches; and difficulty concentrating; skin irritations; and general malaise.

In addition to the SBS risk, the building sector is a source of negative impacts related to energy and climate change. As per the EPA, the continuous upward trend of climate change leads to many other risks that impact the building sector: Chronic risks (such as heat waves and sea level rise), Acute risks (such as intense participation and fires), Market risks (reducing attractiveness of assets that have not incorporated climate adaptation not mitigation), and Policy risks (increasing building related cost due to regulations related to addressing climate change impacts) (EPA, 2021). The building sector is also responsible for about 38% of the greenhouse gases that are directly related to human life; it is also considered one of the sectors sharing in the global energy crisis, as it is responsible for about 30–40% of energy consumption worldwide. Its effect on climate change is clear due to the nature of its relationship with energy consumption, where the decrease of the energy consumption of a building influences global and local climate change and vice versa (Santamouris, 2016). In addition, reducing energy consumption would be undoubtedly beneficial (Alardhi et al., 2022).

The case is not different in Saudi Arabia, where the population increase of its major cities led to a parallel increase in energy consumption (Al-Surf et al., 2021; Algarni & Nutter, 2013). Forty-nine percent of the total energy consumption in the residential sector is related to the increased use of mechanical ventilation systems. In spite of the main purpose of using such "smart" systems to achieve thermal comfort and good IAQ of internal spaces with minimum energy, it has been reported that housing residents in Saudi Arabia are highly exposed to indoor air pollutants due to many factors, such as infiltration, indoor equipment, burning of biomass (Arabian incense), poor ventilation, and occupants' daily activities. The increase in energy consumption and the low IAQ of Saudi housing represent the problem and incentive of this chapter, which aims, through descriptive and experimental methodologies, to overcome the challenge of achieving the balance between energy efficiency and healthy IAQ, using simulation techniques on a proposed hybrid ventilation system. The importance of this subject emerges from the dual effect of its results related to achieving both sustainability and human well-being. In addition, it could be considered as one of the important initiatives to achieve Saudi Vision 2030.

This chapter focuses on using simulation techniques to analyze a proposal of introducing a hybrid ventilation system to a case study of a residential unit in Riyadh city, Saudi Arabia, in a trial to explore its impact on improving the IAQ and BEP. For this purpose, the scope will not include the measurement of the physical properties of the internal air to calculate the concentration of different pollutants and determine its quality; instead, it will depend on the fact that increasing the natural ventilation rate of internal space will improve the IAQ of such space but will increase the energy demand. The use of digital simulation applications will try to achieve the balance between improving the IAQ and energy performance: The IAQ will depend on applying natural ventilation as per the results and recommendations of much research, and the energy performance will depend on building physical properties as per the Saudi Building Code (SBC), which specifies the minimum requirements for designing and constructing energy-efficient low-rise residential buildings.

2. Literature Review

According to Awbi (2015), ventilation philosophy has undergone a few transitions throughout the last few decades. It started with an attempt to fully seal an indoor environment with minimum infiltration of outdoor air to conserve energy. The following decade started to notice a decline in IAQ due to the lack of fresh air flow into the buildings, and this is when the term "Sick Building" came to be a "syndrome" (Awbi, 2003). And since people spend most of their time indoors, this is considered and still being considered a serious issue (Sarkhosh et al., 2021).

Due to the nature of this paper dealing with multidisciplinary subjects, the literature review will handle three issues: foundational concepts of "Ventilation, Indoor Air Quality and Energy Consumption", basics of "Natural, Mechanical, and hybrid ventilation systems", and the role of new technologies in supporting architects during design stages "The role of technology and Energy Simulation to enhance Building Energy Performance" (BEF).

IAQ has been considered a multidisciplinary phenomenon due to its varying factors. According to the US standard ASHRAE 62.2 for ventilation and air quality, an acceptable IAQ is the" air toward which a substantial majority of occupants express no dissatisfaction with respect to odor and sensory irritation and in which there are not likely to be contaminants at concentrations that are known to pose a health risk". As per the EPA, IAQ is defined as the air that is free of harmful concentrations of pollutants and that 80% of its occupants are satisfied with its quality (Qataya et al., 2023; Türk, 2022). The EPA has defined three main elements of good IAQ: providing adequate ventilation, controlling the air contaminants, and maintaining appropriate thermal comfort (Bas, 2004).

As the population's growth continues to escalate in Saudi Arabia, so does the need to provide appropriate homes for its occupants. Houses are responsible for about 50% of the total electricity consumption in the Kingdom and on a global scale as well. In 2019, it was reported by the National Development Program that due to the hot climate in the central region of Saudi Arabia, the energy consumed by air conditioning (AC) reached 64% of the total household electricity usage (Krarti et al., 2020). Although the energy consumption has been declining since 2016, mainly due to the government's effort to enforce new regulation, energy efficiency in Saudi buildings still remains low (Al-Qahtani & Elgizawi, 2020).

There is a reverse relation between the use of natural ventilation and the energy demand in buildings. The increased use of natural ventilation leads to reduced pollutant concentration, which results in enhancing the level of IAQ and increasing the energy demand. The reverse is true: to save energy, the rate of natural ventilation should be decreased, which means low levels of IAQ. This paper tries to overcome the challenge of achieving the balance between energy efficiency and healthy IAQ through a proposed hybrid ventilation system.

This energy efficiency crisis is not only a national issue but a global one that has governments and organizations initiating great efforts to address this problem to find the balance between energy consumption and energy demand while considering environmental consequences as well (Esmaeil et al., 2019).

In many smaller buildings, "forced" or "mechanical" ventilation is not used to introduce ventilation air. Instead, natural ventilation, via openable windows and other openings, exhaust fans, and infiltration, is used to provide ventilation air. Infiltration is required as an input to heating and cooling design calculations. This value is often expressed as the natural (unpressurized) Air Changes per

Hour (ACH) at design conditions. In contrast, the air tightness required by code for single-family homes is expressed as the ACH with the building pressurized at 50 Pa (~0.2 inches' water column) (Henderson & Harley, 2022). The recommended ACH50 value in SBC is (4).

Natural ventilation can be greatly enhanced by applying passive design strategies that lead to a reduction of energy consumption in areas of hot-arid climates. These passive strategies include natural ventilation, well-insulated walls and/or walls, shading devices, green roofs, and window glass type.

The improvement effect of Passive Climate Adaptation Measures (PCAMs) was concluded in Anwar et al.'s (2020) combined shading devices, natural ventilation, and a green front wall that resulted in an increase in the thermal comfort of the interior space. Another study found that blocking up to 80% of sunlight by good shading devices led to lowering indoor temperature and up to 30% of air conditioning load (Alozie et al., 2019). Measuring the potential of energy conservation levels after applying passive cooling techniques was tested by Al-Qahtani & Elgizawi (2020), who applied four techniques, including shading devices in the southern facades, insulated double-glazed windows, heat insulator (mineral wool) in the outer walls and roofs, and green roofs. The use of DesignBuilder to simulate both the current condition and the improved conditions after adding each technique individually showed that wall and roof insulation has the maximum effect on reducing the building's cooling load.

Although natural ventilation provides a qualitative advantage of providing a space with "fresh" outdoor air, as well as helps with the reduction of energy consumption, it is difficult to be controlled due to the natural forces of the wind and its direction and to the lack of filtration capabilities. The potential of a natural ventilation system relies on the design of the natural system and the given climate, and the advantages of mechanical ventilation system can be feasible when combined with a natural ventilation system. Over time, the concept of the hybrid ventilation system emerged with an increasing interest (Emmerich et al., 2001). This led to a parallel increase in the number of studies that were conducted regarding effective ventilation systems. Many trends have emerged through the literature, mainly the efficiency of a hybrid ventilation system regarding energy consumption.

To compare between natural and hybrid ventilation, a simulation plan was done using CONTAMR after defining key variables and concluded that natural ventilation improved the air quality only in some regions, whereas the hybrid ventilation system improved performance in all regions (Emmerich & Crume, 2006). In another study, a proposed hybrid ventilation system was installed in an apartment window and led to a decrease of 20% in energy saving while maintaining the concentration levels of CO_2 below maximum levels (Lim et al., 2015). In a similar experiment, where measurements of IAQ variables were recorded and a questionnaire was applied before and after applying a hybrid ventilation system to determine the perceived IAQ and it was concluded that when the mechanical air supply mode was turned on, it improved ventilation in general and led to a decrease in total volatile organic compounds concentrations (Vornanen-Winqvist et al., 2018).

To meet the new building code related to ventilation, air tightness was enhanced, and a self-regulating air inlet device with filter system intervention was installed in an apartment building. It was found that increasing the airtightness of the apartment does not necessarily improve IAQ and that with passive ventilation, filter replacement is necessary for optimal functioning as well as the maintenance of the passive stack duct (Kravchenko et al., 2022).

As observed from the literature, it seems very important to address the application of a hybrid ventilation system in harsh climates similar to that of Riyadh, Saudi Arabia. It is important to address this issue using the split HVAC systems, which are commonly used in Saudi Arabia.

As shown in Fig. 6.1, the challenge of achieving the balance between improving IAQ (which is hard to control and may compromise thermal comfort) and improving thermal comfort by mechanical ventilation (which leads to increasing energy consumption and leads to compromising IAQ) could be overcome by using a hybrid ventilation system with an intelligent control system that could gather and analyze climate data and decide the timing of switching between natural and mechanical ventilation.

Two rectangles, one for improving IAQ and the other for thermal comfort, with a third rectangle representing an intelligent control system to resolve the challenge of achieving the balance between improving IAQ and thermal comfort by using a hybrid ventilation system with an intelligent control system.

Cooling and heating a building account for about 60–70% of a building's energy consumption and the building sector as a whole consumes 40% of energy, world-wide, annually. As a result, in the efforts to conserve energy, architects and designers made efforts to reduce heating and cooling losses by tightening the building envelope. This resulted in the reduction of the ventilation rate, which eventually led to increased air pollution. As this problem continued to grow,

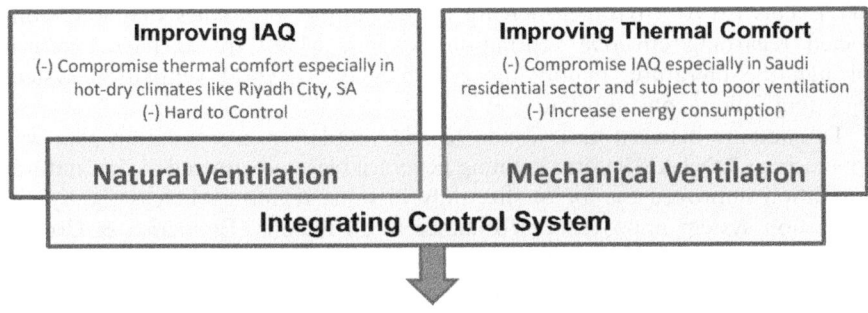

Fig. 6.1. Advantages of Hybrid Ventilation System. *Source:* By authors.

Indoor Air Pollution (IAP) as a study emerged into its own discipline. Computational Fluid Dynamics (CFD) is a simulation application that simulates and measures heat transfer, combustion equipment, turbo-machines, biological flows, and more. It is based on fundamental physics laws that are governed by equations. CFD was not originally invented to study building performances, originally, to estimate the indoor airflow of a building, physical models were made, which were costly and time-consuming. However, since the 1970s, CFD has been used to predict air movement in built environments and, over time has developed into a vital tool to measure IAQ (Shree et al., 2019).

Simulation applications could provide building engineers with information supporting decisions related to energy and thermal comfort, especially when used with Building Information Modeling (BIM) applications during the design, construction, and operation phases, in which the life cycle costs of the building are calculated based on the performance of its systems and materials to achieve a balance between user comfort and energy efficiency and reduce any related cost and time during these stages. Simulation techniques enable the designer to answer questions, graphically and numerically related to different design scenarios, and performance indicators related to many user comfort-related factors such as internal temperature variables, heating and cooling loads, natural lighting, and ventilation levels (Hamdi & Mostafa, 2022; Mostafa & Rashwan, 2022; Talib, 2020; Aljarbou & Mostafa, 2022).

3. Method and Procedures

The chapter adopted a descriptive method in its first part to study the research problem in a theoretical context by reviewing related literature and an experimental methodology in its second part to explore the role of the hybrid ventilation in improving IAQ and the possibility of achieving the balance between natural and mechanical ventilation. The procedures start with choosing both the case study and the appropriate simulation application, then building the case's digital model, inserting it into the simulation application, and then running the simulation before and after applying dual ventilation to achieve the targeted results. Fig. 6.2 shows the procedure of the research.

A flowchart diagram for the research procedures goes from the hypothesis to the software application and case study selection process to the experiment in two steps: the first is a software run for the case baseline, the second is for the proposed hybrid system, and ending with results and recommendations.

The city of Riyadh is the capital of the Kingdom of Saudi Arabia (KSA), the largest in area, the most populous compared to other cities in the Kingdom, and the largest in terms of the number of residential units. Residential buildings of various types, whether apartments or villas, represent about 80% of the total buildings in the city according to land uses (AlJadid & AlHemmedi, 2018). Given that the rate of electrical energy required for air conditioning loads in residential buildings in the city of Riyadh, which amounts to 60.6% of the total electrical energy consumed in the city according to Ministry of Energy reports, exceeds the

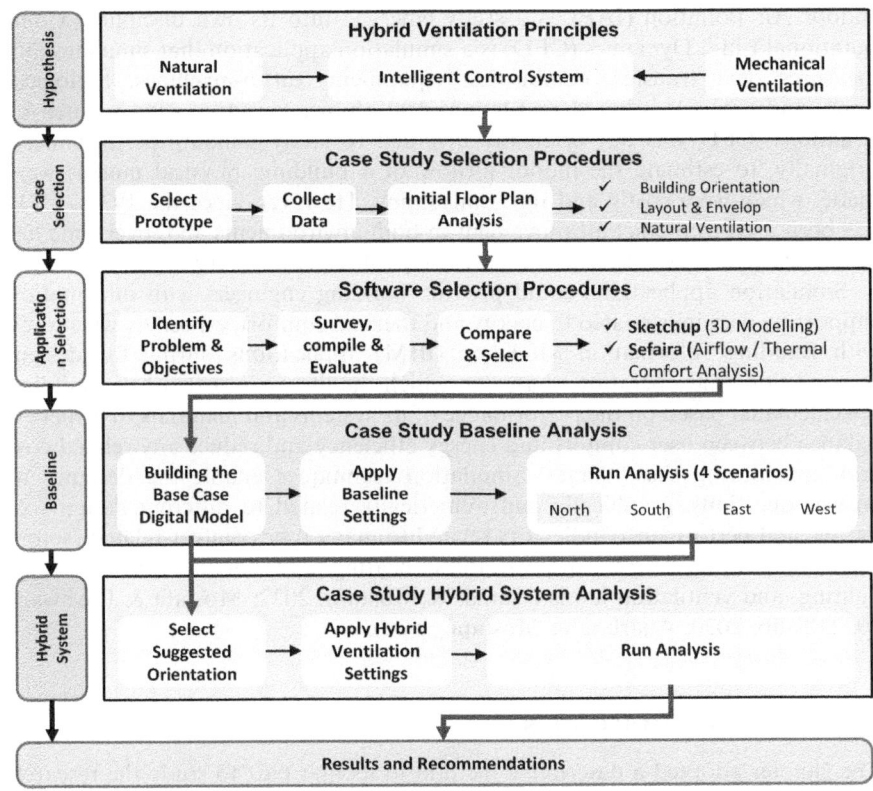

Fig. 6.2. Research Procedures. *Source:* By authors.

rate nationwide, which amounts to 46.9%, one of the models was chosen (Awal Khair). Residential units that were repeatedly selected and implemented within the "Sakani" program initiated by the Ministry of Housing in the Kingdom.

In general, the Kingdom's climate is hot desert, but there is diversity in the nature and characteristics of the climate of each of its regions due to the vast area it covers (shown in Fig. 6.5). The Riyadh region is characterized by a desert climate that is hot and dry in summer and cool and sometimes rainy in winter. With an average annual temperature of 26.6C, it reaches more than 50C in the summer, while it drops to around 0C in the winter. The average relative humidity is 33.1%, and the average rainfall is 84.4 mm annually. The prevailing winds in the city of Riyadh are generally considered to be the northern winds, specifically the northeastern winds, and when they blow actively in the summer or spring, they cause frequent dust and sand storms due to the surrounding desert sand dunes.

To select the most appropriate application for the target experiment, the authors followed the procedures suggested by GoldSim (2017) which begin with clearly defining the problem to be solved and the functional requirements, surveying potential applications, selecting the most suitable applications, conducting a detailed evaluation of each shortlisted application, comparing these applications based on a defined set of criteria, and finally choosing the most suitable application based on the evaluation results.

After well identifying the target objectives, the authors adapt these procedures within three stages: survey and collect related potential applications, filter and eliminate selection, compare and select the suitable application. A survey was done in the first stage to find potential applications that offer CFD and energy analysis simulation, and to review the general features, requirements, and capabilities of each application.

It was noticed from the first round that most of the CFD applications require specialized physics knowledge and are complex and not easy to be used by architects. So, in the second round, a trial to filter and eliminate such complex applications led to three that seem to be more suited for architects and designers: Sefaira, Autodesk CFD, and SIMSCALE CFD. More analysis was done about these three applications to prepare for the third round, in which evaluation criteria were collected from a number of specialized sites, such as (G2, Capterra, and Gartner Peer Insight). The result shown in Table 6.1 led to the selection of Sefaira Systems, which has a plug-in is compatible with both SketchUp and Revit.

To prepare the case digital model for the Sefaira application (Fig. 6.3), the model plane count is required to be less than (<30,000), the plane visibility (as Sefaira analysis only calculates what is visible), and the entity type. After

Table 6.1. The Comparison of the Three Simulation Applications Using Likert Scale (1–5).

#	Criteria	Sefaira	SIMSCALE CFD	AutoDesk CFD
1	User friendly/Easy to learn	5	4	2
2	Popularity in CFD	1	5	3
3	Loading refit model into the application	5	3	5
4	Availability of learning resources	4	3	4
5	License price	4	N/A	2
6	Free educational version	2	4	5
7	Provide split-systems simulation examples	3	4	2
	Average	**3.42**	**3.28**	**3.28**

Source: Authors.

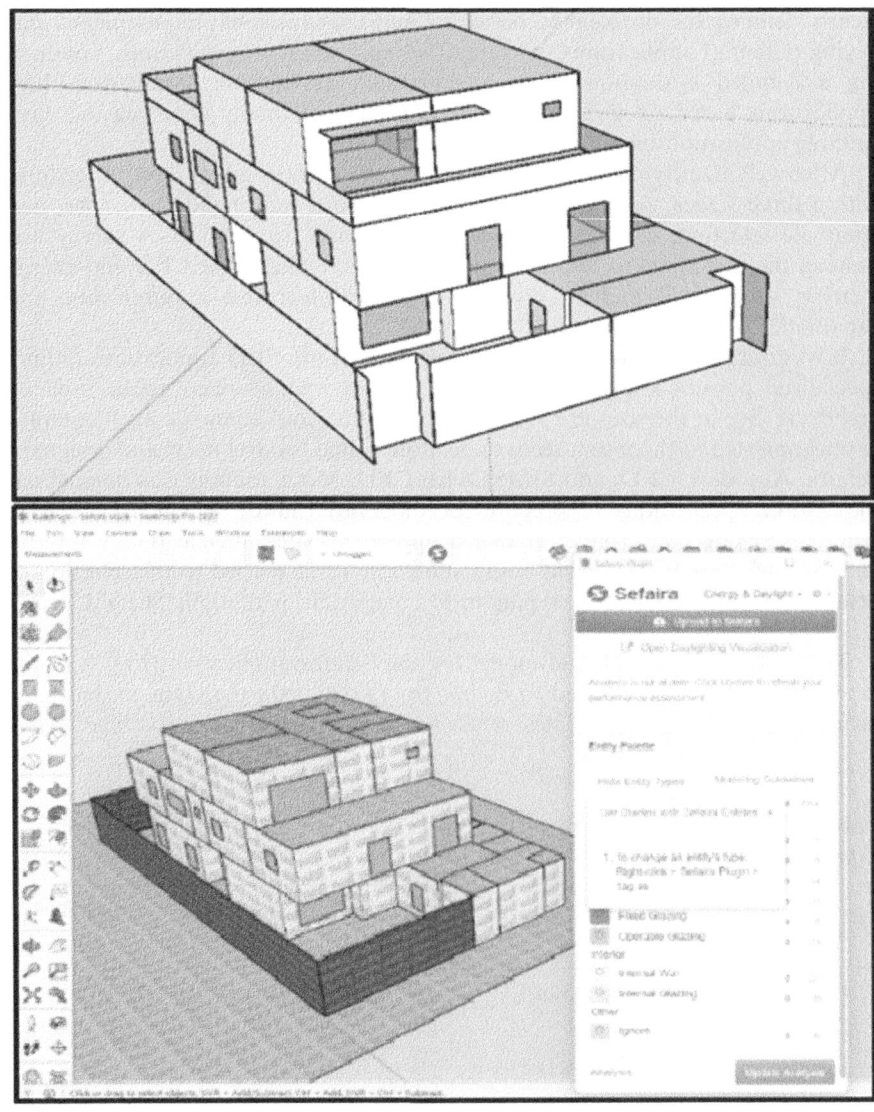

Fig. 6.3 The Progress of Building the Digital Model and Inserting It Into the Simulation Application.

preparing the case digital model up to these considerations, the necessary input information for the plugin was set to get an initial idea of the building performance, and the model was uploaded to the application (Sefaira).

4. Experimental Study and Results

This section includes the application of the experimental simulation for both the case-base unit and the alternative hybrid system proposed to improve the IAQ and BEP.

As a first step, all variables related to the two main components of the case baseline model (shown in Fig. 6.4) were set to the Sefaira application, then the first round simulation run was done, and all related results were documented.

4.1 Round (1) Basic Data

- Occupancy: six people
- Building Orientation: North-West facing (as the case study is a typical unit that is repeatedly used in Riyadh, we used Sefaira application to compare the four directions.

Building Envelope properties: The values highlighted in blue in Table 6.2 are based on an SBC section specifying the minimum requirements for designing and constructing energy-efficient low-rise residential buildings. Of particular focus are the maximum thermal transmittance U-values for residential building envelopes, depending on climatic conditions, where buildings are placed under three climatic zones based on location.

HVAC System Properties: The selected case study uses split units. The related variables of this split are shown in Table 6.3.

- The Ventilation Rate:

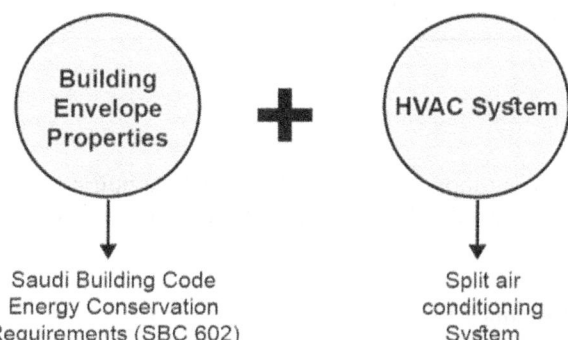

Fig. 6.4.   The Two Main Components of the Case Baseline Model.
Source: By Authors.

Table 6.2. The Building Envelope Values Input Based on the SBC Energy Conservation Requirements for Saudi Climatic Zone (1).

Climate Zone	U-Value (W/m².K)					SHGC Glazing	Infiltration Rate
	Wall	Roof	Floor	Window	Door		
Zone 1	0.342	0.202	0.496	2.668	2.839	0.25	4.0 (ACH50)

Table 6.3. Split System Set Point Values Inputs.

Type	Thermostat Set Point		Operation Time
Split system	For heating: 20 °C	For cooling: 25 °C	24H/7days a week

Table 6.4. Ventilation Rate Calculation.

$Q_{fan} = 0.05\, A_{floor} + 3.5\, N_{oc}$ Where: Q_{fan} = fan flow, L/s A_{floor} = floor Area, m² N_{oc} = Number of occupants **Total Airflow Rate for Whole House –** **≥ The Value in Sefaira is in L/m².s**	Ground Floor: $Q_{fan} = 0.05 \times 224.5 + 3.5 \times 6 = 32.225$ L/s 1st Floor: $Q_{fan} = 0.05 \times 183 + 3.5 \times 6 = 30.15$ L/s 2st Floor: $Q_{fan} = 0.05 \times 91 + 3.5 \times 6 = 25.55$ L/s ≥ 87.925 L/s = 0.18 L/m².s

The minimum outdoor airflow rate for the whole house ventilation is shown in Table 6.4, based on the floor area and number of occupants:

4.2 Results of Round (1)

Running Simulation for the case-based model using the previous input values that were based on the proposed design, location of the building, and the Saudi

Table 6.5. The Energy Consumption Results of the Case Base Model Using Sefaira Web Application (Round1).

Energy Use Per Year (kWh/m²/year): North-West Facing Base-case Building	
EUI	88.53
HVAC energy per unit area	41.44
Annual cooling energy per unit area	26.33
Annual heating energy per unit area	1.48

Building Code Energy Conservation Requirements (SBC 602), Table 6.5 represents the output values of the simulation analysis that was done in Sefaira.

These values will work as a baseline to compare the energy consumption of the suggested intervention strategy, which is the integration of a Hybrid System into the base-case villa.

Through the Sefaira application, a preliminary analysis is possible to investigate the advantages and disadvantages of incorporating a hybrid system into a residential villa. The principles of a hybrid system function by means of an intelligent control system, by which the user can set up the system to automatically switch between mechanical and natural ventilation systems through operable windows and openings to take advantage of the natural passive strategies and save energy. Fig. 6.5 shows the main three components of the alternative model, while Fig. 6.6 shows more details of such an alternative system, highlighting primary components in red and optional components in blue (Heiselberg, 2002).

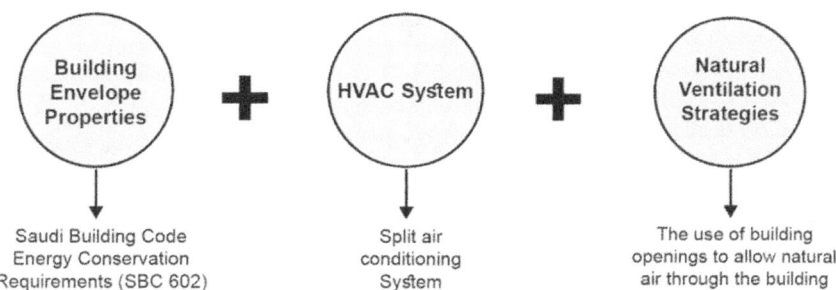

Fig. 6.5. The Three Main Components of the Alternative Model
Source: By Authors.

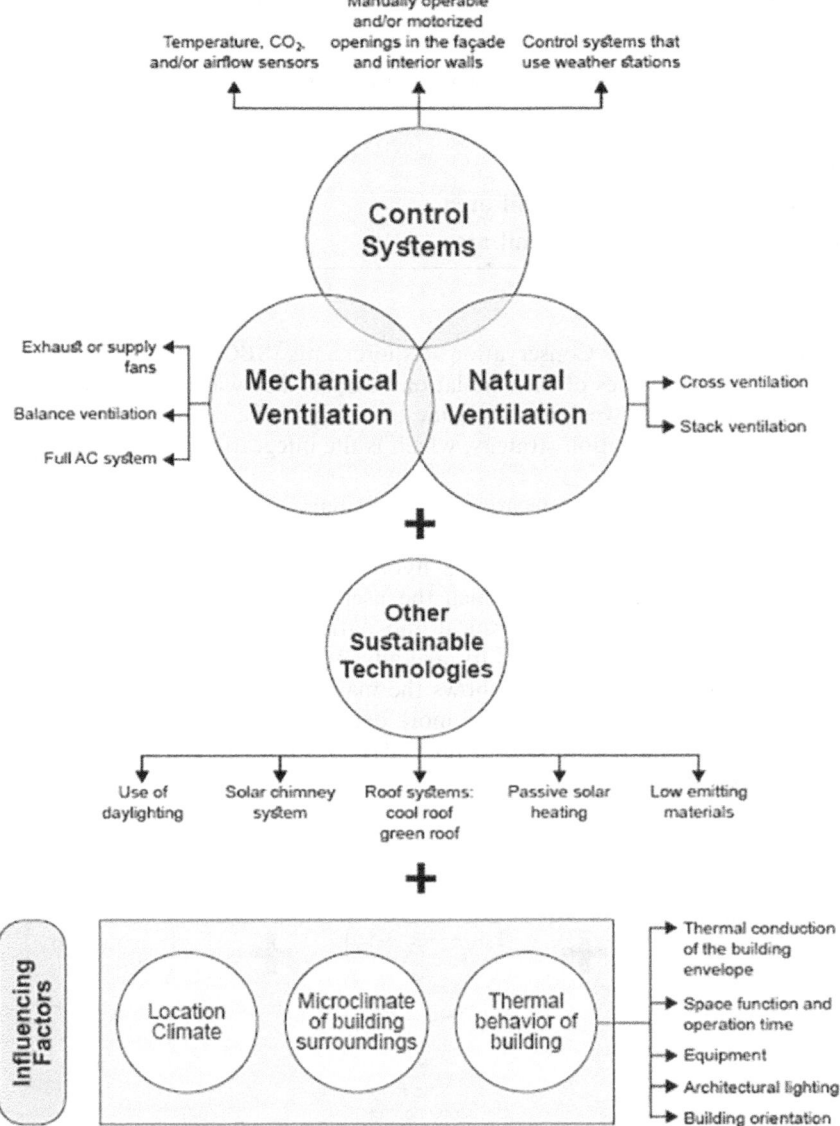

Fig. 6.6. Components of the Hybrid Ventilation System *Source:* By Authors.

Table 6.6. The Input Values for the Building Envelope for the Alternative Model.

Climate Zone	U-Value (W/m².K)			SHGC			Infiltration Rate
	Wall	Roof	Floor	Window	Door	Glazing	
Zone 1	0.328	0.196	0.453	2.668	2.839	0.25	Crack ventilation

Table 6.7. Split System Set Point Values Inputs.

Type	Thermostat Set Point		Operation Time
Split system + Natural ventilation	For heating: 20°C	For cooling: 25°C	24H/7days a week

4.3 Round (2) Basic Data

- Occupancy: six people
- Building Orientation: Northwest-facing
- Building Envelope properties: The values highlighted in blue in Table 6.6 are based on a recent study that was made to analyze the reduction of the u-value of a building envelope that was located in Makkah. This study was chosen due to the similar climate conditions (Alaboud & Gadi, 2022).
- HVAC System Properties: The same split system in addition to using the natural ventilation as shown in Table 6.7.

4.4 Results of Round (2)

In the second round of the simulation analysis, the natural ventilation was incorporated into the base case and the simulation was run. The result is shown in Table 6.8.

5. Discussion and Conclusion

The proposed hybrid ventilation system doesn't have a fixed set, as it should be customized for each climatic zone and building envelope configuration. It also depends on the availability and flexibility of the components.

Table 6.8. The Energy Consumption Results of the Alternative Model Using Sefaira Web Application: Round 2.

Energy Use Per Year (kWh/m^2/year): Northwest-Facing Improved Case Building	
EUI	76.37
HVAC energy per unit area	29.29
Annual cooling energy per unit area	19.98
Annual heating energy per unit area	1.52

For the configuration of physical properties of the building envelope: the minimum requirement of the SBC standards to be used as a baseline for both the IAQ and building envelope performance for energy conservation was (0.342) u-value for the walls, (0.202) for the roofs, (0.496) for the floors, (2.668) for the windows, and (2.839) for the doors, with a (0.25) SHGC for the glazing. The first three values have minimal difference than the case base model.

For the air infiltration rate, the value of the ACH50 for the case base model follows the SBC, which is (4), while in the alternate model, it is considered as a crack ventilation. The introduced natural ventilation in the alternate model could be either manual through operable openings controlled by the user as per the external weather condition (night time as an example) or through a smart system connected to external weather sensors and mechanical control of selected openings in the external envelope to introduce the natural ventilation at the suitable time and period without affecting the internal comfort zone.

As shown in Fig. 6.7, the energy consumption of the AC with the base-case was (41.44 kWh/m2 per year) before intervention and (29.09 kWh/m2 per year) after intervention. The energy consumption of the hybrid system was decreased by 14% compared with the base case. Although the Sefaira program doesn't provide capabilities of measuring the IAQ, the author was able to manually measure the minimum requirement of the ventilation rate, which was entered as data input for the simulation analysis. Previous studies had found that the hybrid ventilation system provides both better quality in the indoor air and energy conservation. Our study found that the hybrid ventilation system improves IAQ and conserves energy as well; however, the amount of energy conserved in the current study was less than that found in previous studies.

The difference in climate and geography between the areas in which previous studies were conducted and those of the current study may explain the variation in results.

One of the advantages of the current study is that it provided preliminary data proving that IAQ can be maintained while conserving energy. This data is necessary since no data regarding this topic in the Saudi local climate zone had previously been available. In the same regard, the current study found that the

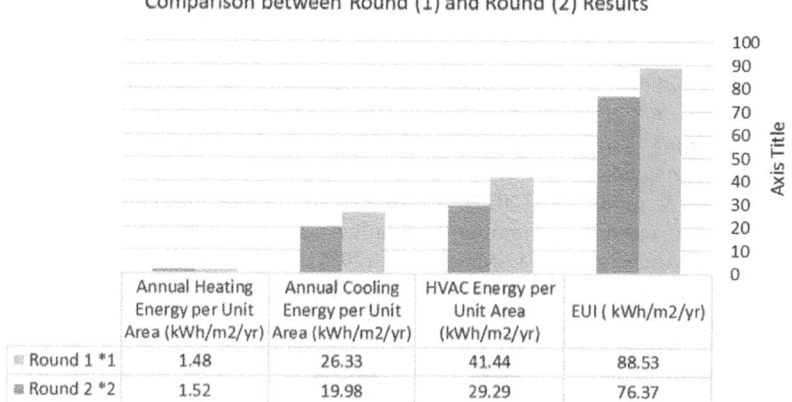

Fig. 6.7. A Comparison of the Energy Consumption Results of the Two Rounds. *1 Northwest-Facing Case Baseline Building. *2 Northwest-Facing Case Baseline Building + Hybrid.

Sefaira application maintains air quality; however, there is no proof that it can actually improve it.

To get the most benefit from this paper, there are some recommendations for some related agencies and bodies: First, the Governmental Agencies should consider, in the code and regulations, varying levels of incentives for applying an intelligent hybrid ventilation systems in existing or new houses. Second, the educational institutions should consider increasing the time allocated for practical applications to enhance students' related knowledge and skills. Third, research bodies should consider the need for IAQ systems' evaluative studies. Fourth, media authorities should work in coordination with related bodies to design advertising campaigns illustrating the advantages and benefits of natural ventilation on health and energy cost. Fifth, engineering consulting offices should encourage owners and users to use intelligent hybrid ventilation and clarify its advantages on health and energy cost (with consideration of dust control). The sixth recommendation is directed to application developers to consider resolving limitations and challenges facing Architects during the process of designing effective hybrid ventilation systems for different types of buildings.

References

Al-Jadeed, M., & Nasser, Al-H. (2018). The effect of thermal insulation in walls on the thermal performance of buildings in the city of Riyadh. *Journal of Al-Azhar University Engineering Sector, 13*(49), 1529–1542.

Al-Qahtani, L. A. H., & Elgizawi, L. S. E. (2020). Building envelope and energy saving case study: A residential building in Al-Riyadh, Saudi Arabia. *International Journal of Low Carbon Technologies, 15*(4).

Al-Surf, M., Balabel, A., Alwetaishi, M., Abdelhafiz, A., Issa, U., Sharaky, I., Shamseldin, A., & Al-Harthi, M. (2021). Stakeholder's perspective on green building rating systems in Saudi Arabia: The case of LEED, Mostadam, and the SDGS. *Sustainability, 13*(15).

Alaboud, M., & Gadi, M. (2022). Evaluation of indoor thermal environmental conditions of residential buildings in Saudi Arabia. *Energies, 15*(5).

Alardhi, A., S Alaboodi, A., & Almasri, R. (2022). Impact of the new Saudi energy conservation code on Saudi Arabia residential buildings. *Australian Journal of Mechanical Engineering, 20*(5), 1392–1406.

Algarni, S., & Nutter, D. (2013). Geospatial representation of the residential energy use in Saudi Arabia. In *Proceedings of the 2013 ASME Early Career Technical Conference (ECTC)*. Tulsa, Oklahoma, USA.

AlJadid & AlHemmedi. (2018). The effect of thermal insulation on the thermal performance of buildings in Riyadh. *Journal of Al Azhar University Engineering Sector (JAUES), 13*(49).

Aljarbou, R., & Mostafa, A. (2022). BIM & BEM for a net zero energy house model case study: A housing unit in Riyadh. SA. *Journal of Engineering Research (JER), 6*(4), 56–66.

Alozie, G., Ifebi, O., & Ukwuoma, E. (2019). Environmental control system (ECS): A review of the effectiveness of shading devices as environmental control system's component in enhancing thermal comfort in buildings. *International Journal of Innovative Research in Education, Technology & Social Strategies* (IJIRETSS), 6(1).

Anwar, M. W., Ali, Z., Javed, A., Din, E. U., & Sajid, M. (2020). Analysis of the effect of passive measures on the energy consumption and zero-energy prospects of residential buildings in Pakistan. *Building Simulation, 14*, 1325–1342.

ASHRAE (2022). *Standards 62.1 & 62.2: Ventilation and acceptable indoor air quality in residential buildings (ANSI approved)*, American Society of Heating, Refrigerating and Air-Conditioning Engineers (ASHRAE), Available on https://store.accuristech.com/ashrae/standards/ashrae-62-2-2022?product_id=2501064 (Accessed on January 6, 2024)

Awbi, H. B. (2003). *Ventilation of buildings (5th ed.*. Routledge.

Awbi, H. B. (2015). Ventilation and air distribution systems in buildings, *Frontiers of Mechanical Engineering*, Available on https://www.researchgate.net/publication/276126485_Ventilation_and_Air_Distribution_Systems_in_Buildings (Accessed on January 6, 2024).

Bas, E. (2004). *Indoor air quality: Guide for facility managers* (2nd ed.).

Emmerich, S. J., & Crume, J. (2006). Simulated performance of natural and hybrid ventilation systems in an office building. *International Journal of Heating Ventilation Air Conditioning and Refrigerating Research, 12*(4), 975.), PP.

Emmerich, S. J., Dols, W. S., & Axley, J. W. (2001). *Natural ventilation review and plan for design and analysis tools*, US Dept. of Commerce, Technology Administration. National Institute of Standards and Technology (NIST).

Esmaeil, K. K., Alshitawi, M. S., & Almasri, R. A. (2019). Analysis of energy consumption pattern in Saudi Arabia's residential buildings with specific reference to Qassim region. *Energy Efficiency, 12*, 2123–2145.

GoldSim Technology Group (2017). *Selecting simulation software* [online] Available from https://www.goldsim.com/Web/Products/SelectingSimulationSoftware/ (Accessed on January 6, 2024)

Hamdi, A. N., & Mostafa, A. O. M. S. (2022). Top trends and challenges of digital technologies to enhance the efficiency of building thermal insulation and the reality of its application in Riyadh, Saudi Arabia. *Emirates Journal for Engineering Research, 27*(2). Article 3.

Heiselberg, P. K. (2002). *Principles of hybrid ventilation. R / Institut for Bygningsteknik No. R0207.* Aalborg Universitet.

Henderson, H., & Harley, B. (2022). Infiltration guidance for buildings at design conditions. *NYS Clean Heat Program.* Available from https://cleanheat.ny.gov/assets/pdf/infiltration-guidance-for-buildings-at-design-conditions.pdf

Krarti, M., Aldubyan, M., & Williams, E. (2020). Residential building stock model for evaluating energy retrofit programs in Saudi Arabia. *Energy, 195.*

Kravchenko, I., Kosonen, R., Jokisalo, J., & Kilpeläinen, S. (2022). Performance of modern passive stack ventilation in a retrofitted Nordic apartment building. *Buildings, 12*(2).

Lim, Y. H., Yun, H. W., & Song, D. (2015). Indoor environment control and energy saving performance of a hybrid ventilation system for a multi-residential building. *Energy Procedia, 78*, 2863–2868.

Mohamed, M. (2019b). Saving energy through using green rating system for building commissioning. *Energy Procedia, 162*, 369–378. https://doi.org/10.1016/j.egypro.2019.04.038

Molina, C. (2020). *A data analysis of the Chilean housing stock and the estimation of uncertainty in indoor air quality in Chilean houses,* PhD Thesis, Available from https://www.researchgate.net/publication/337499017_A_data_analysis_of_the_Chilean_housing_stock_and_the_estimation_of_uncertainty_in_indoor_air_quality_in_Chilean_houses (Accessed on January 6, 2024).

Mostafa, A., & Rashwan, Y. (2022). BIM and digital simulation in assessing window alternatives for enhancing heat performance of building facades - case study: A housing unit in Riyadh, SA. *Journal of Engineering Research (JER), 6*(4), 249–257.

Qataya, R., Mohamed, M. A., AlShanwany, h., & sabbour, S. (2023). A framework for enhancing natural ventilation in hot-arid regions: A bioclimatic design approach. *The Egyptian International Journal of Engineering Sciences and Technology.* https://doi.org/10.21608/eijest.2023.209023.1225

Sakani Portal (2024). *List of design profiles, Awal Khair villa brochure,* Available from https://sakani.sa/app/design-profiles/9 (Accessed on January 6, 2024).

Santamouris, M. (2016). Innovating to zero the building sector in Europe: Minimising the energy consumption, eradication of the energy poverty and mitigating the local cli-mate change. *Solar Energy, 128*, 61–94.

Sarkhosh, M., Najafpoor, A. A., Alidadi, H., Shamsara, J., Amiri, H., Andrea, T., & Kariminejad, F. (2021). Indoor Air Quality associations with sick building syndrome: An ap-plication of decision tree technology. *Building and Environment, 188.*

Shree, V., Marwaha, B. M., & Awasthi, P. (2019). Assessment of indoor air quality in buildings using CFD: A brief review. *International Journal of Mathematical, Engineering and Management Sciences*, 4(5), 1154–1168.

Talib, M. A. (2020). The role of technology in investigating the performance of local architecture, the marsh structures as an example. *Journal of the Association of Arab Universities for Engineering Studies and Research*, 29.

Türk, B. (2022). Important factors affecting the quality of indoor air and a bibliometric analysis. *Sakarya University Journal of Science*, 26(3).

Vornanen-Winqvist, C., Salonen, H., Järvi, K., Andersson, M. A., Mikkola, R., Marik, T., Kredics, L., & Kurnitski, J. (2018). Effects of ventilation improvement on measured and perceived indoor air quality in a school building with a hybrid ventilation system. *International Journal of Environmental Research and Public Health*, 15(7).

Weather Spark (2024). Riyadh climate, *Weather by month, average temperature, Saudi Arabia*. Available from https://weatherspark.com/y/104018/Average-Weather-in-Riyadh-Saudi-Arabia-Year-Round (Accessed on January 6, 2024)

Chapter 7

Differential Pressure Effect on Air Flow Through the "Takhtabush"

Mady Mohamed

Effat University, Saudi Arabia

Abstract

People have tried from ancient times to adapt their buildings to the harsh climate in the hot–dry zone by reducing heat impacts. They used to open their houses onto a private internal open space that was visually and acoustically separated from the outside, called Sahn "The courtyard." The courtyard helps maintain cooled indoor temperatures by employing the stack effect phenomenon. Clean, oxygen-rich air for breathing is human life's most pressing environmental requirement. The Takhtabush, "A covered outdoor sitting area at ground level," was introduced to the traditional courtyard to ensure the airflow. It is located between the courtyard and the back garden, opening completely onto the courtyard and through a Mashrabiya onto the back garden, which ensures a steady flow of air by convection. Since the back garden is bigger and has more sunlight, it will heat up faster than the courtyard. The sun's radiation will make air movement and create a cool air flow in the Takhtabush, leading to the courtyard. However, the orientation of the building is also a big matter when using Takhtabush. Knowing the good wind and the sunlight orientation will surely affect the way it works. This chapter aims to investigate the effectiveness of the size of the backyard and its exposure to solar radiation on the thermal performance of the courtyard on the urban scale. The expected results confirm quantitatively and qualitatively the importance of employing the Takhtabush with the exposed-to-sun backyard to enhance the thermal performance of the open courtyard.

Keywords: Passive cooling; traditional measures; low energy architecture; thermal comfort; hot arid zone; courtyard; thermal performance; Takhtabush

1. Introduction and Research Background

The achievement of adequate Indoor Environment Quality (IEQ) lies at the core of every debate about the built environment of buildings (Fathy, 1986). There are fundamental relationships between climate, comfort, and the role of architecture, as described by the Vitruvian tripartite model of the environment (Hawkes, 2002). This is very important since poor environmental performance of buildings can negatively affect occupants. McMullan (McMullan and Seeley, 2007) identified this effect as a temporary illness that could be called building-related illness, tight building syndrome, office eye syndrome, or, more generally, Sick Building Syndrome (SBS). The latter term is recognized by the World Health Organization (WHO) (WHO, 2003). The SBS is a misnomer because buildings do not get sick, but rather building occupants can exhibit symptoms associated with being ill. The WHO identified a range of symptoms associated with SBS that cause genuine distress to some building occupants but cannot be clinically diagnosed and, therefore, cannot be medically treated. They typically include a stuffy nose, dry throat, chest tightness, lethargy, loss of concentration, blocked, runny or itchy nose, dry skin, watering or itchy eyes, and headache (Mohamed, 2009). Unhealthy spaces with poor environmental quality were found to lead to absenteeism among staff and pupils in school buildings and negatively affect the performance of children and their schoolwork, as well as the whole educational process (McMullan and Seeley, 2007). Several factors contribute to SBS, such as chemical pollutants, microbial growth, and physical discomfort (McMullan and Seeley, 2007). Physical comfort conditions include uncomfortable temperature, low humidity, low air movement and stuffiness, low ventilation rates, insufficient negative air ions, unsuitable lighting and decoration, insufficient daylight levels, uncomfortable seating, excessive noise levels, and high electromagnetic radiation from electrical services and appliances (McMullan and Seeley, 2007). According to Baker (Baker and Steemers, 2002), "the pursuit of comfort is a basic drive in human behaviour, evolved for the purpose of survival, and it is not just a sign of wimpishness." Also, according to the Chartered Institution of Building Service Engineers (CIBSE), the term comfort is defined as "that condition of mind that expresses satisfaction with the environment" (CIBSE, 1999).

The most important environmental requirement for human life is clean, oxygen-rich air for breathing (Allen, 1995). The true role of architects is to design buildings that improve people's lives, and nothing is more vital than natural air. We can achieve good air quality in our buildings by using a variety of environmental design techniques, one of the most well-established and successful being the Takhtabush element, "A covered outdoor sitting area at ground level." It is an important component of the Arab house that ensures a steady flow of air through convection (Figs. 7.1 and 7.2).

Differential Pressure Effect on Air Flow 85

Fig. 7.1. The Takhtabush of Al-Souhimi House, Cairo. *Source:* Mohamed (2018).

Fig. 7.2. Interior Image of the Takhtabush. *Source:* Mohamed (2018).

It is a good thing that our built environments have the Takhtabush as part of many designs in reality, but it is imperative that we know how it operates. It is crucial to comprehend the science underlying these measures in order for them to be effective; otherwise, neither the building nor the people using it will gain. The heated air rises because of the stack effect, which is caused by hot air being lighter than cool air. The phenomenon of the stack effect is employed in the courtyard way to enhance thermal comfort by producing cool breezes (Wazeri, 2002). It is crucial to know that the main driver for the airflow is the difference in air temperature, which causes the differential pressure, where air pressure is caused by the unequal heating of the earth's surface. Low pressure is warm, moist air that rises and forms clouds, while high pressure is cold, dry air that sinks and creates clear skies. The Takhtabush is well-working when the backyard is larger and thus less shaded than the courtyard, and the air heats up more readily there than in the courtyard. The heated air rising in the backyard draws cool air from the shaded

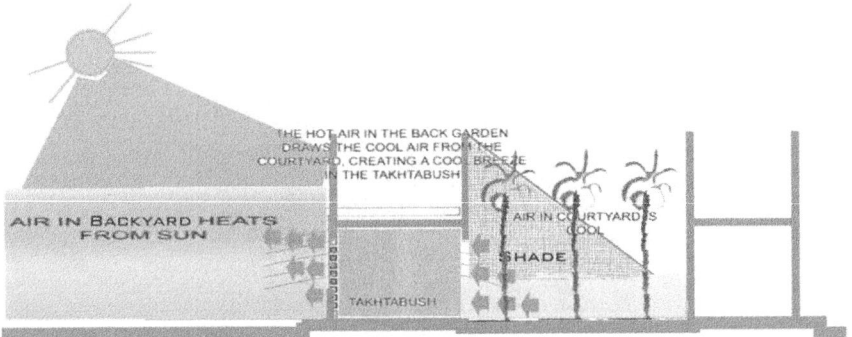

Fig. 7.3. The Airflow From the Shaded Courtyard to the Backyard Through the Takhtabush. *Source:* Mohamed (2018).

courtyard through the Takhtabush, creating a steady cool breeze (Fathy, 1986). Fig. 7.3 illustrates the created airflow through the Takhtabush. The idea of the Takhtabush, in case there is not enough area for a large backyard, could be replaced by another design measure (tool), such as the solar chimney.

The current research aims to investigate the effectiveness of the size of the backyard and its exposure to solar radiation on the thermal performance of the courtyard on the urban scale. The research tries to achieve this through defining the design properties of the courtyard and the Takhtabush through an analytical literature review and through conducting a field study using two scenarios of the courtyard/backyard in the urban context.

2. Literature Review

Many attempts have been made to look into traditional ways of dealing with climate in the hot–dry zone. Several factors control human comfort and make what is known as the "human thermal environment." Mohamed (Mohamed, 2009) conducted a wide review of these factors and found that they can be divided into two main categories: factors related to the individual and other factors related to the environment. The human factors include clothing level and activity level. Environmental factors "which could be lie partially under the architect's control" include air temperature, Mean Radiant Temperature (MRT), relative humidity, and air velocity (McMullan and Seeley, 2007). According to Givoni (Givoni, 1998), several design details affect the thermal performance of buildings in the hot–dry zone, which in turn affects human thermal comfort. These are (i) internal and attached open spaces, (ii) orientation of main spaces and windows, (iii) window size, location, and details, (iv) the layout of the building's plan, (v) shading devices, (vi) the color of the building's envelope, (vii) building's materials, and (viii) vegetation around and inside the buildings.

Ventilation devices, roof construction, and humidification strategies can also be added to the above list (Mohamed, 2009). The passive cooling devices that can enhance the state of thermal comfort inside buildings are (Fathy, 1986; Givoni, 1998; Mohamed, 2010; Oliver, 1997, 2003):

Sahn/hosh: The Courtyard.
Malkaf: A wind catcher.
Nafora: The Fountain.
Shesh: The Venetian blinds.
Takhtabush: A covered outdoor sitting area at ground level.
Mushrabiya: Open wooded lattice screens.
Rasha/taka: A small opening at the upper level of a wall.
Salsabil: A water-fed cooling plate.
Shuksheika: The vented or fenestrated lantern over the main hall.

Oliver (1997, 2003) presented and discussed the main features of traditional buildings in Egypt in terms of structure, materials, and styles. He also mentioned some passive ways that the Egyptians adopted in their buildings, such as the Mashrabiya, hosh, durqa'ah, and courtyard. Fathy (1986) discussed the principles and presented examples of natural energy and vernacular architecture in hot arid climates. He categorized the passive techniques into three main categories based on three main strategies; passive solar, natural ventilation, and evaporative cooling. The environmental performance of government primary schools in Egypt was investigated, and it was found to be very poor (Mohamed et al., 2005). In a following study, Mohamed (2009) confirmed that using some appropriate passive strategies and measures within the façade skin could enhance the thermal performance of the case studies by 13%. Mohamed et al. looked into the technical and social factors that led to the decline of earth architecture in the Sahara desert (Mohamed et al., in review). The results suggested a strong possibility of reusing earth architecture from the environmental point of view. However, a number of limitations were identified, including durability, buildability, and the attractiveness of the mud architecture to the locals. Filippi (2006) analyzed the main characteristics of the urban pattern and buildings' typologies of the traditional earth architecture in two settlements of El Dakhla oasis. Iscandar (Iscandar, 2006) presented some neo-vernacular case studies of Michael Graves, Hassan Fathy, and Ramses Wissa Wassef Iscandar suggested that those examples show respect to the site, the natural environment, and the climate, and were successful in mixing traditional techniques with contemporary requirements.

Houses represent the background or framework for human existence (El-Shorbagy, 2010). Throughout history, people have tried to adapt their buildings to the harsh climate in the hot–dry zone by reducing heat impacts (Mohamed et al., 2010). They used to open their houses to a private internal open space that was visually and acoustically separated from the outside, called the Sahn "courtyard" (Afify, 2002), which serves a variety of social and cultural needs (Al-Naim, 2006). Akbar (Akbar et al., 1982) claimed that the courtyard in

Islamic culture helped maintain a balance between privacy and socialization, as the public and private worlds were intertwined. Consequently, it serves as a focal point of family gatherings that provides a link between the family and the community, operating as an outdoor space and allowing interaction with private visitors (Bahammam, 1987).

In the Saudi context, a typical traditional Saudi dwelling—in the Najdi and Al-Ah'saa' regions—is compacted and adjacent to one another, conveying the impression that these homes are clustered together, and close proximity is considered a key characteristic of traditional settlements located in a desert environment (Al-Naim, 2023). As a rule, cities consist of residential blocks with several houses in each block, and because these buildings are adjacent in each block, the residents establish a binding agreement through the use and construction of common and shared walls in each block (Akbar, 1998; Husin, 2016). The social factors played a significant role in shaping the dwelling and the surrounding built environment, as the tribal social system contributed to the adhesion and dialogue between the buildings. In addition, the layout of each traditional dwelling was oriented entirely inward, with the courtyard being the main private interior space of the dwelling (Al-Naim, 2023).

With some modifications to the courtyard, such as using water and vegetation in its landscape, the benefits can be maximized, particularly the thermal performance benefits. In the evening, the warm air of the courtyard, which was heated directly by the sun and indirectly by the warm buildings, rises and is gradually replaced by the already-cooled night air from above. This cool air accumulates in the courtyard in laminar layers and seeps into the surrounding rooms, cooling them (Wazeri, 2002). In the morning, the air of the courtyard, which is shaded by its four walls, and the surrounding rooms heat slowly and remain cool until late in the day when the sun shines directly into the courtyard (Fathy, 1986). Three factors influence the capability of the courtyard (Wazeri, 2002): the depth of the form, defined by the ratio of the courtyard's perimeter to its height; the elongation of the plan, determined by the length-to-width ratio; and the openness to the sky, measured by the ratio of the top area to the bottom area of the courtyard.

Previous studies (Wazeri, 2002, 2003) show that the rectangular shape of the courtyard's plane is better than the square one. They also recommended that the ratio between the length, width, and height must not be less than 1:2:1.4. Moreover, they said that the best orientation to the courtyard is by orienting the long side to the east-west. In addition, it can decrease the air temperatures of the courtyard by shading the plane with wide canopy trees, shading the walls by climbing plants, and moistening the floor. A recent study (BMT Fluid Mechanics, 2007), concerned with the effects of surface openings on the airflow caused by wind in courtyard buildings, suggested that openings should be in the upwind and downwind surfaces to achieve maximum air velocity. It added that the larger the upwind surface openings, the more the velocity increases significantly.

In a previous research, the author of the current research (Mohamed, 2017) confirmed in a previous work the effectiveness of utilizing the idea of the stack effect phenomenon with other passive strategies. The results of this work revealed an enhancement of 16% over the total hours of the year for human thermal comfort, while energy consumption was reduced by 12%. In another work by the author, Mohamed (Mohamed, 2018), which examined the effect of the Takhtabush on the internal courtyard thermal performance, he confirmed a significant enhancement for the courtyard when attached to the Takhtabush. The Predicted Mean Vote (PMV) and the Predicted Percentage Dissatisfied (PPD) were much better when utilizing the Takhtabush by 25%, which confirms the effectiveness of employing the concept of the Takhtabush in today's designs in the hot zones of the world.

3. Research Methodology

In order to achieve the goal of the research, theoretical and field studies have been adopted from a well-designed scientific research methodology that has been published by the author (Mohamed, 2009, 2010, 2013; Mohamed et al., 2010; Mohamed and Gado, 2006, 2014). This methodology is concerned with the process of quantifying the effectiveness of passive techniques. It includes three main studies: a theoretical study, a field study, and a computer-based study.

The theoretical study is employed in order to identify the design targets and propose successful strategies and measurements for achieving design goals. An intensive descriptive and analytical theoretical study is conducted. The different types of courtyards and Takhtabush are analyzed, where design lessons could be extracted. The parameters that govern the airflow inside these amazing architectural elements are analyzed to identify the significance of each one of them.

The field study is employed to measure and quantify the effectiveness of the current passive techniques. Full-scale experimentation is the oldest method used to assess a physical phenomenon and supplies unarguable information. Collecting information to assess the environmental performance or comparing a mathematical model with in-site measurements was appropriate. The advantage of the experimental approach is that it deals with reality, and therefore, errors are limited to experimental procedures. Effat University campus—Jeddah, KSA—has been chosen for this study. Two different courtyards with the same orientation, size, and specification are chosen. The only difference between them will be their connectivity with the Takhtabush. Two similar shaded courtyards were selected, while the backyard for each is different (Figs. 7.4 and 7.5).

For Case #A, its backyard is bigger in size and sunny most of the time.
For Case #B, its backyard is also shaded most of the time.

Environmental equipment and data loggers for air temperature, humidity, MRT, and air velocity were utilized (Fig. 7.6).

Fig. 7.4. The Selected Location of the Two Case Studies by the Author After "Google Earth".

Fig. 7.5. Pictures for the Selected Locations Captured by the Author.

To test the performance of the two courtyards, the following were applied by the students of the Energy & Design Course "ARCH 453" (Fig. 7.7).

- Choosing the three different points in each space based on the following:
- One main central point in both spaces. There are two points, one in the courtyard and another in the backyard, with the same distance in each space.
- Measuring the air temperature, CO_2 level, MRT, humidity, and wind speed by using data loggers and handheld equipment.
- Writing the results in a printed table at every measuring time from 9:00 a.m. to 5:00 p.m.

As mentioned in the introduction, it is crucial to know that the main driver for the air flow is the difference in air temperature, which causes the differential pressure where air pressure is caused by the unequal heating of the earth's surface. Fig. 7.8 illustrates the average air temperatures of the two spaces over the selected three locations of measurements. It is very clear from the figure that the air temperature of the third point in scenario A (31.11 C°) is much higher than

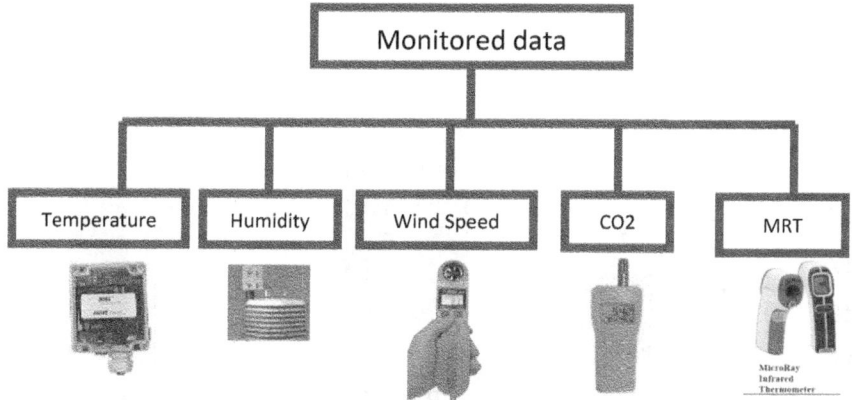

Fig. 7.6. Environmental Equipment and Data Loggers Utilized in the Field Study.

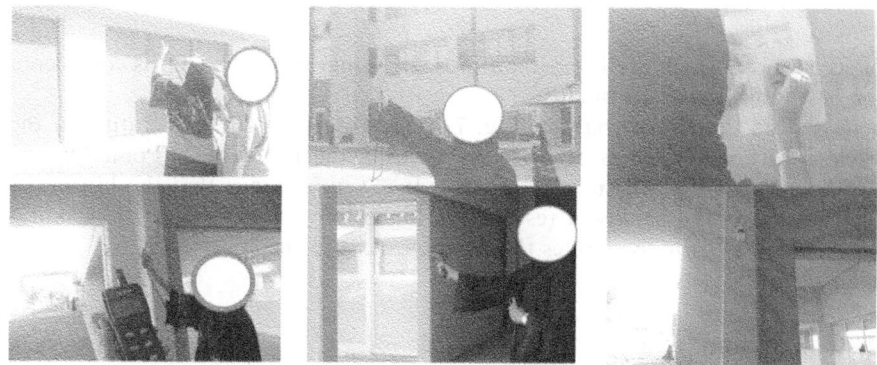

Fig. 7.7. Monitored Data in the Field Study.

the same point in scenario B (28.6 C°), with more than a 2-degree difference, while it is slightly higher for the second point and less for the first point. This is because the backyard in scenario A is bigger and more exposed to the sun without enough shading compared to scenario B.

Fig. 7.9 illustrates the analysis of the average humidity, air velocity, and CO_2 levels in the two scenarios over the selected three locations of measurements. It is noticeable that the average humidity levels of scenario A at the three points are less than those of scenario B. This is explained by the levels of the air velocity for the same three points of scenario A, which are higher than those of the three points of scenario B. The levels of CO_2 also confirm this for the same three points

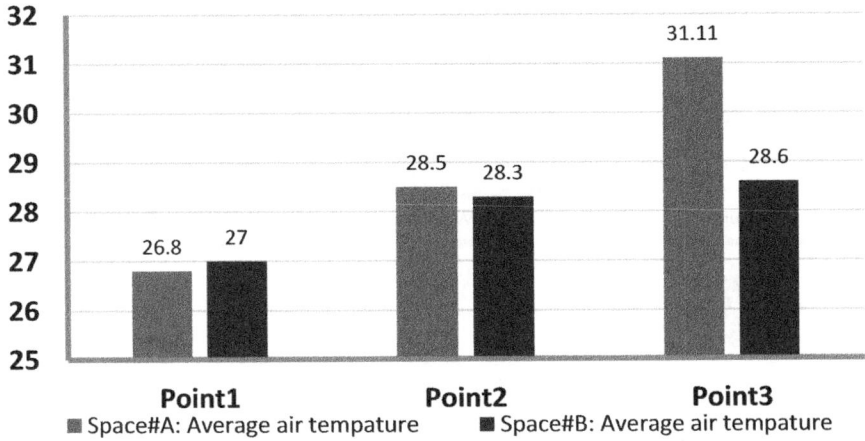

Fig. 7.8. Average Air Temperatures of the Two Spaces Over the Selected Three Locations of Measurements.

of scenario A, which are lower than those of scenario B. The CO_2 is considered the best indicator of air quality.

Based on the above analysis, Fig. 7.10 illustrates the air temperature of the backyards (Point 3) against the air velocity inside the Takhtabush (Point 2) in the two courtyards over the monitored day. It is very obvious that the higher air temperature in the backyard results in a higher air velocity inside the Takhtabush, which in turn accelerates the air movement in the courtyard.

4. Conclusion

The significant effect of the size and the exposure to the sun in the backyard, which resulted in differential air pressure and, in turn, affected the air velocity, has been tested and proved on the urban scale in this research. The results of the field study confirmed that the Takhtabush is well-working when the backyard is larger and thus less shaded than the courtyard; air heats up more readily there than in the courtyard. The heated air rising in the backyard draws cool air from the shaded courtyard through the Takhtabush, creating a steady cool breeze. It is concluded that the higher air temperature in the backyard results in a higher air velocity inside the Takhtabush, which in turn accelerates the air movement in the courtyard.

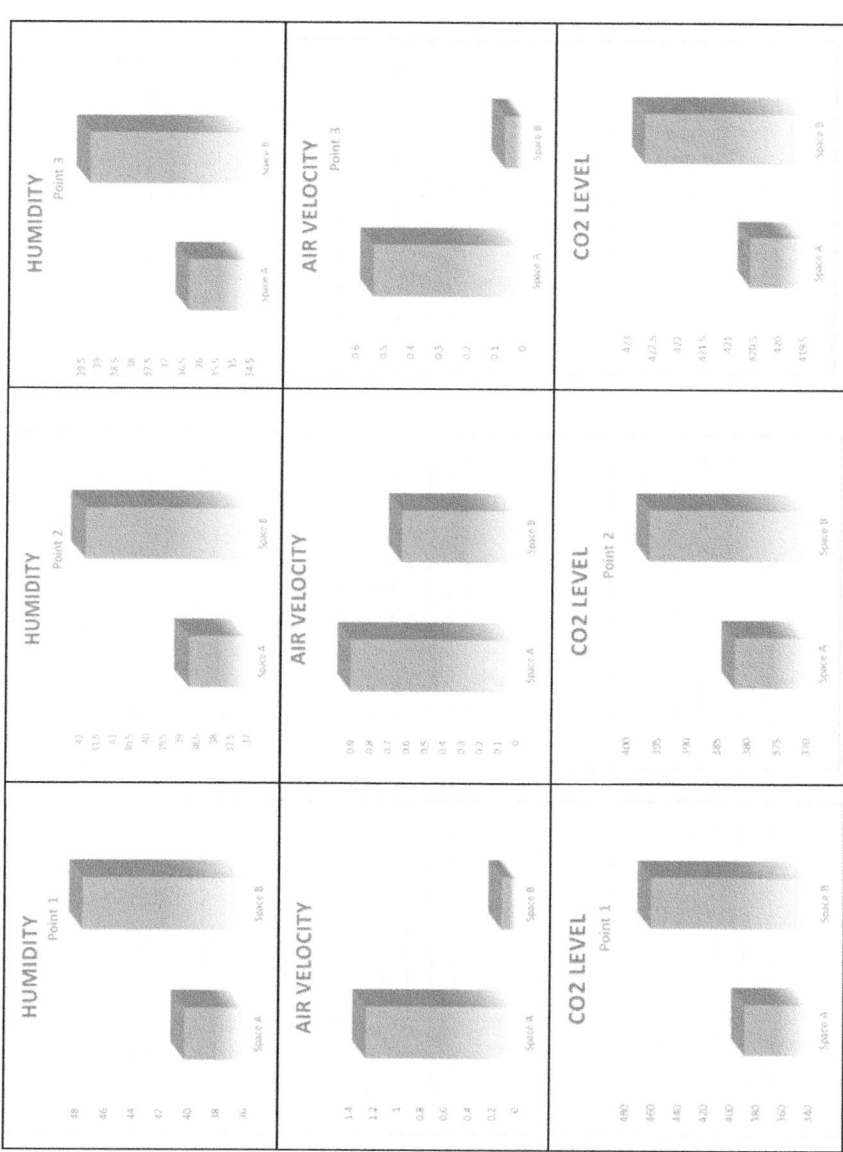

Fig. 7.9. The Analysis of the Humidity, Air Velocity and CO_2 Levels in the Two Courtyards Over the Selected Three Locations of Measurements.

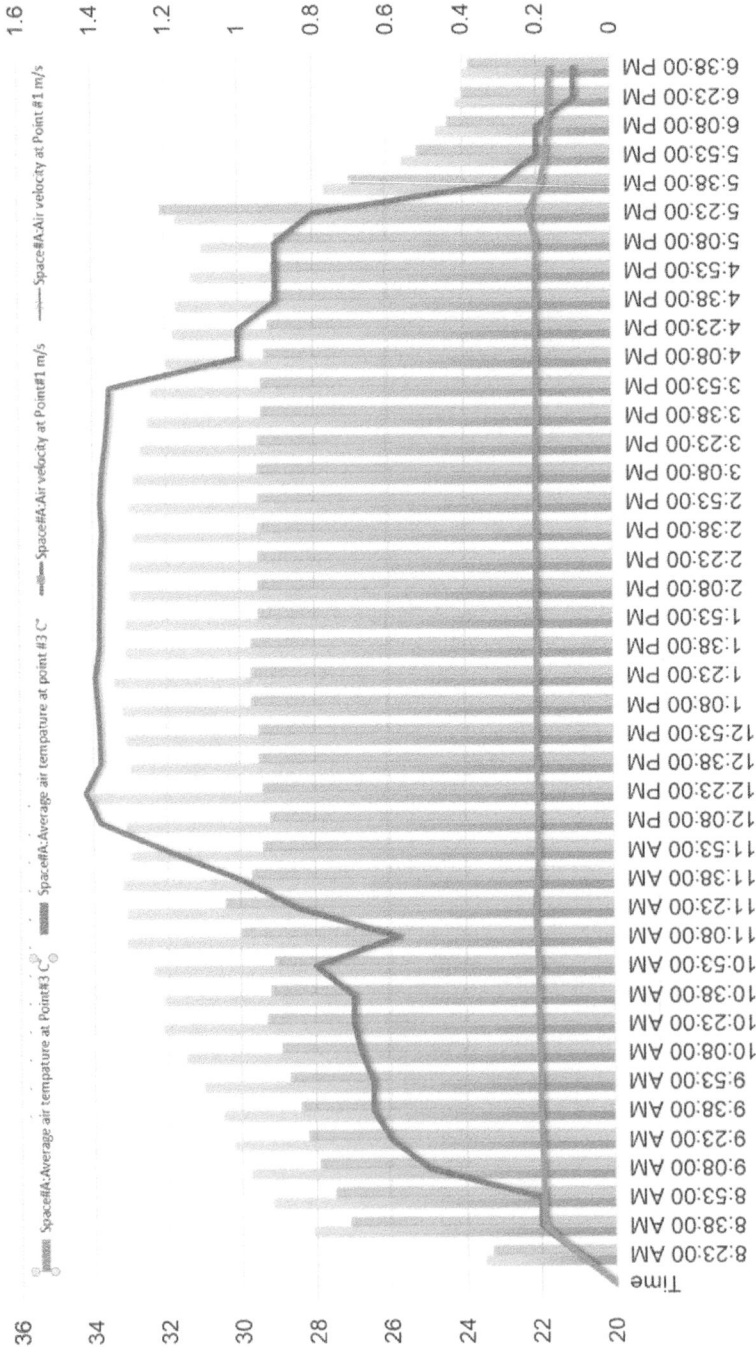

Fig. 7.10. The Relationship Between the Air Temperature in the Backyard and the Air Velocity at the Takhtabush.

References

Afify, H. (2002, February 2–4). Courtyard house as a prototype in desert environments. In *Urban development in the desert and its building problems*. Housing and Public Works Ministry.

Akbar, J. (1998). *Crisis in the built environment: The case of the Muslim city*. Concept Media Pte Ltd, A Mimar Book.

Akbar, J., Serageldin, I., & El-Sadek, S. (1982). Courtyard houses: A case study from Riyadh, Saudi Arabia. In *Arab city: Its character and Islamic cultural heritage* (pp. 162–176). Proceedings of a symposium held in Medina, Kingdom of Saudi Arabia, 28 February–5 March, 1981. IUCN Library System.

Al-Naim, M. A. (2006). *The home environment in Saudi Arabia and Gulf state: Growth of identity crises and origin of identity*. Working Articles.

Al-Naim, M. A. (2023). The typology of courtyard space in Najdi architecture, Saudi Arabia: A response to human needs, culture, and the environment. *Journal of Asian Architecture and Building Engineering*, 1–20.

Allen, E. (1995). *How buildings work, the natural order of architecture*. Oxford University press.

Bahammam, A. S. (1987). *Architectural patterns of privacy in Saudi Arabian housing*. School of Architecture, McGill University.

Baker, N., & Steemers, K. (2002). *Daylight design of buildings*. James & James.

BMT Fluid Mechanics. (2007). *Large boundary layer wind tunnel*. [Online]. http://www.bmtfm.com/?/335/219/123. Accessed on January 18, 2008

CIBSE. (1999). *Environmental design, CIBSE Guide A*. Yale Press Ltd.

El-Shorbagy, A.-M. (2010). Traditional Islamic-Arab house: Vocabulary and syntax. *International Journal of Civil & Environmental Engineering (IJCEE-IJENS)*. https://doi.org/https://api.semanticscholar.org/CorpusID:11380972

Fathy, H. (1986). *Natural energy and vernacular architecture: Principles and examples with reference to hot arid climates*. University of Chicago Press.

Filippi, F. D. (2006). Traditional architecture in the Dakhleh Oasis, Egypt: Space, form and building systems. In *PLEA2006 - The 23rd conference on passive and low energy architecture*. Geneva, Switzerland.

Givoni, B. (1998). *Climate consideration in building and urban design*. Van Nostrand Reinhold.

Hawkes, D. J. M. A. K. S. (2002). *The selective environment: An approach to environmentally responsive architecture*. Spon press.

Husin, Z. (2016). *The role of domestic courtyard in Islamic teachings and practices: Oman as a case study*. https://api.semanticscholar.org/CorpusID:210707238

Iscandar, M. F. (2006). Neo-Vernacular architecture in Egypt. In *3rd international conference ArchCairo 2006*. Cairo.

McMullan, R., & Seeley, I. H. (2007). *Environmental science in building*. Palgrave Macmillan.

Mohamed, M. (2009). *Investigating the environmental performance of government primary schools in Egypt: With particular concern to thermal comfort*. PhD thesis, Dundee University

Mohamed, M. (2010). Traditional ways of dealing with climate in Egypt. In S. Lehmann, H. A. Waer, & J. Al-Qawasmi (Eds.), *The seventh international conference of sustainable architecture and urban development (SAUD 2010)*. The Center for the Study of Architecture in Arab Region, Amman, Jordan.

Mohamed, M. (2013). An approach to integrate the environmental impact assessment process in the early stages of design. In *The first international engineering conference hosting major international events innovation, creativity and impact assessment*. Housing & Building National Research Center, Cairo, Egypt.

Mohamed, M. (2017). Green building rating systems as a design target for public building - Case study analysis. *Progress in Industrial Ecology, An International Journal, 11*, 118–134.

Mohamed, M. (2018). The mastery of the Takhtabush as a paradigm traditional design element in the hot zone climate. *EQA – Environmental quality/Qualité de l'Environnement/Qualità ambientale, 28*, 1–11.

Mohamed, M., & Gado, T. (2006). Application of computer-based environmental assessment and optimization tools: An approach for appropriating buildings. In *3rd international conference ArchCairo 2006, appropriating architecture taming urbanism in the decades of transformation*, Cairo.

Mohamed, M., & Gado, T. (2014). Investigating the process of exporting autodesk ecotect models to detailed thermal simulation software. *Environment and Ecology Research, 2*.

Mohamed, M., Gado, T., & Osman, M. (2010). Investigating the intelligence of the low-tech earth architecture of the Sahara: A feasibility study from the western desert of Egypt. *Intelligent Buildings International, 2*, 179–197.

Mohamed, M., Gado, T., & Unwin, S. (2005). The environmental performance of classrooms in Egypt: A case study from El-Minya governorate. In P. C. O. Egbu & M. K. L. Tong (Eds.), *The second Scottish conference for postgraduate researchers of the built & natural environment (PRoBE 2005)*. Glasgow Caledonian University.

Mohamed, M., Osman, M., & Gado, T. (in review). *Investigating the revitalisation of the intelligent earth architecture of the Sahara: A case study from the western desert of Egypt*. IBI.

Oliver, P. (1997). *Encyclopaedia of vernacular architecture of the world*. Cambridge University Press.

Oliver, P. (2003). *Dwellings*. Phaidon Press Limited.

Wazeri, U. (2002). *Practices on environmental architecture - The sunny design for the interior court - Studies on Cairo and Toshki*. Madboli.

Wazeri, U. (2003). *Friendly architectural design to the environment - Towards green architecture*. Madboli.

WHO. (2003). *Technical meeting on exposure-response relationships of noise on health*. World Health Organization Regional Office for Europe, European Centre for Environment and Health, Bonn Office.

Part II

Architecture and Design in the Context of Heritage Protection

Chapter 8

Using Computer Applications to Measure the Efficiency of Environmental Design in Heritage Buildings

Reem Elhaddad

Jazan University, Saudi Arabia

Abstract

Al Dosariyah Castle is a heritage building located in Jazan Province (KSA). It is perched atop a mountain with a view of the Red Sea harbor. The main aim of the chapter is to investigate the efficiency of the environmental design of heritage buildings. The building was designed with very thick walls and an internal courtyard, which protects from high outdoor temperatures and saves natural ventilation. The building rooms have been selected to represent two different scenarios. The scenarios are concerned with the level of protection from sunlight and saving natural ventilation that influences the value of thermal comfort in indoor spaces. Design Builder simulation was conducted to investigate the thermal comfort of indoor spaces throughout the whole year to determine the highest and lowest quantities with and without these passive techniques. The findings of the chapter motivate old self-used building methods, which have positive effects on improving thermal comfort and reducing total energy consumption.

Keywords: Energy saving; passive techniques; heritage buildings; Design Builder; energy efficiency

1. Introduction

Despite the limitations of advanced technologies at their disposal, the ancient architects were interested in achieving energy efficiency within architectural spaces.

Even though significant and quick changes have occurred since the start of the second half of the 20th century and continue to this day in all domains, it is difficult to attain thermal comfort in interior spaces, particularly in the field of architecture, and these advancements have become evident in engineering applications. The chapter examines passive building methods used in historic architecture, evaluates their effectiveness in design builder applications, and establishes whether thermal comfort would have been possible in the absence of these methods. The number of urbanized areas has increased globally, and by 2050, more than 70% of the world's population is predicted to live in urban centers, according to the United Nations (Puteh et al., 2012).

According to international development statistics, 85% of people would reside in underdeveloped countries by 2030 (Zomorodian et al., 2016). The characteristics of indoor environments, which depend more and more on artificial systems to function properly, are being influenced by the growth of urban density of buildings, particularly in the city center. There has been a notable increase in the amount of time individuals spend indoors. Architects and engineers must take into account the fact that people spend between 80% and 90% of their time indoors when they are devising strategies to enhance environmental comfort for users while simultaneously improving building performance (Pedersen et al., 2024). Between 20% and 40% of total energy consumption is accounted for in the building sector (residential, commercial, and public) in developed countries (Mahmoud et al., 2019). Buildings use artificial lighting and air conditioning to account for nearly 70% of global final energy consumption (Rupp et al., 2015). Air conditioning uses a lot of energy because the temperature inside the building is always controlled, despite the location (Tang et al., 2024). The increased public discussion about climate change has likely contributed to the global interest in the field of thermal comfort research in recent years (Romero et al., 2013). The evaluation of indoor environmental quality and overall thermal comfort are not exclusively based on physical characteristics. The physiological and psychological reactions of the human body to its surroundings are dynamic and incorporate a range of physical phenomena (such as light, sound, vibration, temperature, and humidity) that interact with the surrounding space (Mishra et al., 2016).

Many environmental solutions can be found in heritage buildings, which generally respect the environment and even turn environmental factors into advantages for users. The majority of traditional architecture solutions fall under the category of passive solar architecture. Despite the lack of mechanical means in those eras, the ancient architects were able to successfully control the climate by utilizing the building's body and elements to bring the building closer to thermal comfort. Heritage buildings effectively harnessed these solutions to serve aesthetic, sensory, and social functions, even though they offered excellent solutions to the majority of environmental factors, particularly the climate factor (Jo et al., 2023).

A crucial passive strategy is a thick wall. Any building's walls, floor, windows, doors, ceiling, and other components make up the building envelope, which is essential because it regulates the amount of energy that enters and exits the structure as well as the indoor temperature. The analysis of building energy efficiency for new construction starts during the building's design phase because a well-designed building can result in significant energy savings for heating and cooling requirements, which can be translated into lower operating costs and a minimal environmental impact (Paraschiv et al., 2020). Thick walls act as insulation for buildings, lowering the amount of energy needed to heat and cool the space and, consequently, the energy costs and greenhouse gas emissions. Buildings with high thermal performance envelopes can lower their energy consumption for heating and cooling while increasing the building's overall energy efficiency. Consequently, the building envelope's thermodynamic parameters enhance the energy efficiency of already-existing structures and provide crucial information for energy simulations of the buildings (Sharples & Bensalem, 2001).

Additionally, building courtyards use less energy. When the courtyard form was first used in ancient Greece and Rome, an internal roof opening was left uncovered to let light in and smoke from fires out. The extent of the uncovered form was typical of Arab architectural space. Buildings with courtyards use wind and stack forces to create airflow through the rooms that surround the courtyard (Dwidar, 2020).

Based on the findings of Srivastav's research, conventional passive techniques can reduce energy consumption while maintaining a high level of comfort for an extended period. Adopting passive strategies in the current context was found to have certain issues. The usage of conventional building materials, like earth, is limited, but there are easily adaptable substitutes with comparable qualities that can be used to achieve the same result (Srivastav & Jones, 2009).

The aim of the chapter is to illustrate the efficiency of passive techniques used in historic buildings when compared to current practices by utilizing simulation tools.

2. Method and Materials

To achieve the chapter goal, the paper examines a specific case study: Al Dosariyah Castle in Jizan Province (KSA), using the Design Builder simulation tool. It compares two architectural scenarios and looks at three parameters: thermal comfort, energy efficiency, and adequate natural ventilation. As seen in Fig. 8.1, the chapter has demonstrated the methodologies that were used (see Fig. 8.1).

The case study is Al Dosariyah Castle, which is located in the Jazan province KSA extreme southwest, between the latitudes of 16° 20' and 17° 40' and the longitudes of 41°20' and 43°20' east. It is bordered on the north and east by Assir, on the south and western south by Yemen, and on the west by the Red Sea (see Fig. 8.2) (Hamoda, 2002) (Alhumrani et al., 2002) (see Fig. 8.2).

Jazan has a wide range of terrain, which contributes to the diversity of the climate in the region. Some areas of the region are suitable for winter resorts, while others are considered to be beautiful summer resorts. Surrounded by mountains to the east and the sea to the west, the lowlands experience extremely hot summers,

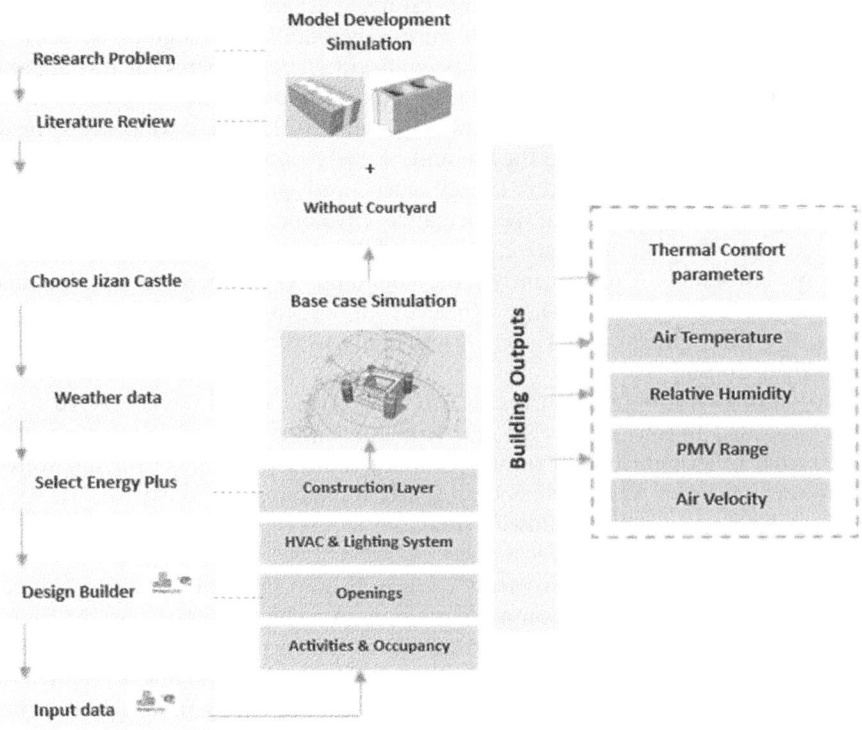

Fig. 8.1. Flow-Chart of Methodology. *Source:* author.

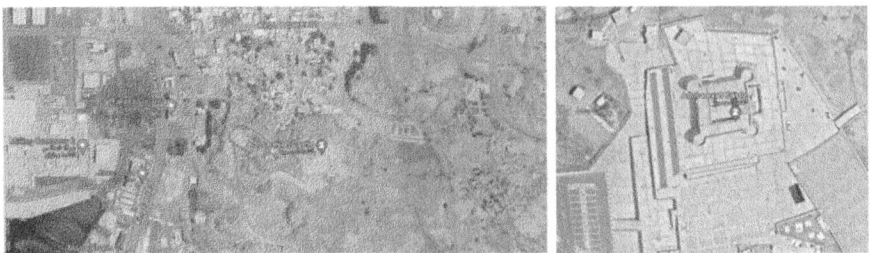

Fig. 8.2. Building Location of the Castle of Jazan in Kingdom of Saudi Arabia. *Source:* Google Map, https://www.google.com/maps/dir/16.8871302,42.5445208

with an average summer temperature of more than 30°C. The average annual temperature of Jizan is 31°C, while the highest temperature is 34°C in June and the lowest temperature is 26 °C in January. People experience discomfort and find

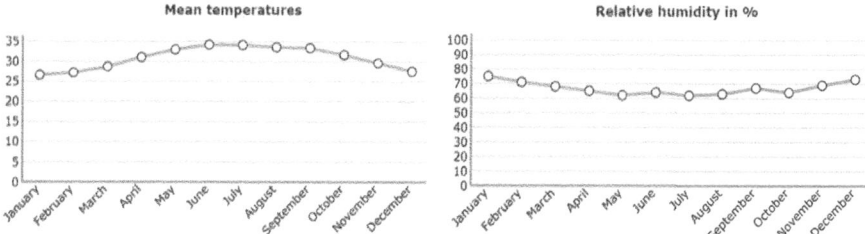

Fig. 8.3. Diagram for Maximum and Minimum for Air Temperature and Relative Humidity in Jazan. *Source:* Climate: Jizan in Saudi Arabia (world data. Info) (Srivastav & Jones, 2009)

high humidity to be depressive. A relative humidity of 40–60% is generally comfortable. It is most uncomfortable in June due to the average humidity of 65%. Conversely, it is more tolerable in January (See Fig. 8.3).

Al Dosariyah castle consists of a square-shaped area with a side length of 34 meters, in the middle of which is an open courtyard, and on its edges are four circular towers, each tower having a diameter of 17.60 meters. The building consists of a basement, ground, and roof floor. The study simulates the ground floor, while it was for living, which on the master plan has the chosen room colored as shown in Abdelhafez et al. (2023) (see Fig. 8.4).

Design Builder V7 is a popular simulation tool among many professionals, including architects and building services engineers, that offers an intuitive interface to the EnergyPlus simulation engine. Al Dosariyah castle in Jizan, Saudi Arabia, was simulated using Design Builder, a dynamic simulation tool, in order to examine the building's energy efficiency. Design Builder created a model drawing of the castle based on the materials, activities, and orientations (see Fig. 8.5).

Fig. 8.4. Architecture Drawings of the Castle (a) Ground Floor Plans, (b) Castle Photos. *Source:* Saudi Ministry of Culture.

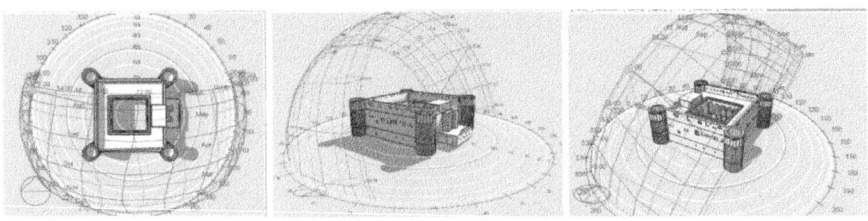

Fig. 8.5. Model Drawing in Design Builder Simulation. *Source:* Design Builder Screenshot.

The natural world, inspired by Leonardo DaVinci's 15th-century bird imitation, has significantly influenced human fields like medicine, engineering, and sustainable design. Bioengineered materials, which can self-heal, adapt, and regenerate in response to environmental changes, are crucial in this field.

Description of the Al Dosariyah Castle: It was constructed without any additions, while the modified case includes a courtyard and modern technology that is used in Saudi Arabia. A courtyard can be modeled using the "Draw void perimeter" toolset included with Design Builder. Thus, this chapter examines the use of methods to model the courtyard space as a passive strategy in order to ascertain the viability of using Design Builder for simulating courtyards. The following Fig. 8.5 shows the chapter methodologies used. Additionally, it includes practical built-in features that make it easier to compare thermal comfort parameters and energy performance of the building in detail, as well as natural ventilation. These features allow renewable energy systems to be optimized for better building energy performance (see Fig. 8.5).

The primary research method utilized in the chapter is the energy simulation software to test the thermal comfort parameters and total latent load. It is used in two main scenarios. The first scenario focused on the output simulation of the base case of the castle without any development, as shown in Fig. 8.6. The second scenario of the simulation assessed the modern technique of the building (cement bricks stuffed with cork and closed the courtyard) and compared the base case of the castle with the current situation. Fig. 8.6 represents the specifications of wall building materials used in the simulation; the buildings' envelopes, roof, and interior partitions are constructed as illustrated (see Fig. 8.1).

3. Results and Discussion

The simulation output displays the thermal comfort parameters, such as air temperature, relative humidity, PMV, air velocity, and total annual energy consumption in kWh, after the parameters are defined using the input data provided in Fig. 8.7 and the construction details of the building elements.

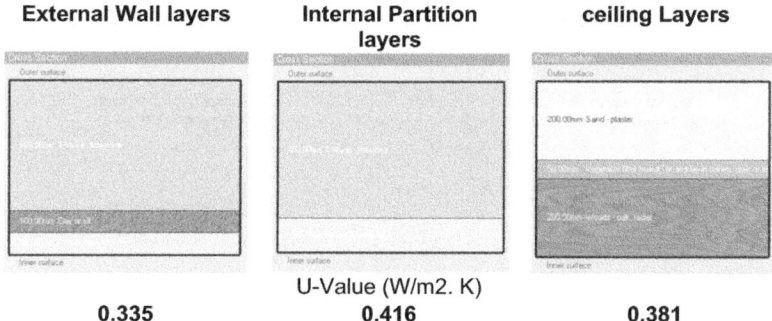

Fig. 8.6. Original Case External Wall, Internal Wall and Ceiling Materials (Design Builder Screenshot).

Building internal air temperature, lighting, ventilation, and relative humidity all have a substantial impact on occupants' thermal comfort. Fanger, however, has developed a model to assess occupant comfort while considering parameters. Offering a technique that could forecast the actual thermal sensation by generating values for the predicted mean vote (PMV) (Zomorodian et al., 2016) and the predicted percentage of dissatisfaction (PPD) increased the utility of the research. Acceptable PMV and PPD ranges:

According to the ASHRAE 55 standard, the suggested temperature limit for.

Fig. 8.7 indicates that the comfort analysis in the base case building shows that the the Air Temperature achieved the highest value in June at 38.5 °C, while Relative Humidity reached the highest value in June at 47.9%; however, the Fanger PMV attained the highest value at 4.47.

Fig. 8.7 illustrates the comparison of the thermal comfort parameters, including air temperature, relative humidity, and final PMV range, which shows that the minimum air temperature in January was 31.04°C compared to the developed case with the current cement block, which assessed 34.85°C. On the other hand, the maximum air temperature is attained in June at 39.34°C which is the most uncomfortable month all over the year, compared to the development case, which reached 45.19°C. There is about a 6°C reduction in the air temperature with the traditional materials of the castle. It was simulated that the base case's relative humidity in the winter was 59.15%, and in the summer, it was 49.98%. Nevertheless, in winter or summer, the evaluated value was better than the simulated developed case studied.

To evaluate thermal comfort, a reliable and accurate model is necessary. Fanger's predicted mean vote (PMV) was employed in this chapter to assess the building's thermal performance. The results show that there are significant differences in PMV prediction among all simulated scenarios.

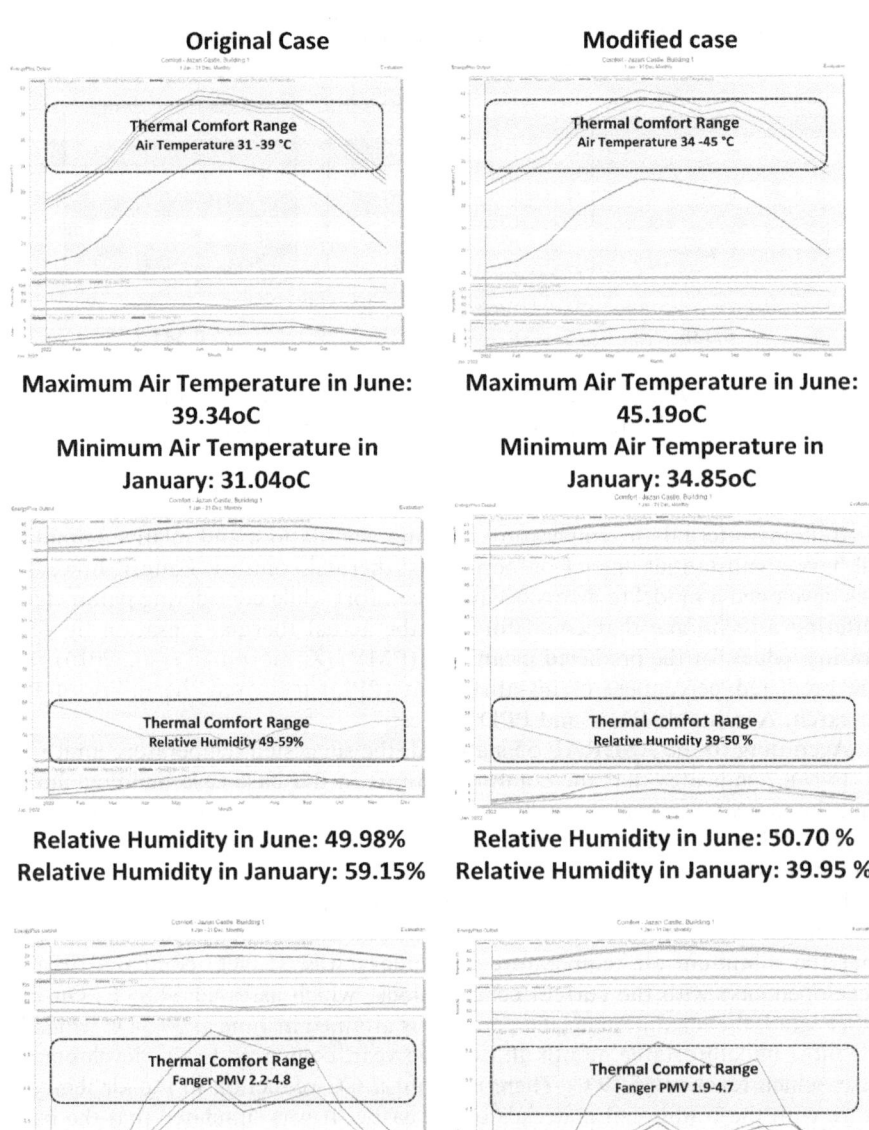

Fig. 8.7. Model Drawing in Design Builder Simulation.

Finally, the graph in Fig. 8.7 shows a comparison of the examined buildings concerning PMV. The base case was determined to be the most successful situation with the lowest PMV values when compared to the Developed Case studied. The current situation of the castle achieves PMV values ranging from the minimum and maximum values of 2.21 and 4.85, respectively.

To assess the effect of particular passive design strategies on lowering energy demand, a variety of retrofitting measures have been developed for the building envelope. Two scenarios are created from these measurements: The first is the baseline scenario, which depicts the actual state of performance of the building. The other scenario will be measured against the standards set by this case. In contrast, the second scenario uses cement bricks stuffed with cork in place of brush stone and carved and punctuated by crusts to fill small gaps, and mortality consists of sand and plaster with the courtyard closed.

According to the zone's latent load at its peak, reasonable load, Fig. 8.8 shows the total latent load of the simulated cases. Otherwise, compared to the cement block technique, which achieves 8012.567 kWh, the base case achieves 5678.829 kWh, the highest value of the total latent load. This suggests that the most effective method for saving energy is the traditional approach that has been employed in the past, as shown in Fig. 8.8.

4. Conclusion

Reducing the environmental impact of building design is one of the main advantages of adaptive reuse of heritage buildings. It can conserve energy, resources, and emissions that would otherwise be needed to demolish and construct new buildings by reusing existing materials and infrastructure. The chapter emphasized the importance of simulation programs in assessing thermal comfort in heritage buildings. It emphasized the necessity of reusing traditional passive techniques in heritage buildings in the Kingdom of Saudi Arabia. Reference to old self-used building methods has positive effects in lowering temperatures and reducing relative humidity to the required limit for feeling thermal comfort and reducing the total energy used in the building for comfortable human living.

Acknowledgments

The author would like to acknowledge the Saudi Heritage Commission and the Saudi Ministry of Culture for supporting this chapter with important data. The author would like to thank JAZAN University for their continuous support and encouragement in conducting this research.

108 Reem Elhaddad

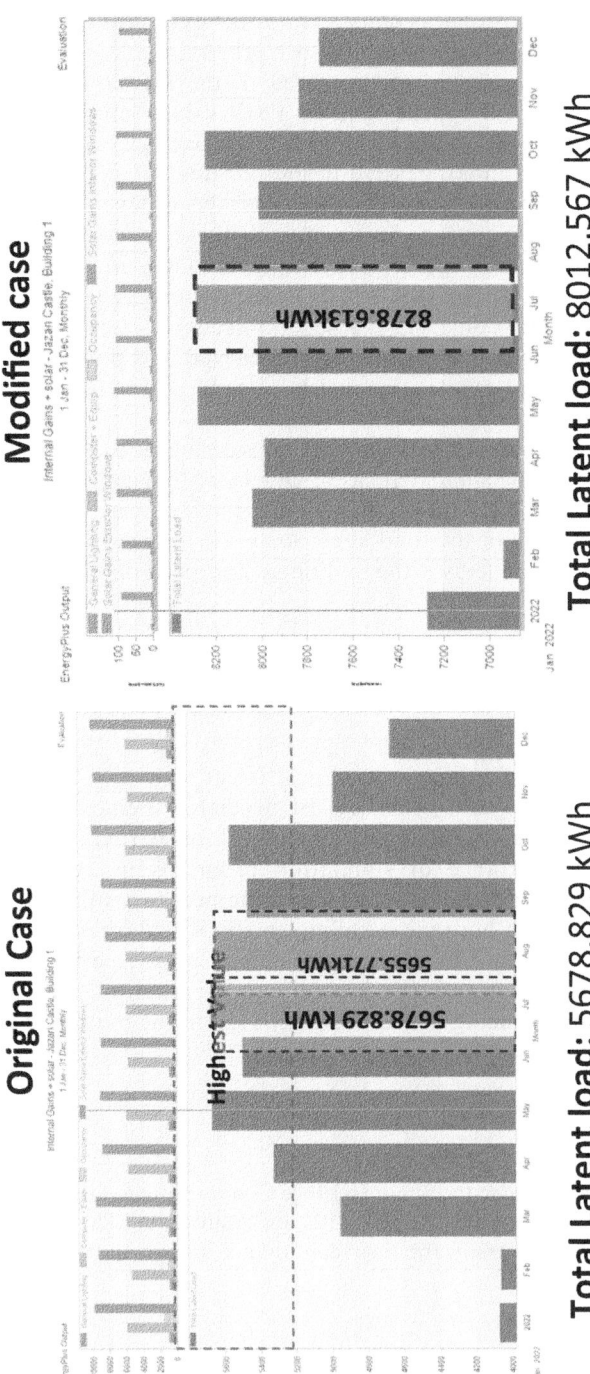

Fig. 8.8. Internal Gain of the Original Case and Modified Case (Design Builder Screenshot).

References

Abdelhafez, M. H. H., Aldersoni, A. A., Gomaa, M. M., Noaime, E., Alnaim, M. M., Alghaseb, M., & Ragab, A. (2023). Investigating the thermal and energy performance of advanced glazing systems in the context of Hail City, KSA. *Buildings, 13*(3), 752. Available at: https://doi.org/10.3390/buildings13030752

Alhumrani, A., Suhai, M. B., Al-Ban, A., & Alzahrani, M. R. Regions in Saudi Arabia.

Design Builder. (2021). *Design Builder [online]*. Available at: http://www.designbuilder.co.uk/

Dwidar, S. I. (2020). Classification and analysis of urban and architectural heritage buildings in Emarite of Jazan in Kingdom of Saudi Arabia. *Journal of Engineering Science, 48*(1), 65–81. Available at: https://doi.org/10.21608/jesaun.2020.130276

Hamoda, N. (2002). Solar radiation and architecture in desert areas. *Symposium on urban development in desert areas and building problems*.

Jo, H. H., Yuk, H., Kang, Y., & Kim, S. (2023). Conservation of architectural heritage: Innovative approaches to enhance thermal comfort and promote sustainable usage in historic buildings. *Case Studies in Thermal Engineering, 51*, 103500. Available at: https://doi.org/10.1016/j.csite.2023.103500

Mahmoud, S., Zayed, T., & Fahmy, M. (2019). Development of sustainability assessment tool for existing buildings. *Sustainable Cities and Society, 44*, 99–119. Available at: https://doi.org/10.1016/j.scs.2018.09.024

Mishra, A. K., Loomans, M. G. L. C., & Hensen, J. L. (2016). Thermal comfort of heterogeneous and dynamic indoor conditions—an overview. *Building and Environment, 109*, 82–100. Available at: https://doi.org/10.1016/j.buildenv.2016.09.016

Paraschiv, L. S., Acomi, N., Serban, A., & Paraschiv, S. (2020). A web application for analysis of heat transfer through building walls and calculation of optimal insulation thickness. *Energy Reports, 6*, 343–353. Available at: https://doi.org/10.1016/j.egyr.2019.08.047

Pedersen, M., Hognestad, H. M., Helle, R., & Jelle, B. P. (2024). The challenge of rehabilitating relocated listed heritage buildings: Requirements and opportunities. *Energy and Buildings, 303*, 113577. Available at: https://doi.org/10.1016/j.enbuild.2023.113577

Puteh, M., Ibrahim, M. H., Adnan, M., Che'Ahmad, C. N., & Noh, N. M. (2012). Thermal comfort in the classroom: Constraints and issues. *Procedia - Social and Behavioral Sciences, 46*, 1834–1838. Available at: https://doi.org/10.1016/j.sbspro.2012.05.389

Romero, R. A., Bojórquez, G., Corral, M., & Gallegos, R. (2013). Energy and the occupant's thermal perception of low-income dwellings in hot-dry climate: Mexicali, México. *Renewable Energy, 49*, 267–270. Available at: https://doi.org/10.1016/j.renene.2012.01.053

Rupp, R. F., Vásquez, N. G., & Lamberts, R. (2015). A review of human thermal comfort in the built environment. *Energy and Buildings, 105*, 178–205. Available at: https://doi.org/10.1016/j.enbuild.2015.07.047

Sharples, S., & Bensalem, R. J. S. E. (2001). Airflow in courtyard and atrium buildings in the urban environment: A wind tunnel study. *Solar Energy, 70*(3), 237–244. Available at: https://doi.org/10.1016/S0038-092X(00)00146-6

Spiru, P., & Simona, P. L. (2017). A review of interactions between energy performance of the buildings, outdoor air pollution, and indoor air quality. *Energy Procedia, 128*, 179–186. Available at: https://doi.org/10.1016/j.egypro.2017.09.036

Srivastav, S., & Jones, P. J. (2009). Use of traditional passive strategies to reduce energy use and carbon emissions in modern dwellings. *International Journal of Low Carbon Technologies, 4*(3), 141–149. Available at: https://doi.org/10.1093/ijlct/ctp022

Tang, X., Zhang, J., & Liang, R. (2024). The design of heating, ventilation, and air conditioning systems based on building information modeling: A review from the perspective of automatic and intelligent methods. *Journal of Building Engineering, 82*, 108200. Available at: https://doi.org/10.1016/j.jobe.2023.108200

Zomorodian, Z. S., Tahsildoost, M., & Hafezi, M. (2016). Thermal comfort in educational buildings: A review article. *Renewable and Sustainable Energy Reviews, 59*, 895–906. Available at: https://doi.org/10.1016/j.rser.2016.01.033

Chapter 9

Enhancing Building Climatic Performance Using AI-Assisted Facade Design: Evidence From the Literature

Tarek Saad Ragab, Marah Aljassem and Jury Aboanoor

Effat University, Saudi Arabia

Abstract

This chapter delves into the corpus of research concerning the employment of artificial intelligence (AI) in the realm of building design, particularly focusing on the myriad AI methodologies applicable for optimizing building facades to enhance climatic performance. The primary objective is to identify pivotal factors influencing indoor air quality and assess the feasibility and relevance of AI implementation to ameliorate these factors. Notwithstanding the recent emphasis on optimizing architectural configurations, there exists a notable dearth of scholarly inquiry in this domain. This chapter endeavors to augment the understanding of how AI can be leveraged to enhance building facade design and promote the sustainability of built environments. The methodology entails a thorough examination of extant literature pertaining to the utilization of AI during the pre-building design phase, with a particular emphasis on the optimization of facade components and materials. Furthermore, the chapter scrutinizes case studies and practical applications of AI in facade design, illustrating its potential to enhance environmental performance and foster innovative design solutions. However, given the nascent nature of this field, further research and development are still required.

Keywords: Artificial intelligence; building facades; cross ventilation; temperature; humidity; energy efficiency; sustainable design

1. Introduction

The domain of technology has undergone significant expansion since the onset of the industrial revolution (citation). Technological advancements have largely supplanted numerous labor-intensive manual tasks, yielding substantial benefits to humanity. Among these advancements is artificial intelligence (AI), developed to automate various manual functions across diverse industries. This chapter investigates the corpus of research pertaining to the utilization of AI in building design, specifically focusing on the multitude of AI methodologies applicable to optimizing building facades for optimal climatic performance. The chapter aims to identify the key factors influencing indoor air quality and assess the feasibility and relevance of employing AI to enhance these aspects. The methodology employed adopts a mixed approach, encompassing both qualitative and quantitative methods. Qualitative data is derived from an exhaustive literature review on the evolution, development, and capabilities of AI in architectural design, which includes publications on case studies and software manuals. Quantitative data is gathered through surveys and semi-structured interviews conducted with architects engaged in AI-related design processes, supplemented by desktop analyses for qualitative and quantitative data synthesis. The chapter delineates four primary objectives. First, to contribute to the enhancement of both internal and external built environments by employing AI to optimize thermal comfort through thermal-based facade design. Second, to investigate the plausibility of employing AI for the improvement of indoor air quality. Third, to facilitate the design decision-making process for architects and designers through AI-driven pre-design data analysis. And fourth, to streamline the architectural design workflow by utilizing advanced AI tools for 3D modeling and rendering software, thereby saving time and effort for architects and designers.

Contemporary research, as highlighted by Pena et al. (2021), predominantly emphasizes the optimization of architectural form. Conversely, this chapter aims to augment understanding regarding the utilization of AI to enhance building facade design and promote sustainable built environments. The chapter methodology entails a thorough review of extant literature focusing on the integration of AI within the pre-building design phase, specifically emphasizing the optimization of facade elements and materials within buildings. AI, a multidisciplinary field of science and technology, pertains to the development of intelligent machines and computer programs capable of executing tasks that typically require human intellect. It encompasses systems capable of simulating various human abilities, facilitated by the utilization of external data sources such as big data. Initially a concept relegated to science fiction and philosophical debates surrounding the impact of technology, AI has now become deeply ingrained in contemporary society, serving as a cornerstone in numerous technical and non-technical domains. Industries ranging from manufacturing and healthcare to supply chains and architecture have experienced significant transformations owing to AI's integration. The versatility of AI lies in its capacity to perform tasks beyond human capabilities, thereby facilitating enhanced efficiency and productivity across a diverse array of applications.

2. Literature Review

The integration of AI into architectural practice traces its origins to the 1960s and 1970s, when researchers commenced exploring its potential applications within the architectural domain. During this era, AI primarily served in data processing and decision-making capacities across various fields, including finance and engineering. Notably, one of the earliest manifestations of AI in architecture materialized through the development of expert systems. These systems, characterized by their utilization of a knowledge base and rule set, were instrumental in furnishing design recommendations informed by specific criteria such as building codes, environmental considerations, and user requirements.

Advancements in the 2000s saw the emergence of evolutionary algorithms as a key tool in architectural optimization endeavors. Employed to enhance building designs with respect to parameters like energy efficiency and structural robustness, evolutionary algorithms marked a significant stride in computational design methodologies within architecture. In more recent years, the scope of AI applications in architecture has expanded to encompass multifaceted processes such as building information modeling (BIM), generative design, and computational design. BIM, a comprehensive digital modeling approach, facilitates the management of project information throughout the entire lifecycle of a building—spanning from initial design phases to construction and ongoing operation. Generative design and computational design leverage AI algorithms to generate and refine building designs, taking into account diverse criteria such as cost-effectiveness, energy efficiency, and user preferences (Böke et al., 2019). These advancements underscore the evolving synergy between AI technologies and architectural practice, promising enhanced efficiency, sustainability, and innovation within the built environment. Technology is undoubtedly one of the key forces at work among the variables that will have a long-term effect on our field. Architecture has gone through a considerable transformation as a result of the introduction of technological solutions at each stage of the value chain. In truth, a gradual shift in how buildings are designed has already begun. First, new construction techniques were used, then appropriate software was created, and finally, today, statistical computing skills (including Data Science & AI) were introduced. Here, we want to observe continuity that guided architecture through its various iterations till the present, not a disturbance. We consider the four complex phases of a slow transition to be Modularity, Computer Aided Design, Pragmatism, and eventually AI (no bold wording). We assert that, beyond the historical context, this progression represents the framework of a gradual changeover. In addition to the historical context, we assert that this evolution is the blueprint for a fundamental upgrade in architectural conception (Artificial Intelligence and Architecture, n.d.).

Modularity revolutionized architecture in the early 20th century, with German architect Walter Gropius developing theories to simplify construction processes and reduce costs. Baukasten, a kit of parts, was introduced in 1923, reducing detail-solving difficulties. American architect Buckminster Fuller expanded modularity by integrating HVAC, water pipelines, and other networks into the modules in his Design House.

Gropius developed the idea of adaptable, commercially available construction kits based on these experiments. fundamental reorientation of the entire construction sector in an industrial direction. The intended product is the home, which will be constructed from components of a highly adaptable construction kit. "Industrial to stock production in large establishments of residential buildings that are no longer built at the construction site, but are produced as assembly-ready components in specialized factories," says Gropius. For Example: The housing complex "Habitat 67" was constructed in 1967 by Israeli-Canadian architect and urban planner Moshe Saf-Yutut (1895–1983) (Artificial Intelligence and Architecture, n.d.; Chaillou, 2020).

A user-friendly user interface for designers. SketchPad has provided drafters with a previously unheard-of level of comfort and flexibility with a pencil and greatly simplified controls. 3D modeling moves from 2D drawing. Thanks to the work of mathematician and computer scientist Pierre Bezier, CAD advances significantly in France. Bezier's research on intricate bends "allows designers to draw ever-difficult 3D shapes with computers, giving CAD software new impetus." Renault, a car manufacturer, utilized the UNISURF program to model the design of some prototypes before the launch of Bezier in 1966. This unexpected advancement had an effect on design software across a wide range of industries, in addition to vehicle design.

By employing software to optimize designs and translate them directly into a process of fabrication and construction in the 1990s, Frank Gehry established a second generation of "smart" digital design in architecture. Jim Glymph, Gehry's "office hippie," used CATIA, a C++ software application created by an aerospace company. It was initially utilized by the maker, Dassault Systems, in 1977 to create the Mirage fighter plane.

Founder of the Parametric Technology Corporation (PTC), who released Pro/ENGINEER in 1988, the first program offering users complete access to geometric parameters. As the program is made available.

We can identify a select group of influential people who have influenced the development of parametric, from the invention of parameters through their translation into advancements across the industry. The work of Zaha Hadid Architects serves as the best initial example of this parametrization of architecture. The aim of Mrs. Hadid's profession was to combine math and architecture using parametric design. She is an Iraqi architect who received her training in the United Kingdom. Typically, the program's algorithms would determine her designs, giving it unheard-of degrees of control over the geometry of the structures. Each design decision would be turned into a specific tuning of factors that would produce a certain building shape. To this day, the designs of Hadid serve as the ideal representation of what is architectural design quantification into parameterized arrays. But David Rutten's 2000s program, Grasshopper, is what made it possible for her to do what she did. Grasshopper, a visual programming interface, makes it simple for architects to identify the key design factors and iteratively fine-tune them. A whole generation of "parametric" designers has been motivated by the interface's ease of use, the intelligence of the built-in features, and how most buildings are designed today.

The BIM movement, which was sparked by parametrization and began in the early 2000s, is still going strong today, going beyond the immediate advantages of Grasshopper for building design. The development of BIM, spearheaded by Philip Bernstein, then Vice President of Autodesk, has raised the bar for reason and viability in the construction sector. The fundamental tenet of BIM is that each component of a 3D model of a structure is a function of parameters, or "properties," which determine how each object looks and are recorded. From Sutherland's SketchPad to Autodesk Revit, the current industry standard BIM software.

According to John McCarthy's 1956 definition of AI, computer logic is modeled after the human brain. Solutions that replicate the statistical distribution of information are made possible by AI, which enables computers to construct intermediary parameters from data or human input. Through the paradigm change from heuristics to stochastic-based decision-making, machines may now discover underlying phenomena and even replicate them.

The URBAN V system makes use of a machine assistant to optimize lighting and space arrangements. It makes a distinction between implicit and explicit dimensions, allowing for the complementarity of machines and people. The implicit parameters are where the machine's AI is developed, allowing for modifications and corrections. Later, Cedric Price, who created the GENERATOR in 1976, embraced this idea.

Furthermore, AI is not just the outcome of a sudden upheaval. It is the culmination of 70 years of advancements and inventions. We see in AI the potential for rich solutions that will complement our practice and address some of our field's blind spots, since it can strike a balance between efficiency and organicity while offering a staggering variety of relevant design alternatives. We don't view AI as a new architectural dogma, but rather as a discipline that presents fresh challenges and exciting opportunities (Chaillou, 2020).

Building design and construction have significantly improved in the contemporary world as a result of the interaction between architecture and technology. AI is now being used in architectural design, particularly in the creation of building facades, as one such innovation. A building's facade, a key element, affects factors including humidity, temperature, and cross-ventilation in addition to contributing to the structure's aesthetic appeal and environmental performance. In this chapter, AI is investigated as a viable tool for facade design optimization, emphasizing its propensity to handle massive data sets, build predictive models, and work in tandem with BIM tools to produce digital twins.

Rhino is another example of an architecture program that has been around for a while and uses AI in its design. Rhino is a 3D modeling software that has been widely used in architecture since its release in 1998. The software was developed by Robert McNeel & Associates and has since become a popular tool for architects, designers, and engineers due to its versatility and ease of use. Rhino's history in architecture can be traced back to its early days when it was primarily used for creating 3D models of buildings and other architectural structures. The software quickly gained popularity due to its ability to handle complex geometries and its support for various file formats. Over time, Rhino has evolved to include a range of advanced features and tools that are specifically geared toward architecture. For example, Rhino's Grasshopper plugin is a visual programming language that allows users to create parametric designs, complex algorithms, and other advanced features.

In recent years, Rhino has also incorporated AI algorithms into its software to enhance its capabilities in architecture. For example, the software includes tools for generative design, which uses AI algorithms to generate and optimize building designs based on specific criteria such as cost, energy efficiency, and user needs. Rhino has also been used in conjunction with other AI tools to improve the design process in architecture. For example, researchers have used Rhino and other AI tools to develop predictive models that can simulate the performance of building designs under different conditions. These models can help architects and designers optimize their designs for various factors such as energy efficiency, structural stability, and user comfort. Overall, Rhino has a rich history in architecture and has continued to evolve alongside advancements in AI technology. Its incorporation of AI tools and algorithms has further enhanced its capabilities in architecture and has opened new possibilities for the design and construction of buildings and other architectural structures (Chaillou, 2019).

Midjourney is a design and technology company that has been working on developing innovative solutions for the architecture industry since its founding in 2014. The company specializes in the use of digital technologies, such as AI, machine learning, and computer vision, to create new design possibilities for architects and designers. One area where Midjourney has focused its efforts is the design of building facades. Building facades are an important aspect of architecture, as they play a key role in defining the visual identity of a building and can have a significant impact on its energy efficiency and environmental performance. Midjourney has developed a range of tools and techniques that can be used to enhance the design of building facades. For example, the company has developed a machine learning algorithm that can analyze images of building facades and identify patterns and features that can be used to inform the design process. Additionally, Midjourney has developed a tool called Facade Designer that allows architects and designers to create parametric designs for building facades. The tool uses a combination of digital modeling and simulation to optimize the design for factors such as energy efficiency, lighting, and ventilation. Overall, Midjourney has been at the forefront of using digital technologies to enhance the design of building facades in architecture. Its innovative tools and techniques have opened new possibilities for architects and designers and have helped to push the boundaries of what is possible in building design. In general, it is expected that as AI technology develops, its applications in architecture will grow and become simpler (Jaruga-Rozdolska, 2022).

A cloud-based tool called another program that makes use of AI to improve the design process for architects and designers is Autodesk Generative Design. This program generates and optimizes design possibilities based on input criteria, including materials, manufacturing processes, and performance requirements, using AI algorithms. To produce and optimize design solutions that satisfy performance requirements, generative design can examine data on building design and performance, such as energy consumption, structural performance, and thermal comfort. The app may also use cloud computing to quickly produce and test thousands of design choices, giving architects and designers a large selection from which to choose. Using Generative Design, architects and designers can investigate novel design options and improve building performance in ways that using conventional design techniques would be challenging or time-consuming. The software may also aid in streamlining the creative process and enhancing client, designer, and architect communication.

In general, Autodesk Generative Design is a potent tool for architects and designers who want to use AI to optimize building design and performance. Its use of AI algorithms to create and optimize design options based on performance criteria might aid architects and designers in exploring new design possibilities and improving building performance in ways that were not feasible using conventional design methodologies.

The second app is Autodesk Insight, which analyzes data on building design, occupant behavior, and environmental factors to offer insights into the performance of buildings. To make suggestions for improving building design and occupant comfort, the software can analyze data on energy use, thermal comfort, daylighting, and more (kietzmann, paschen, 2018). Building designers and architects may swiftly produce 3D models of their designs using Autodesk Insight and test several design possibilities in real-time. The program offers suggestions for increasing building performance and occupant comfort by analyzing the effects of various design alternatives on energy use, thermal comfort, and daylighting (Nguyen and Amoah, 2019).

3. Application Tools

Building envelope design decisions should be made with the support of AI, which can be utilized as a pre-design tool by architects and designers. AI can analyze complex data and provide insights that enhance energy efficiency, thermal comfort, and overall building performance.

As a pre-design tool, AI can analyze environmental data by assessing factors such as terrain, climate, and building orientation. This allows architects and designers to optimize building envelopes for energy efficiency, thermal comfort, and natural illumination. By processing vast amounts of environmental data, AI helps in making informed decisions that align with sustainable design principles.

AI-powered tools can also generate 3D models of building envelopes, enabling architects and designers to experiment with various design possibilities. These models allow for visualizing how different design choices affect a building's performance, facilitating a more efficient and informed design process (Ploennigs & Berger, 2022).

Material selection is another critical area where AI can contribute. AI algorithms can analyze data on different building materials, providing insights into their impact on energy efficiency and thermal comfort. This assists architects and designers in selecting materials that optimize building performance while maintaining sustainability and cost-effectiveness.

Furthermore, AI can examine energy use patterns in buildings and suggest improvements in building envelope designs to reduce energy consumption. By integrating AI-driven recommendations, architects and designers can develop designs that minimize energy waste while maximizing efficiency.

Lastly, AI can enhance occupant comfort by analyzing data on thermal conditions, indoor air quality, and natural lighting. These insights allow architects and designers to refine building envelope designs to create healthier and more comfortable indoor environments. AI-driven design strategies ultimately support the development of spaces that prioritize both performance and occupant well-being.

For architects and designers who wish to maximize building envelope design for energy economy, thermal comfort, and occupant comfort, AI can be a potent predesign tool. AI-powered systems can offer insightful analysis and suggestions for enhancing building envelope design and performance by examining data on environmental conditions, building performance, and occupant comfort (kietzmann, j., paschen, j..est 2018).

The process of design exploration is generative design. The design goals, as well as characteristics like performance or spatial requirements, materials, manufacturing processes, and cost limitations, are entered by designers or engineers into generative design tools. The program swiftly generates design alternatives by investigating every variation of a potential solution. It experiments with each iteration, learning what works and what doesn't.

The use of generative design enables a more seamless workflow between people and machines, allowing architects and designers to create optimized and sustainable solutions tailored to specific project needs.

The process begins by defining the design problem, which involves identifying key goals and constraints such as energy efficiency, structural integrity, and user experience. Establishing these parameters ensures that the design aligns with performance objectives and project requirements.

Next, relevant data is collected to inform the generative design algorithm. This includes information on the building site, climate conditions, and user needs, which play a crucial role in shaping the design outcomes. By integrating these factors, designers can ensure that the generated solutions respond effectively to environmental and functional demands.

Using a visual programming language like Dynamo, a generative design algorithm is then created. This algorithm generates thousands of design options, evaluating each one based on its performance in relation to the defined problem. By automating this process, generative design enables rapid exploration of multiple possibilities, helping designers identify optimal solutions efficiently.

Once the algorithm has produced a set of potential designs, the next step is to evaluate and refine them. This involves analyzing the performance of each option and adjusting the algorithm as needed to enhance the results. By iterating through different configurations, designers can improve efficiency, sustainability, and feasibility.

Finally, the selected design is implemented in the Revit environment, where further refinements ensure that it meets construction requirements and regulatory standards. This integration streamlines the transition from concept to realization, making generative design a powerful tool for modern architectural practice.

Overall, generative design software facilitates an innovative approach to problem-solving, allowing architects and designers to develop optimized, data-driven solutions that enhance both functionality and sustainability.

The AI-powered platform Midjourney was created with architects and other building industry professionals in mind. The platform offers perceptions and suggestions for building design and construction using machine learning algorithms and data analytics. In order to help architects optimize building designs and raise energy efficiency, Midjourney uses a number of data sources, such as building performance data, energy usage data, and environmental data. The software also makes use of predictive analytics to identify potential problems early on and suggest fixes.

Midjourney is an AI-powered software that can assist in designing and building facades by generating optimized design options based on user-defined parameters. The process begins with inputting building parameters, including size, shape, and location. These details provide the software with essential information to tailor facade designs to the specific project context.

Next, the user selects a design style, such as modern, traditional, or minimalist, guiding the AI in generating designs that align with aesthetic and functional preferences. This customization ensures that the generated facades fit the desired architectural vision. Once the parameters and style preferences are set, Midjourney generates multiple design options using machine learning algorithms. These algorithms analyze the provided inputs to produce innovative and visually compelling facade solutions tailored to the project's unique requirements.

After the software generates various design options, the user evaluates and refines the selections. This involves reviewing the generated facades, making necessary adjustments, and fine-tuning elements to ensure that the final design meets performance, aesthetic, and contextual needs. By leveraging AI-powered tools like Midjourney, architects and designers can explore a wide range of facade design possibilities efficiently, streamlining the design process while maintaining creative control.

For example, input text data to the Midjourney software (to design a layout for an office for 100 people that included desks, focus rooms, meeting rooms, and boardrooms, as well as plants and lots of light), and Midjourney came up with the following variations:

Overall, using Midjourney for facade design involves inputting building parameters, selecting a design style, generating design options using AI, evaluating and refining the designs, and implementing the final design in your project (MSA Engineering Journal, n.d.).

A multi-story structure just west of Denver's central business center is the subject of the case study. As part of the project's design, it is important to consider solutions that will maximize inside light, adhere to specific window-to-wall ratios, and use rooftop solar panels to generate renewable energy (MG AEC | Architecture | Autodesk, 2021). The goal of the design is maximizing indoor light, achieving ideal window-to-wall ratios, and utilizing renewable energy sources, such as rooftop solar panels, which are all objectives of the project design. The workflow begins with the input of fixed constraints, including floor heights, property and zoning limits, and other limitations. Building orientation and any other "must-haves" or "nice-to-haves" can be included, prioritized, and sorted by designers. These inputs offer versatility, which expands the range of possible design strategies. Then, set parameters by using Dynamo: Once the data has been input, you will need to set parameters for the generative design algorithm. This will involve specifying the design constraints, such as material properties, structural requirements, and energy efficiency goals. The workflow begins with the input of fixed constraints, including floor heights, property and zoning limits, and other limitations. Building orientation and any other "must-haves" or "nice-to-haves" can be included, prioritized, and sorted by designers. These inputs offer versatility, which expands the range of possible design strategies. The outcomes increased the amount of optimism that they would satisfy the project's initial sustainability goals: maximizing the solar exposure on the floors and rooftops, reducing the window-to-wall ratios on each façade, and making sure the floor area ratio was at its highest.

Data-driven processes like generative design in Revit and Dynamo workflows help people make better decisions (MG AEC | Architecture | Autodesk, 2021).

4. Discussion

The synthesis of evidence from the literature presents compelling insights into the potential of AI-assisted facade design to enhance building climatic performance. Across various studies, the utilization of AI in optimizing building facades emerges as a promising approach to address contemporary challenges related to energy efficiency, indoor environmental quality, and overall sustainability in the built environment.

The reviewed literature demonstrates that AI-driven facade design strategies offer multifaceted benefits, encompassing improved thermal comfort, enhanced daylighting, optimized ventilation, and reduced energy consumption. Notably, AI algorithms facilitate the analysis of complex climatic data and building parameters to inform design decisions, thereby enabling the creation of facades tailored to specific environmental conditions and user requirements. A key finding from the literature is the capacity of AI-assisted facade design to optimize various climatic variables, such as temperature regulation, humidity control, and natural ventilation. Studies show that AI algorithms can iteratively refine facade configurations to achieve optimal performance, resulting in buildings that are responsive to climatic fluctuations and conducive to occupant comfort. Furthermore, the literature highlights the role of AI in expediting the design process and fostering innovation in facade design. AI-powered design tools enable architects to generate and evaluate a multitude of design options rapidly, facilitating iterative design exploration and optimization. This iterative approach not only enhances design quality but also enables architects to explore novel design solutions that may not be feasible using conventional methods. Moreover, evidence suggests that AI-assisted facade design has the potential to contribute to the broader goals of sustainability and environmental stewardship.

By optimizing building performance and reducing energy consumption, AI-driven facade design strategies can mitigate the environmental impact of buildings and contribute to global efforts to combat climate change. However, despite the promising findings, several challenges and limitations associated with the adoption of AI in facade design are evident in the literature. These include technical barriers such as data availability and computational complexity, as well as practical considerations related to integration with existing design workflows and industry standards. Addressing these challenges will require interdisciplinary collaboration and ongoing research efforts to refine AI algorithms, develop user-friendly design tools, and enhance industry adoption. In conclusion, the evidence from the literature underscores the transformative potential of AI-assisted facade design in enhancing building climatic performance. By leveraging AI algorithms to optimize facade configurations and inform design decisions, architects can create buildings that are not only aesthetically pleasing but also environmentally responsive, energy-efficient, and conducive to occupant well-being. However, realizing this potential will necessitate concerted efforts to address technical challenges, foster interdisciplinary collaboration, and promote the widespread adoption of AI in architectural practice.

Furthermore, the literature indicates that AI-assisted facade design has the potential to revolutionize the architectural profession by facilitating a shift toward data-driven and performance-based design methodologies. By harnessing the power of AI to analyze vast amounts of climatic and building data, architects can make more informed design decisions that prioritize both environmental sustainability and occupant comfort.

Moreover, the evidence suggests that AI-assisted facade design can lead to cost savings and improved project outcomes. By optimizing building performance and reducing energy consumption, AI-driven design strategies can result in lower operating costs over the lifespan of a building. Additionally, the ability to simulate and evaluate different design scenarios using AI can help architects identify potential performance issues early in the design process, reducing the need for costly revisions during construction. However, while the literature presents a compelling case for the benefits of AI-assisted facade design, it also highlights the need for caution and ongoing research. Concerns have been raised regarding the potential for AI to perpetuate biases in design outcomes, as well as the ethical implications of AI-driven decision-making processes. Additionally, the complexity of AI algorithms and the reliance on data inputs raise questions about transparency, accountability, and the need for robust validation and verification processes. In conclusion, while AI-assisted facade design holds great promise for enhancing building climatic performance, it is essential to approach its adoption with careful consideration and attention to ethical, technical, and practical considerations. Continued research, interdisciplinary collaboration, and industry engagement will be crucial in realizing the full potential of AI in architecture and ensuring that its benefits are equitably distributed across society. By leveraging AI to optimize facade design, architects can create buildings that not only respond to their environmental context but also contribute to a more sustainable and resilient built environment for future generations.

5. Conclusion

Evidence from literature underscores the transformative potential of integrating AI into architecture, heralding a paradigm shift toward buildings that excel in aesthetics, functionality, durability, and ecological integrity. The literature elucidates current applications of AI in architecture, delineating its role in enhancing building performance and streamlining the design process.

Specifically, the literature review illustrates how AI is presently employed to optimize key variables such as humidity, temperature, and cross-ventilation in building facade design. Furthermore, it highlights the potential of AI-driven design tools to expedite architectural workflows, enhance construction quality, and foster the development of environmentally conscious and sustainable structures. However, despite the promising prospects, the literature underscores the need for further investigation to fully capitalize on AI's potential in architecture. Challenges pertaining to the integration of AI with existing design tools and methodologies are acknowledged, necessitating concerted research efforts and collaborative endeavors to surmount. In summation, the application of AI in architecture holds immense promise for revolutionizing the sector, yielding visually captivating, high-performing, and sustainable buildings. Realizing these potential demands requires continued study and cooperation, as underscored by insights gleaned from surveys and literature reviews, which shed light on both the obstacles and opportunities associated with AI adoption in architecture.

References

Alışık, E. (2022). All compressed and rendered with a pathetic delicacy that astounds the eye: Midjourney renders ambergris as Constantinople. *CyberOrient*, *16*(2), 76–88.

Artificial Intelligence and Architecture (no date) *Google Books*. Available at: https://books.google.com. Accessed December 12, 2024

Artificial Intelligence Applied to Conceptual Design. (2021). A review of its use in architecture. *ScienceDirect*. Available at: https://www.sciencedirect.com. Accessed December 12, 2024

Beyan, E. V. P., & Rossy, A. G. C. (2023). A review of AI image generator: Influences, challenges, and future prospects for the architectural field. *Journal of Artificial Intelligence in Architecture*, *2*(1), 53–65.

Böke, J., Knaack, U., & Hemmerling, M. (2019). State-of-the-art of intelligent building envelopes in the context of intelligent technical systems. *Intelligent Buildings International*, *11*(1), 27–45.

Byrne, U. (2023). A parochial comment on Midjourney. *International Journal of Architectural Computing*, *21*(2), 147–160.

Caulfield, J. (2019). How to cite a book in APA style. *Scribbr*. Available at: https://www.scribbr.com. Accessed December 12, 2024

Chaillou, S. (2020). The advent of architectural AI. *The Medium*. Available at: https://medium.com. Accessed December 12, 2024

Chaillou, S. (no date) 'The advent of architectural AI: A historical perspective', *Academia.edu*. Available at: https://www.academia.edu (Accessed: 12 December 2024).

Di Blasi, G., Gallo, G., & Petralia, M. P. (2006). Smart ideas for photomosaic rendering. In *Eurographics Italian Chapter Conference* (pp. 267–272).

Günay, E., & Mayuk, S. G. (2022). A research on the use of machine learning on building facades. *European Journal of Respiratory Diseases*. (Vol. 2, 2, pp. 224–240). Academia+1ResearchGate+1.

Holm, L. (2022). Dali server: Structural unification of protein families. *Nucleic Acids Research*, *50*(W1), W210–W215.

Jaruga-Rozdolska, A. (2022). Artificial intelligence as part of future practices in the architect's work: MidJourney generative tool as part of a process of creating an architectural form. *Architectus*, *3*(71), 96–105. https://doi.org/10.37190/arc220310

Kietzmann, J., Paschen, J., & Treen, E. (2018). Artificial intelligence in advertising: How marketers can leverage artificial intelligence along the consumer journey. *Journal of Advertising Research*, *58*(3), 263–267.

Library Guides. (2019). *APA 7th referencing: Overview*. Victoria University. Available at: https://libraryguides.vu.edu.au. Accessed December 12, 2024

Masuch, M., Schlechtweg, S., Schönwälder, B., & Magdeburg, D. (1997). *DALI! Drawing animated lines!* (pp. 87–95). SimVis.

McCarthy, J., Minsky, M., Rochester, N., & Shannon, C. (1956). *A proposal for the Dartmouth summer research project on artificial intelligence*. Dartmouth College.

MG AEC. (2021). *Architecture | Autodesk*. Autodesk. Available at: https://www.autodesk.com. Accessed December 12, 2024

MSA Engineering Journal. (no date). *MSA engineering journal*. Available at: https://msaengjournal.org. Accessed: December 12, 2024

Nguyen, T. V., & Amoah, E. K. (2019). An approach to enhance interoperability of building information modeling (BIM) and data exchange in integrated building design and analysis. *Proceedings of the International Symposium on Automation and Robotics in Construction*, *36*, 876–883.

Pena, M. L. C., Ye, M., & Xu, L. (2021). Artificial Intelligence applied to conceptual design: A review of its use in architecture. *Automation in Construction*, *129*, 103749.

Ploennigs, J., & Berger, M. (2022). AI art in architecture. *arXiv Preprint arXiv:2212.09399*. Available at: https://arxiv.org. Accessed December 12, 2024

Tan, T. E., Anees, A., Chen, C., Li, S., Xu, X., Li, Z., Xiao, Z., Yang, Y., Lei, X., Ang, M., Chia, A., Lee, S. Y., Wong, E. Y. M., Yeo, I. Y. S., Wong, Y. L., Hoang, Q. V., Wang, Y. X., Bikbov, M. M., Nangia, V., & Ting, D. S. W. (2021). Retinal photograph-based deep learning algorithms for myopia and a blockchain platform to facilitate artificial intelligence medical research: A retrospective multicohort study. *The Lancet Digital Health, 3*(5), e317–e329.

ZDNet. (no date). *What is AI? Everything to know about artificial intelligence.* ZDNet. Available at: https://www.zdnet.com. Accessed December 12, 2024

Chapter 10

Investment of the Historic "Mount Uhud" to Establish Mountain Resorts, Overlooking the Prophet's Mosque in Al-Madinah

Nusaibah Mohammed Abdualhammed Al-shabi and Marwa Hussein Tawfik Hussein

Taibah University, Saudi Arabia

Abstract

Al-Medinah in Saudi Arabia, a prime religious destination for Muslims visiting the Prophet's Mosque, faces overcrowding in nearby hotels. This chapter explores why Mount Uhud has not been utilized to build hotels and resorts to support religious and cultural tourism. The objective is to examine the potential of investing in Mount Uhud for touristic resorts while preserving its religious identity, aligning with the "Saudi Vision 2030" goal of increasing accommodation capacity for Pilgrimage and Umrah performers. The chapter hypothesizes that developing mountain resorts on Mount Uhud will reduce hotel congestion around the Prophet's Mosque, attract religious tourism, and provide opportunities to enjoy Al-Madinah's natural scenery and historical sites. Researchers used historical, descriptive, and deductive methods, including a questionnaire given to Al-Madinah residents and visitors. Based on the outcomes, a proposed design for a tourist resort on Mount Uhud was developed. Key findings indicate the feasibility of investing in Mount Uhud as a religious and historic site to establish temporary resorts, accommodate Pilgrimage and Umrah performers, and entertain Al-Madinah residents simultaneously.

Keywords: Religious tourism; interior design; mountain resorts; Mount Uhud; historic sites

1. Introduction

Al-Madinah, one of the holiest cities in Islam, attracts millions of pilgrims annually who visit the Prophet's Mosque as part of their religious journey. This influx of visitors has led to significant overcrowding in the city's hotels, especially those near the mosque. Despite this challenge, Mount Uhud—a site of great historical and religious significance—remains underutilized in the development of accommodations and touristic facilities.

This chapter investigates the potential of Mount Uhud as a strategic location for developing touristic resorts that can support religious and cultural tourism while maintaining the site's spiritual integrity. The study aligns with the objectives of *Saudi Vision 2030*, which aims to expand accommodation capacity for Pilgrimage and Umrah visitors. By analyzing the feasibility of establishing mountain resorts, the chapter explores how such developments could alleviate congestion around the Prophet's Mosque, diversify tourism experiences, and enhance Al-Madinah's appeal as a destination that blends religious, cultural, and natural heritage.

To achieve this, the chapter employs historical, descriptive, and deductive methods, including a questionnaire distributed to Al-Madinah residents and visitors. Based on the findings, a proposed design for a tourist resort on Mount Uhud is introduced. The study ultimately demonstrates that investing in Mount Uhud for temporary resorts is not only viable but also beneficial in improving visitor experience, accommodating religious travelers, and offering leisure opportunities for local residents.

2. Literature Review

Mount Uhud is one of the main significant natural landmarks in Al-Madinah; it is the most renowned mountain in the Arabian Peninsula due to its status as a sacred Islamic site. There are three explanations for its name "Uhud": that it was named "Uhud: single & integral" because it stands as one undivided piece of land separated from other mountains; that this is the name of its first inhabitant; and that it is called "Uhud: individual" as a reference to the Unitarian concept of Allah (Was, 2014).

Mount Uhud extends as a series from east to west with a slight northern inclination in the northern part of Al-Madinah. The mountain spans 7 kilometers with an elevation reaching 1,077 meters; its width varies between 2 and 3 kilometers, and it is situated 5 kilometers away from the Prophet's Mosque. In its vicinity, there are several smaller mountains, with Mount Thawr to the north and Mount Aynayn to the west-south. Mount Uhud is strategically located; it oversees the convergence of the city's valleys and its green oases. It is bordered by the University Road to the north, the Southern Ring Road to the south, the Airport

Road to the east, and the Tia'b and Thawr mountains to the northwest (Al-zaidy, 2007).

The rocks of Mount Uhud belong to the Precambrian era (690–800 million years ago); they are acid to medium "fire-born" igneous rocks with a fine-crystallized structure, among various collateral Clastic rocks, which are distinct with high solidity and minimum distortion. The massive geological part of Mount Uhud consists of rose Rhyolite and light gray Dacite rocks; in addition to indurated volcanic projectiles, including Breccia and indurated volcanic ashes. Mount Uhud also contains granite rocks, which mostly tend to be dark red with veins of different colors such as blue and black (Al-Shohrany).

One of the distinct features of Mount Uhud is the many concaved hollows which retain rain water; they are called "Maharees"; as well as many caves and cracks, some of which exceed 1.5 meters high and 10 meters deep; also, many metals exist in Mount Uhud.

Rhyolite is a pale, fine-grained volcanic rock that is usually pale in color. It is commonly used as an acoustic and thermal insulator for walls, in the road industry, and as decorative rocks in landscapes, jewelry, and interior design.

Dacite is a fire-born, fine-grained rock that is also usually pale in color and exists in large quantities on Mars. Crushed dacite is added to backfill for construction projects, used for entrances and interior decor, and utilized for sidewalks and garden decorations.

Breccia is a composite or concrete rock consisting of different sharp-edged rock pieces. Ancient Egyptians used it to build statues, while Romans considered it a precious stone and used it to construct public buildings, pillars, and walls.

Granite is an underground fire-born rock that has become a key material for construction and massive architectural arts. It is used internally for floors, stairs, and other decorative purposes.

The Indian almond, also known as the Olive Bark tree, lawz Bajali, or hindibedm, is a decorative tree that can grow up to 20 meters high. It is suitable for providing shade in gardens and parks, serves as a good source of profit, and is useful for sand dune fixation.

The Bladder Dock, or Sorrel humeidh, is an annual herbaceous plant native to the Arabian Peninsula. It is a fast-growing plant that can reach up to 50 cm in height and spread. It is used to cover open areas and stabilize slopes for environmental architecture purposes. Additionally, it is useful in rehabilitating natural vegetation cover and can be planted on roadsides, as it is a winter annual plant.

The twisted Acacia, or Samur, is a flat-top desert tree that grows in Africa and the Kingdom of Saudi Arabia. It is resistant to severe desert weather, important for soil fertilization, and used as wind barriers to resist desertification. However, it is unsuitable for planting on roadsides due to its sharp thorns.

The Selim Acacia, or salam, is a tall desert tree widely spread across the Arabian Peninsula. It has high drought tolerance and can be planted on a wide scale within design plans targeting desert arrangements. It has the ability to block wind and alter weather.

The wide jujube, or sidr, nabak, is a desert weather-tolerant tree spread in the northern and middle regions of the Arabian Peninsula. It has very high tolerance to desert weather, supports the environmental system, and aids in rehabilitating natural vegetation cover. It can be planted on roadsides and in parks as a wind barrier.

Natural building materials are defined as materials used in their original state and shape as found in nature, without undergoing industrial processes such as reshaping, trimming, cutting, or processing (Abdel Fattah, 2018). These materials are categorized into four main types. Earth's raw materials include stones, marble, limestone, and cement, which are commonly used for structural and finishing purposes. Botanical raw materials consist of wood, bamboo, reeds, and cotton, offering sustainable and renewable options for construction and insulation. Animal raw materials, such as leather, wool, and feathers, are often used for decorative and comfort-enhancing applications. Finally, metal raw materials, including iron, copper, and gold, play a crucial role in structural support, electrical systems, and aesthetic detailing in architecture.

Stones are among the most commonly used and weather-resistant building materials. Designers and researchers aim to improve the properties of stones by maintaining their natural state while providing features to protect them from weather elements. They achieve this by recycling quarry residues to produce stone plates, which are more solid than natural stone and possess various aesthetic and economical aspects (Youssef, 2020).

Clay is one of the oldest local building materials, known for being cheap, available, and easy to transfer and use due to its light weight. It has been used across civilizations, suiting both economic and environmental conditions. Clay's flexibility allowed nations to use it in artistic forms. Through engineering developments, clay transitioned from a folk building material to an engineering constructional material, addressing issues related to energy and pollution.

Concrete is a highly efficient aesthetic building material. It is easy to shape, and recent developments, including the introduction of computers and CNC machines, have enabled the creation of various shapes, especially in prefabricated concrete. This material is distinct for its accuracy and execution speed. Technological advancements in NANO techniques have improved concrete performance by reducing air pollution from concrete-sun interactions, making it self-cleaning and ideal for organic architectural facades.

Wood is a natural building material with renewable sources. It is considered the most important organic material due to its various types. Wood's organic cell composition gives it specific beauty through its fibers, veins, interlocks, and colors, enhancing both internal and external spaces.

Mountain tourism, or natural scenery tourism, started in the 19th century. It introduced mountains as places for relaxation, activities, and nature sightseeing; this type of tourism helps highlight the traditional, cultural, and geological features of the mountains (Attia, 2015).

The visual image of the mountain environment is influenced by both natural and human elements, and studies have identified key principles that should be followed when constructing buildings in mountainous areas (Attia, 2015). First, buildings should be distributed harmoniously with the land formation, ensuring that their purposes and heights blend seamlessly into the landscape. Entrances should reflect the local spirit, incorporating indigenous design styles, and be surrounded by native shrubs that are compatible with the area's climate. The finishing materials used in mountain buildings should be sourced locally, align with the intended functions of the spaces, and preserve the architectural identity of the region. Additionally, lighting elements should be strategically placed in spaces and pathways to emphasize movement and orientation. Furthermore, the local climate must be considered when determining the building's orientation, as well as the shape and size of its openings. Beyond environmental factors, social considerations also play a crucial role in the design and planning of touristic resorts. Essential aspects include providing tranquility and, if needed, isolation from daily life routines, ensuring that rooms offer individual services for both personal and family use, and incorporating a dedicated "business center" to meet the needs of business travelers and officials.

3. Practical Framework

The objective of this analytical chapter is to identify the design fundamentals applied in selected projects and to understand their creative approaches. The examples chosen for analysis adhere to specific criteria to ensure relevance and applicability. First, the selected resorts must be located in mountainous environments similar to Al-Madinah, allowing for a meaningful comparison in terms of geography and climate. Additionally, these resorts should draw inspiration from their natural surroundings and cultural heritage, ensuring that their architectural identity aligns with the local context. Lastly, the selected case studies must be five-star resorts that integrate contemporary design principles while maintaining sustainability through organic construction methods. This approach ensures that the analysis highlights innovative yet environmentally responsible solutions for mountain resort development.

The "Desert Rock" project, located on the west coast of Saudi Arabia, is designed by Oppenheim Architecture in collaboration with the Red Sea Development Company. The design aims to merge the unique hospitality of ancient mountains with nature, creating a global trademark. It is part of Saudi Arabia's ambitious plan to promote environmental tourism, covering an area of 11,000 square miles that includes islands, beaches, mountains, and volcanic locations, engaging the glorious granite mountains and legendary desert scenery.

Natural illumination is maximized by installing full-wall windows, providing light and the opportunity to enjoy the scenery. Construction within the mountain itself provides shade and reduces hot temperatures. Artificial lights are used in a direct and focused manner to highlight interior decor and materials. The internal and external spaces are situated within mountain cracks and caves or above shaded slopes to cope with cold night weather and reduce heat gain during the day. Consequently, the construction is hidden during the day and glows like small lanterns at night (Luxigon, 2019).

Materials generated from drilling processes at the resort location are used in its infrastructure. Stone pieces decorate internal and external walls and floors, while earth, stone, and sand are used to make rubble concrete, the main construction material. The road network leading to the resort is built at the edges of the main valley, hidden behind the existing natural landscape, reducing noise and light pollution and allowing visitors to fully immerse themselves in the surrounding desert scenery.

The analytical chapter yielded several key design principles essential for developing mountain resorts in environments similar to Al-Madinah. Large windows should be incorporated extensively to maximize natural illumination, while artificial lighting should be used strategically to enhance decorative elements and add an artistic touch. Natural features such as water and plants play a dual role, aiding in ventilation and providing protection from high temperatures. Additionally, the existing land formations should be leveraged to create natural barriers against harsh climate conditions. Horizontal construction is recommended to ensure privacy and optimize views of the surrounding landscape. To maintain harmony with nature and highlight the cultural identity of the area, natural building materials like stone, wood, and granite should be prioritized (Mohammad, 2017).

As part of the study, a questionnaire titled *"Utilizing Mount Uhud to Build Mountain Resorts Overlooking the Prophet's Mosque"* was conducted to gather insights from the local community regarding construction on Mount Uhud. The objective was to assess public opinion and support the research findings. A total of 241 participants took part in the survey, providing valuable perspectives on the feasibility and desirability of such developments (see Table 10.1).

Table 10.1. Questionnaire Analysis (by Authors).

1. Age Group		2. Gender	
21–35	**66%**	Female	85.5%
36 and Above	**17.4%**	Male	14.5%
15–20	**14.5%**		
3. Academic qualification		**4. Are you a citizen, resident or visitor?**	
University	**70.5%**	Citizen	**68.5%**
Bachelor	**12%**		
Secondary school	**10.8%**	Resident	**27.4%**
Masters	**4.1%**		
Middle school	**1.7%**	Visitor	**4.1%**
Doctorate	**0.8%**		
The questionnaire outcomes show that the highest ratio of participants was the university students, followed by bachelor's degree holders; thus,		The questionnaire outcomes show that the highest ratio of participants was Saudi citizens, while the lowest ratio was the visitors; thus, most of	

Table 10.1. *(Continued)*

most of the participants are of higher education.		the participants are the people of Al-Madinah.	
5. Did you visit Mount Uhud and climbed to its top?		**6. Would you like to develop Mount Uhud to accommodate performers of Pilgrimage & Umrah?**	
Yes	49.4%	Yes	85.5%
No	36.5%	No	14.5%
Only Jabal Al-Rumah	14.1%		
The questionnaire results reveal that most participants have climbed Mount Uhud, encountering issues with difficult-to-access roads and insufficient seating areas. Those who didn't climb cited the lack of attraction sites and road conditions, with a minority fearing heights.		Based on the majority of opinions, development of Mount Uhud is preferred due to its historical and religious significance, which can attract visitors, given that its identity as a sacred site for Muslims is preserved.	
7. In your opinion; which constructions will be the best utilization of Mount Uhud?		**8. Do you think that constructions on the mountain could decrease the over crowdedness in the hotels around the Prophet's mosque?**	
Temporary resorts	40.2%	Yes	58.1%
Parks	34.4%	No	41.9%
Permanent resorts	14.9%		
Based on the majority of opinions, temporary resorts were chosen to accommodate Pilgrimage and Umrah performers. These resorts will also be open to locals, offering various activities and educational opportunities about Al-Madinah, alongside the construction of parks.		The questionnaire results indicate that 58.1% of participants believe that building on Mount Uhud could reduce hotel overcrowding around the Prophet's mosque, provided transportation is available. This is considered a satisfactory percentage.	
9. How would you prefer the constructions on the mountain be?		**10. If resorts are built; which style would you prefer to be used in this location?**	
Within the mountain itself	68.9%	Both styles	52.7%
Bungalows	31.1%	Environmental style	34.9%
		Hijazzi style	12.4%

(Continued)

Table 10.1. *(Continued)*

Based on the majority of opinions, the preferred construction is within the mountain itself.	Based on the majority of opinions, both the environmental and Hijazzi styles were combined in the design to maintain the nature and culture of the mountain.
11. In your opinion; what are the best colors for resorts?	**12. Which size do you prefer for the resort slots?**

Neutral colors	**84.6%**	Full wall slots	**57.7%**
Cool colors	**10%**	Medium slots	**38.2%**
Warm colors	**5.4%**	Small slots	**4.1%**

Based on the majority of opinions, neutral colors were selected for the proposed design.	Based on the majority of opinions, full-wall slots were selected for the proposed design.
13. Which materials would you prefer to be used in the design?	**14. Would you prefer to enhance the internal and external spaces using plants and water; or keep the mountainous stone nature?**

Natural materials	**53.1%**	Plants & water	**43.2%**
Modern materials	**29%**	The mountainous nature	**38.2 %**
Traditional materials	**17.8%**	Plants only	**10.4%**
		Water only	**8.3%**

Based on the majority of opinions, sustainable natural materials were selected for the proposed design.	Based on the majority of opinions, both elements of water and plants were selected for the internal and external design while maintaining the mountainous nature.
15. Which type of illumination would you prefer for the design?	**16. What is your preferred style for furniture distribution inside residential constructions?**

Natural & artificial	**78.8%**	Spacious space	**61%**
Natural	**18.7%**	A lot of details	**3.9%**
Artificial	**2.5%**		

Based on the majority of opinions, both natural and artificial illumination were used in the proposed design.	Based on the majority of opinions, the comfortable and spacious design was selected for the proposed project.

17. Recommendations and opinions of the local community according to the questionnaire:

Table 10.1. *(Continued)*

There were 66 answers for this question; summarized in the following points:

To provide a variety of activities for the visitors, e.g., accommodations, seating areas, and parks, at the bottom of the mountain to serve different categories of visitors, in order not to deprive the local inhabitants of the leisure of enjoying the mountain.	To limit the proposed project to be for religious purposes only and provide accommodation for the performers of Pilgrimage and Umrah in order for them to closely recognize the sites of Al-Madinah and Mount Uhud without turning it into a place for leisure
To utilize and develop Mount Uhud but at the same time maintain its identity and religious status.	To build subway routes to facilitate reaching the Prophet's mosque
To utilize sustainable building and furniture materials that don't deteriorate with time.	To use natural colors in the proposed design, with hints of warm or cool colors to draw attention to the design details
To utilize large slots, but the design should apply the required processes to provide privacy and resist hot temperatures.	To preserve the mountainous nature, while integrating green areas and water in the design to satisfy all tastes

4. Results

The proposed design for Mount Uhud resorts aims to balance religious tourism with environmental and cultural preservation. Temporary resorts will be constructed to provide accommodation for Pilgrimage and Umrah performers, alongside seating areas overlooking the Prophet's Mosque, accessible to all visitors. The architectural style will integrate environmental and Hijazi influences, ensuring that the resorts blend seamlessly into the mountain while maintaining its natural and cultural essence.

Natural brown hues will dominate the color palette, complemented by sustainable materials to reinforce the project's ecological commitment. The design will incorporate full-wall openings oriented according to their optimal directions for natural lighting and ventilation. Additionally, plants and water features will be integrated both internally and externally, enhancing comfort while preserving the mountain's rocky terrain. A combination of natural and artificial lighting will be employed to create a visually appealing and health-conscious environment. Most importantly, the project will uphold the spiritual significance of Mount Uhud by centering on religious tourism, ensuring that any development respects and enhances the site's historical and cultural identity.

5. Application

The objective of this project is to integrate the religious background of Al-Madinah with Mount Uhud's rocky nature to establish resorts built within the mountain itself in order to provide accommodation for the visitors and give them the chance to enjoy the spirituality of the place and discover the historical sites of Al-Madinah.

The proposed project also aims to accomplish one of the "Saudi Vision 2023" objectives, which is to increase the accommodation capacity to facilitate hosting performers of Pilgrimage and Umrah.

The objective is to maintain the mountain's name due to its distinct importance for Muslims and to affirm the sense of authenticity of the chosen site which we love and it loves us back. According to Anas (may Allah be pleased with him), Prophet Mohammed said, "Mount Uhud loves us, and we love it." The logo was drawn based on the mountain's curvatures, forming the name "Uhud" (see Fig. 10.1).

The main idea was to integrate the natural elements (rocks, water & plants) with the cultural Hijazzi style of Al-Madinah to provide the chance to experience the essence of nature and learn more about the history of the city, as well as to save energy by focusing on utilizing natural illumination and cooling the premises using water and vegetation. The materials proposed for this project are those extracted from the mountain itself, e.g., stones and granite, natural wood, and fabrics designed according to the Hijazzi style.

The design of the reception area is based on the nature of the site by integrating natural materials with water and plants, a variety of seating areas, and a lot of natural illumination in addition to artificial light to decorate the place.

Second space (accommodation rooms): The room's front side is designed in the shape of a "Mashrabiya"; rooms are distributed across the mountain top in the shape of an old Hijazzi house so that during the day rooms look like they are windows inside the mountain and as lit lanterns hanging on the mountain during night-time.

Fig. 10.1. The Resort Logo. *Source*: by Authors.

The design includes various seating areas, including floor seating inspired by Arabian culture and decorated with Hijazzi motifs, and a relaxing area. The design of the floor-bed includes a desk as its headboard, taking into consideration that both the bed and the desk have two views: of the mountain and the pool. There is also a designated room to change clothes and a bathroom designed by integrating nature with Hijazi motifs.

The project design includes an outside seating area on the top of the mountain overlooking all of Al-Madinah and the Prophet's Mosque. The objective is to provide both the people of the city and its visitors the chance to learn more about it and key sites and at the same time, enjoy the refreshing weather at the mountain top. The seating areas are designed to accommodate large numbers of people, so they are convenient for groups as well as individuals, who are welcome to enjoy the nice weather and beautiful scenery in a full-service area. The reception is located at the bottom of the mountain; accommodation rooms on top of the mountain can be reached using the elevator, while moving between the rooms is available through the two side elevators. Source: Authors.

Every three cafes serve a group of seating areas in order to provide the most possible services; the images also show the motion pathways between the project spaces. Source: Authors.

Barcode for the project demonstration video

6. Conclusion

Mountain resorts play a crucial role in attracting tourists by offering an escape into nature's tranquility. Establishing a resort on Mount Uhud aligns with this objective, particularly by drawing religious tourists who seek both spiritual and peaceful experiences in Al-Madinah. The findings from the questionnaire indicate that while the residents of Al-Madinah are open to the idea of developing Mount Uhud, there is a strong concern about preserving its religious significance as a sacred Islamic site. Given the mountain's rich historical, geographical, and geological elements, any development must ensure that its sanctity remains intact. This can be achieved by constructing temporary resorts that accommodate Pilgrimage and Umrah performers while also allowing residents and visitors to appreciate the mountain's historical importance and scenic beauty.

To ensure the successful and culturally sensitive development of Mount Uhud, several key recommendations should be considered. First, any development should prioritize the preservation of Mount Uhud's religious and historical significance while enhancing its role as a cultural and religious tourism destination in alignment with Saudi Vision 2030. Second, architects, engineers, and interior designers should be encouraged to create designs that harmonize with the natural landscape, incorporating sustainable materials and reflecting the region's architectural heritage. Finally, the Saudi Heritage Commission should take an active role in developing infrastructure and transportation services that facilitate religious tourism while maintaining the sacred character of the site.

References

Abdel Fattah, M. (2018). The technical and aesthetic impact of nanotechnology applications on the design of architectural facades. *Journal of Architecture, Arts, and Humanities*, 3(11(2)), 689–707. https://doi.org/10.12816/0046912

Al-Shohrany, A. A. *Mount Uhud at Al-Madinah: A monument which tells the prophetic history*. Saudi Press Agency.

Al-zaidy, K. (2007). Uhud: A mountain which loves us and we love it. *Al-Riyadh Newspaper*. Available at: https://www.alriyadh.com/294638. Accessed November 17, 2007

Attia, A. (2015). The remedy of visual pollution on circulation axes in mountain environment: An applied study on Al-Hada Ring Road -Taif. *Journal of Urban Research*, 18(1), 38–57. https://doi.org/10.21608/jur.2015.89777

King, H. M. (n.d.). *Geology and earth science news and information*. Dacite. Available at: https://geology.com/rocks/dacite.shtml

Luxigon (2019). Desert rock. *Oppenheim Architecture*. Available at: https://oppenoffice.com/works/desert-rock/

Mohammad, H. (2017). Design basics of touristic buildings. *Almohandes com*. Available at: https://www.eng2all.com/أسس-التصميميه-للمنشات-السياحيه-design-basics-of-tou. Accessed February 10, 2017

Was (2014). Mount Uhud: An interval odyssey between the expansion of Islam and Hijrah. *Almadinah Mobasher*. Available at: https://web.archive.org/web/20160304120502/http://www.almadina.com/node/563006?live. Accessed: October 14, 2014

Youssef, M. M. A. (2020). *Touristic sustainability in mountainous regions*. Arab Journal for Scientific Publishing.

Part III

Case Studies: An Insight Into the Day-to-Day Practice of Architecture in the Arab World

Chapter 11

Developing a Sustainable Mountain Resorts Design Framework for Aseer, Saudi Arabia

Haifa Al-Harbi[a] and Mostafa Sabbagh[b]

[a]King Saud University, Saudi Arabia
[b]King Abdulaziz University, Saudi Arabia

Abstract

Vision 2030 aims to put the Kingdom of Saudi Arabia on the world tourism map. Over 30 licenses have been issued to establish touristic hospitality accommodation facilities in the Aseer region alone. However, none of the projects have been completed so far. Sustainable Tourism Development in Aseer should integrate environmental sensitivity and community consideration and aim to save natural resources. Additionally, the natural mountainous topography of Aseer can be an ideal location to construct sustainable resorts that can revive the tourism industry. Given the lack of sustainable resorts in Aseer, this chapter offers insights into developing a sustainable mountain resort design framework. A qualitative approach involving the analysis of five case studies from different countries was used to identify the principles of the proposed design framework. The framework was categorized as follows: landscape integration, sustainable construction, water and energy efficiency, and local community engagement. The framework offers stakeholders and architects essential guidance for designing sustainable resorts in the mountainous area of Aseer.

Keywords: Sustainable tourism; Saudi tourism; design framework; natural heritage; mountain resorts

1. Introduction

The Kingdom of Saudi Arabia's (KSA) Vision 2030 represents an ambitious initiative to diversify the nation's economy and reduce its dependence on oil. Central to this vision is the development of the tourism sector, aiming to position Saudi Arabia as a premier global destination (Hassan, 2019). The Vision 2030 framework emphasizes sustainable development, integrating environmental sensitivity, community engagement, and the conservation of natural resources. Within this context, the Aseer region, known for its moderate climate and stunning mountainous topography, presents a unique opportunity for developing sustainable mountain resorts that can invigorate the tourism industry. Saudi Arabia's geographical diversity, which includes vast deserts, pristine coastlines, and mountainous regions, offers an array of natural and cultural attractions. Despite this potential, significant development and infrastructure are required to make these areas accessible and attractive to tourists. The Aseer region, in particular, remains underdeveloped in terms of tourism infrastructure, highlighting the need for a comprehensive framework that guides sustainable resort development. If unchecked, development at sites that are predominantly natural and virgin may lead to the interruption of fragile ecosystems and loss of habitat.

Vision 2030 places a strong emphasis on sustainability as a cornerstone of national development. This commitment is reflected in various initiatives aimed at enhancing environmental protection, resource conservation, and the promotion of sustainable building technologies. For instance, KSA has invested in advanced waste management systems, integrated recycling projects, and efforts to combat desertification and reduce pollution. Water scarcity is addressed through measures such as resource conservation, seawater desalination, and treated wastewater reuse. Additionally, there are robust efforts to protect marine and coastal ecosystems and expand the network of natural reserves.

Developing a sustainable tourism infrastructure in Aseer requires a delicate, nuanced approach that balances environmental conservation with economic development. Green building standards and regulatory frameworks are considered new and under development (Sabbag et al., 2019), lacking principles tailored to the Aseer region, facilitating tourists' connection with nature, promoting culture exchange, and/or enhancing quality and comfort with minimum impact to the environment.

The tourism sector, which has been significantly impacted by the COVID-19 pandemic, now faces the dual challenge of recovery and the need for sustainable practices. Restrictions on international travel created a unique opportunity for stimulating local tourism. The pandemic has underscored the importance of resilient local tourism infrastructure that can adapt to health and environmental considerations.

Research by E. Crossley (2020) has highlighted the interplay between the pandemic and climate change, emphasizing the need for sustainable tourism practices that promote environmental healing (Arnoult, 2020). Similarly, J. Mair and Smith (2021) have explored the critical role of community well-being in the postpandemic tourism recovery, advocating for development strategies that integrate local community engagement. Another study highlighted how the pandemic would possibly affect future pro-environmental travel behavior and provide essential management substances for sustainable tourism. These studies underscore the importance of regulatory frameworks and stakeholder engagement in achieving sustainable tourism development.

Aseer, located in the southwestern corner of KSA, is poised to become a focal point for tourism. The region's natural beauty, moderate climate, cultural heritage, unique topography, and stunning mountains make it an ideal candidate for the development of sustainable mountain resorts. The tourism infrastructure in Aseer is inadequate and in need of major development. To develop the infrastructure, a framework is required that can help and support the local economy, preserve heritage sites, and revive the vernacular architecture, while conserving energy, natural ecology, and resources.

This chapter aims to propose a design framework for sustainable mountain resorts in Aseer, aligning with the goals of Vision 2030. By analyzing best practices from sustainable mountain resorts globally, this chapter seeks to identify principles that can be adapted to the context of Aseer. The proposed framework will address key areas such as landscape integration, sustainable construction, water and energy efficiency, and local community engagement, providing essential guidance for architects and stakeholders.

To achieve this aim, the chapter sets forth several key objectives. First, it explores best practices by investigating sustainable mountain resorts worldwide, focusing on strategies that effectively preserve environmental, cultural, and social aspects. Second, it aims to develop a comprehensive design framework tailored specifically to the unique context of Aseer, ensuring that sustainability principles are seamlessly integrated into the region's mountain resorts. Finally, the chapter provides actionable recommendations for architects and stakeholders involved in the development of these resorts, ensuring that their designs align with Vision 2030's sustainability goals while maintaining the region's natural and cultural integrity.

This chapter is the first to propose a detailed framework for sustainable mountain resorts in Aseer, offering a foundational guide that supports the region's tourism development in harmony with its natural and cultural heritage.

2. Literature Review

The aim to diversify KSA's economy and reduce dependency on oil has led to the prioritization of and improvements to domestic industries, such as tourism. According to the Arab Travel Market Forum, the number of international arrivals to KSA is expected to increase by 5.6% annually from 17.7 million in 2018 to 23.3 million in 2023. This number is expected to rise to 30 million by 2030 (Invest Saudi). The National Transformation Program 2020 (2016) has over 23 initiatives, including developing tourism and the national heritage sector (Oxford, 2017) (National Transformation, 2017), ensuring the sustainability of vital resources, and supporting the resettlement of jobs, and foreign investment.

One such initiative focused on tourism and heritage was Saudi Seasons, an initiative launched by the Saudi Commission for Tourism and National Heritage via which 11 festivals were planned for different Saudi regions in 2019. Saudi Seasons should help achieve goals from the overlapping National Transformation Program 2020 as well, particularly those related to reviving tourism. While it has been difficult to gauge the full extent of the impact of COVID-19 on the tourism sector in KSA as of March 2020, it is clear that the pandemic has significantly affected tourism figures not only in KSA but also worldwide (Saudigazette, 2023). The National Transformation Program 2020 and Vision 2030 focus on developing tourism and all related sectors. Such integrated development will create opportunities and a better quality of life for Saudi youth and make the cultures of Saudi regions known worldwide.

Vision 2030 emphasizes the importance of developing the tourism and entertainment sector. This includes encouraging private sector investment, developing tourist sites, facilitating procedures for issuing visas to visitors, and developing historical and heritage sites. It aims to enable the tourism sector to contribute 6% of the gross domestic product (GDP) by the end of 2023 (Person, 2022). Vision 2030's tourism agenda merely marks the beginning of the development of the KSA tourism infrastructure. It encourages private investment to enable tourism growth by promoting domestic tourism that focuses directly on leisure. The developed tourism sector will also provide employment opportunities for Saudi youth. in fact, the tourism sector will create one every three jobs in the upcoming years (Person, 2022). The country plans to encourage public and private investment in roads, airports, and hotels to support tourism. Offerings include international events, luxury destinations, heritage sites, and ecotourism, in addition to government agencies announcing major agreements with travel agencies, real estate and retail companies, as well as major hotel groups. These types of offerings and other strategies have created new momentum in the construction sector; with tourism capital investment expected to rise to over US$53.3 billion over the next 10 years, KSA aims to become a major tourist destination by 2030 (Som and Al-Kassem, 2013). As part of developing tourism, maximizing KSA's rich cultural heritage is emphasized by the Vision 2030 agenda for social and economic transformation. Under this plan, KSA wishes to double the number of Saudi heritage sites registered with UNESCO. KSA is relying on the benefits of the registered sites to promote international tourism, as 10 sites are already included on the tentative list to be considered by the UNESCO for nomination. To date, there are 1073 registered sites from around the world on the World Heritage list. Compared to other Arab countries, KSA already has five registered sites, namely Al-Hijr Archeological Site (Madâin Sâlih), At-Turaif District in ad-Dir'iyah, Historic Jeddah (the Gate to Makkah), Rock Art in the Hail Region of Saudi Arabia, and Al-Ahsa Oasis (an Evolving Cultural Landscape), which are expected to increase inbound tourism competition with similar historic sites in the region. In 2020, the Saudi representative to UNESCO launched the "13-in-one" initiative to highlight the cultural diversity of the various regions of KSA. She explained that this initiative mainly relies on members of local society in all its spectrums to enrich local content that showcases cultural heritage and regional diversity. One of the most important economic benefits of the Vision 2030 strategies is implementing Sustainable Tourism Development, which includes the three primary dimensions of tourism development: economic, social and cultural, and environmental.

The *Aseer* province is located in KSA southwestern corner, between *Wadi Al-Dafaat* in the north and the Red Sea in the west. *Aseer* is named after the confederation of families that lived there. The capital of *Aseer*, *Abha*, is located 2000 meters above sea level. The western part of the city lies on the ridge of an escarpment, and the terrain then falls to the lowland of *Tihama*. A road runs up into the *Sawdah* Mountains, located 3,000 meters above sea level in the north. The east and the south lie on 1,850-meter-heigh terrain, encompassing *Kamis Mushayt* and *Ahad Rafidah* (Al-Yami & Price, 2006).

Sustainable tourism development requires a balanced approach that integrates environmental, economic, and social sustainability. The World Tourism Organization (UNWTO) defines sustainable tourism as development that meets the needs of present tourists and host regions while protecting and enhancing opportunities for the future (UNWTO, 2020). This concept is particularly relevant for the Aseer region, which offers unique ecological, cultural, and economic opportunities. KSA has taken extensive steps to protect the environment and natural resources (UNWTO, 2020). KSA has initiated several regulations that play critical roles in achieving its sustainability values of Vision 2030. Promoting domestic tourism is required in order to achieve sustainability, and diversification of tourism is not undertaken in terms of market, product, and geographical areas. This is particularly relevant given that the *Aseer* region is a unique tourist destination and has vast unrealized potential in terms of ecology, culture, and economy.

2.1 Ecology

The Saudi Commission for Tourism and Antiquities and the Ministry of Municipal and Rural Affairs are jointly planning to prepare a checklist for construction and building in mountainous areas. The checklist will offer a scientific methodology to guide the municipalities of the mountainous areas to embark on the construction in a manner that accommodates the mountainous nature and the limited land available for urban development (GOV.SA.). These checklists will help achieve environmental sustainability to construct mountain resorts in *Aseer* that are blended with nature and preserve the land sensitivity, which in turn, will protect the wildlife and vegetation without damaging the surrounding environment.

2.2 Culture

Sustainable sites are rich with natural areas for experiencing unique features and cultural values. Tourism development in KSA focuses on promoting cultural values and promoting cultural tourism to explore the various cultures in KSA by identifying opportunities for tourism that can revive the culture, heritage, and traditions supported by the conservation of tourism sites, handicrafts, local markets, and any related events. The attractions in *Aseer* are not limited to its historical buildings—also notable is the artwork, called El-Got El*Aseer*i, that *Aseer*i ladies used to decorate the interior walls of homes for over four hundred years; this art is no longer a common practice in contemporary homes, except for exhibitions and forums. UNESCO listed El-Got El*Aseer*i as part of the Intangible Cultural Heritage of Humanity. *Aseer*, with its native culture, is aware of *El-Got ElAseeri's* concept and details. The best proof of this is the old and new houses, which are still experiencing their remains, and creations shaped in paintings and murals with engravings and attractive colors created by *Aseeri* women. The society of *Aseer* has traditionally encouraged all the members of the family to work. Although women in *Aseer* support men in the family by carrying out the domestic tasks and helping men during the harvesting season (since the primary source of livelihood is agriculture), they also took on the responsibility of creating these highly structured interior wall decorations that have proved to be the most outstanding architectural feature of *Aseer*i houses (Al-Hababi, 2012).

2.3 Economy

According to a report published by the World Travel and Tourism Council (WTTC), the tourism sector in KSA grew rapidly between 2009 and 2018. Although Vision 2030 affects the tourism and travel industry in KSA, tourism targets have been set outside the Vision 2030 statement as well. Some of the goals of Vision 2030 and the Saudi Authority for Tourism and National Heritage that could drive growth in the travel and tourism were embarked upon by issuing visas to visitors. Supporting the tourism sector will help move KSA from its current position as the world's 19th largest economy to the top 15 economies. Additionally, an increase in nonoil government revenues from US$43.44 billion to US$226.58 billion is expected due to the contribution of nonoil revenues to total revenues increasing from 12% in 2014 to 32% in 2018, an average growth of 20% during this period. In fact, the total contribution of travel and tourism to the GDP reached US$73.06 billion, or 9.5% of the total GDP in 2019, confirming the increasingly important role of the sector in KSA's economic development (Economic Impact Reports). With government investment supporting the rapid growth in this sector, the tourism economy is expected to grow to nearly US$106.66 billion over the next 10 years. According to Rochelle Turner, Research Director at WTTC, tourism is positioned as a pillar of the future Saudi economy (Economic Impact Reports). Moreover, KSA is seeking to attract foreign investment, which will create opportunities for companies outside KSA to invest in the country, such as in inbound international commercial travel, as part of a strategy to enhance the contribution of tourism to a diversified national economy within the framework of Vision 2030 for economic and social transformation. The government-owned Public Investment Fund injected US$2.67 billion into a leisure investment company to develop KSA entertainment infrastructure and is expected to create nearly 22,000 jobs by 2030. The Tourism Authority in *Aseer* should develop tourist areas and programs accessible throughout the year. This would play a major role in attracting the investment capital to this sector needed to provide stability and durability, growth, and alternative tourist attractions. To be sure, the private sector plays a role in sustainable development, and thus the tourism sector deserves attention in considerations of how to achieve sustainability. Allowing foreign investors to invest in the tourism sector will positively influence this goal. Therefore, the Saudi Commission for Tourism and Antiquities should sponsor such investments by providing the necessary assistance to prepare studies that contribute to attracting specialized investment owners. Because the strategic objective of the *Aseer* region is linked with successful investing in tourism activities, it encourages the creation of a set of sub-objectives that include building year-round tourist attractions, creating permanent and seasonal job opportunities in the sector, and achieving a comprehensive human resource development in local communities that would be best integrated in the revival of tourism in the region.

In 2013, KSA agreed to implement the Future of Saudi Cities Program (FSCP), which was launched by the Ministry of Municipal and Rural Affairs in collaboration with UN-Habitat. FSCP seeks to achieve sustainable urban development in Saudi cities through effective planning and management, including enhancing and supporting economically productive cities and improving urban legislation and institutional frameworks (WTTC). This program is fully in line with Vision 2030 and the National Transformation Program, and it responds to the global urban development agenda that the KSA has committed to implement. More specifically, the agenda aims to develop cities that are prosperous, productive, fair, socially inclusive, and environmentally sustainable and that boast adequate infrastructure and a high quality of life. Aboneama studied the current situation in *Abha* city, the capital of the *Aseer* region, by applying the principles of sustainable design in its architecture and proposed categorizing *Abha* as a sustainable city (Aboneama, 2018). To be sure, *Abha* is an excellent candidate for a sustainable city, given that it is home to reasonably moderate-to-cool climatic conditions throughout the year and adequate precipitation relative to its surroundings. Notably, Aboneama proposed establishing a sustainable transportation plan in the city by installing trolleybus and tram lines between *Abha* and *Khamis Mushait* and using zero-emission buses that generate energy from renewable resources. Moreover, he suggested applying passive design techniques to buildings. Most buildings in *Abha* have neither the spirit of the famous vernacular architecture of *Aseer* nor do they use local building materials, building techniques, aesthetics, and cultural elements; all the buildings are similar and built with cement. Additionally, developing new water and drainage systems strategies is required. In fact, the future of rainwater harvesting in *Aseer* is promising to be adequate for the local population's domestic use and irrigation. Transforming *Abha* into an eco-city is a great solution and could offer guidance for many Middle Eastern cities facing the same challenges.

Since the establishment of the Saudi Commission for Tourism and National Heritage in 2000, KSA has pursued the facilitation of tourism development at the national level. Development in the Saudi tourism sector has focused on areas with great potential to be a large tourism market, taking advantage of sites with natural beauty and cool climate (Jaber and Marzuki, 2018). The impact of tourism development on the environment has not been adequately assessed. In fact, unsustainable tourism activities have degraded natural resources that the tourism industry relies on. Tourism leads to negative impacts when the level of tourist use is greater than the environment's capacity, which adjusts gradually to changes. Traditional tourism has potentially damaged many natural areas. It can pose tremendous stress on an area and lead to soil erosion, pollution, loss of natural habitat, and threats to endangered species. It usually demands natural resources and can force local people to compete over natural resources (World Travel). The National Tourism Development principles focus on the compatibility of tourism with the special characteristics of the community and its values; sustainability; economic, social, cultural, and environmental advantages; and the actual and effective contribution of tourism to comprehensive national development in general. Additionally, KSA is rich with extradentary natural elements and historical sites, such as in *Aseer*, which will become national and international tourist destinations if the National Tourism Development principles are implemented effectively. Furthermore, domestic tourism has risen in recent years. More than four million domestic trips were reported in 2010. Domestic tourism revenues increased by 80% between 2013 and 2014, with a total increase of US$4.93 billion (Zawy). *Aseer* is now considered one of the most famous tourist destinations in KSA. Local and international tourists visit the region every year. The COVID-19 pandemic of 2020 increased domestic tourism in *Aseer*, and 100% of *Abha*'s accommodation facilities and *Khamis Mushait* were occupied, and more than 70% in *Tanuma, Al-Namas,* and *Bani Amr* in August 2020 (Ministry of Tourism).

According to the secretariat of the Aseer region, the Ministry of Agriculture, in collaboration with the Tourism and Antiquities Authority, has begun to establish natural resort sites in Aseer (Mane'a, 2015). The conditions to be considered, especially in areas near natural sites, were noted. Sustainability principles need to be implemented at design stages, given that the authorities choose the areas where resorts should be established through a geographical survey to allocate eligible sites. Nevertheless, no projects have been completed so far.

According to Booking.com, the highest star ratings for the accommodation facilities are three stars, and 176 facilities are unrated (Booking.com). Finally, most of the hotels are located in Abha, followed by Kamis Mushayt, Mahayil Aseer, Qal' at Bishah, Tanmah, and Al-Namas, respectively.

Example of Family Lodge in Aseer. Although *Aseer* does not have any sustainable resorts, many families have started family resorts to accommodate tourists. These resorts offer activities for all members of a visiting family. The host family offers tour-guided trips to explore the landmarks and introduce the visitors to the local *Aseer* cuisine. In the summer of 2020, due to the COVID-19 pandemic, a very large number of Saudi families visited *Aseer*, compelling more local families to begin offering their farms to visitors either for day trips or night stays.

On the road between Abha and Al-Souda Park, one of the prominent tourist attractions, which has become a landmark although it was recently started, is a farm that a family in the village of Bani Mazen (southwest of Abha) has turned into a rural lodge to attract many tourists and visitors (Al-Bridi, 2019). The family has maintained the farm well. The project is a first in the domain of investment in rural lodges, and its success can inspire the undertaking of similar projects. The owner of the farm and rural lodge, which he called "Shmoukh," which means altitude or height, said that the idea had been borrowed from some European countries and developed to suit the specificities of Gulf life. Initially, they started by working on the farm as a family. Keeping the farm intact, with its trees and big fruit trees such as peaches, figs, and cherries, they took part of the farm (an area of 4,000 m^2) and established family gathering areas. One area is approximately 16 meters and large enough for a family of 8–10 people to travel between farms and experience nature and fresh air while enjoying a variety of services, food and beverages, and the famous *Aseer*i cuisine. The team that takes care of the farm includes 25 family members. The tourist season for the resort is the summer, in order to allow all the family members to host the visitors to the lodge.

Most of the accommodation facilities in *Aseer* are not inspired by the vernacular architecture of *Aseer*. *Aseer*'s houses represent a distinctive type of vernacular architecture in KSA (Arab News, 2018). The vernacular architecture in *Aseer* respects the mountainous nature, socio-cultural values, and the use of local materials. *Aseer*'s architectural heritage is unique. Therefore, sustainable development should aim to ensure that new buildings respect the mountainous topography and the regional heritage. However, contemporary development in *Aseer* does not respect the natural mountainous topography. Most construction work starts by demolishing the mountain instead of adapting to it. In many cases, the decision to level the topography supersedes the initiation of design. Valley and mountain houses embody the ideal concept of respecting the nature of the land by designing houses of sizes that fit the site without damaging nature. Moreover, this is also reflected in the choice of material type; in the mountains, the locals build their houses with stone, and in the valley, they build them with mud. Traditions and cultural values are reflected well in the planning of these houses, the narrow roads, and the green surroundings that blend perfectly with nature. The houses are usually multi-stories and have small, colorful rooms and narrow windows for passive natural ventilation. In terms of the construction, social practices and environmental conditions are demonstrated in the material characteristics, as materials with high thermal conductivity are chosen. Therefore, local materials help achieve the balance between the cold winters and hot summers. Based on the climatic zone of the mountain, in the winter, the lowest air temperature is 13.8 °C in December, and the maximum solar radiation is from the south direction [116,756 Wh/m^2]. In the summer, the highest air temperature is 23.3°C in June, and the minimum solar radiation is from the south [44,557 Wh/m^2] (Shawk,

2018). Walls gain heat throughout the day which guarantee warmer nights without using heater systems.

Building materials are chosen based on the location of the house. The primary natural building materials are stone, wood, and mud. Other materials, such as iron, are used as secondary materials for manufacturing doors and windows (Abu-Ghazzeh, 1997). For example, the valley houses are constructed using mud, whereas the prevalent material in the highlands is local stone. For the roof, timber is used, which grows in the valley, and big rocks can be included in the walls. The colors used for decoration are mixed with limewash. *Aseer*i citizens appreciate the mud houses for their passive ventilation techniques. Mud maintains the thermal comfort of the occupants in the summer and the winter without air conditioners and heating systems, respectively, which indicates the durability and effectiveness of the choice of material.

3. Methodology

This chapter adopts a qualitative research design to explore the principles of sustainable mountain resort design and develop a framework applicable to the Aseer region. The qualitative approach is suitable for this chapter, as it allows for an overall understanding of complex phenomena through the analysis of multiple case studies. The analysis focuses on how they adapt to the mountainous topography, how they empower the local community's engagement, and the smart solutions applied to achieve sustainability. The chapter findings are expected to help identify how sustainability can be implemented in the context of Aseer. The essential criteria of assessment were chosen based on Purandare (Purandare, 2009). He divided the sustainable criteria into three global categories: economic sustainability, community engagement sustainability, and environmental sustainability.

Saratu (Saratu, 2012) identified categories that were used to frame the case studies; some of the principles he formulated can be applied in the case study assessment of this research, which will investigate the applicability of the categories identified. The first category of landscape integration includes the site planning of the landscape that can integrate the built area with the natural landscape. The spatial organization and design of the building, how the local culture and heritage inspire the design, and the level of applying sustainable techniques are then analyzed in greater detail. The second category is the water and energy efficiency category, which is used to identify methods and systems applied to save water and energy. The third category is sustainable construction, which assesses the extent of use of local and sustainable materials and methods in constructing the building. The last category is social, economic, and cultural engagement to support the local community. This category evaluates the manner of engagement adopted by the resort to support local societies. Tourist areas, which have carried out capacity studies, are included in the process of design, construction, and operation. This chapter identified only five relevant case studies.

The selection of case studies was based on criteria relevant to the Aseer region, including climate, topography, and community engagement level. Five sustainable mountain resorts from various parts of the world were selected to provide diverse insights and best practices that could be adapted to the context of Aseer. The case studies were chosen to represent different geographic regions and sustainable practices, ensuring a comprehensive analysis.

4. Case Study Analysis

The analysis of case studies based on applying the identified principles of sustainable design revealed a certain degree of distinction at the application level between all the case studies. Case study selection was based on similarities to the Asser region in terms of climate, topography, and community engagement level. The analysis involved collecting data on the case sites from the web. The four categories mentioned in the previous section were rated based on their sustainability as follows. Excellent: the solution could be easily integrated with the local context; very good: the solution could be integrated with the local context; good: the solution demonstrated a weak compatibility with the local context, but could be developed to facilitate integration; not applied: no sustainable solution was applied. Analyzing the five case studies (Table 11.1) shows that the application of sustainable principles varies based on each case study's location.

4.1 Case Study One

Limalimo Lodge is very well integrated with the landscape, located in the Simien Mountains National Park, a UNESCO World Heritage site. Following a low-impact design strategy, the lodge adapts to the mountainous topography, fitting well with the surrounding environment. In terms of water and energy efficiency, the lodge uses an extremely efficient renewable energy source to provide electricity by utilizing solar-motorized smart lighting to illuminate the corridors at night and solar heating to heat the water. The onsite bio-waste system is an excellent solution to minimize waste that recycles used water and utilizes greywater for irrigation. Moreover, the lodge was constructed using a low-impact construction method, and they worked closely with the community to upskill them to use the construction method. Local materials such as rammed earth, wood, and thatch were used. Rammed earth was assembled from the site, demonstrating an excellent use of sustainable material and local building methods. The community was a part of all the stages, starting from planning to design to construction of the building; even in the operation stage, the majority of the staff are locals. The lodge involves the surrounding villages in the guest activities, demonstrating remarkable local community engagement.

Table 11.1. Case Study and Analysis Category Summary, by Authors.

Category	Landscape Integration	Sustainable Construction	Water and Energy Efficiency	Local Community Engagement
Limalimo lodge, Ethiopia	Low-impact design, blends with topography, uses indigenous plants	Local materials (rammed earth, wood, and thatch), low-impact construction	Solar-powered lighting and water heating, a bio-waste recycling system	Employment, involvement in planning and operations, cultural preservation
Alila Jabal Akhdar resort, Oman	Inspired by Omani village architecture, restores indigenous plants	Local stone, LEED certified, minimal environmental footprint	Aflaj irrigation system, sewage treatment plant, solar panels	Local sourcing of materials and food, employment, cultural activities
Kasbah Bab Ourika, Morocco	Integrates with surrounding villages, maintains natural landscape	Traditional Berber techniques (rammed earth, limestone, and clay bricks)	Solar panels, biodigester system, greywater recycling	Employs locals, sources materials and food locally, supports community development
Aristi Mountain resort, Greece	Harmonizes with traditional stone-built villages	Local stone and wood, passive design techniques	Waste heat recovery, LED lighting with sensors, sewage treatment plant	Employment, promotion of traditional activities (e.g., mushroom hunting)
Topas Ecolodge, Vietnam	Blends with mountainous terrain, uses local granite and palm leaves	Local materials, traditional building techniques, and respects topography	Hydroelectric system, air heating system, well water filtration	Employment, partnerships with local communities, cultural exchange

4.2 Case Study Two (Alila Jabal Akhdar Resort, Oman)

Alila Jabal Akhdar Resort is well integrated with the landscape. The suite clusters are inspired by the local Omani village located on the mountain. The design of the resort was inspired by Omani Vernacular Architecture. The resort uses an Aflaj water system, which is a traditional irrigation method that has been in use for 5,000 years, minimizing the ecological impact on the surrounding environment. The Aflaj consists of canals that carry water up from subterranean water springs, storing it in ponds that passively produce a natural evaporative cooling effect. Additionally, an onsite Sewage Treatment Plant recycles gray and black water through the biosystem and uses the recycled water for irrigation. Energy-saving lighting and movement response control systems and dimmers are used for the resort pathways for energy efficiency, and all indoor lighting is energy efficient (light-emitting diode (LED) lighting system). Installing solar panels (photo-voltaic modules) provides up to 60% of the energy required for hot water supply and energy-saving lighting. Engaging with the surrounding villages allows for promoting the local architecture. The local stone material creates a harmony between the resort and the surrounding landscape. Maximizing the use of local materials in the construction phase minimizes the ongoing energy usage footprint. The cement and steel were extracted locally. The resort involves the locals and employs them from the surrounding villages. Most of the raw materials are obtained from local suppliers that include supplies during the construction phase and food for the resort.

4.3 Case Study Three (Kasbah Bab Ourika, Morocco)

The integration of the destination with the surroundings is stable in Kasbah Bab Ourika, especially with the surrounding villages. A biodigester system generates electricity that turns waste products into electricity, gas, and compost for the garden, and solar panels produce hot water for the hotel and the under-floor heating. Greywater is recycled and used for irrigation. The resort was constructed following the traditional Berber building technique by using rammed earth, limestone, and clay brick walls. The thick walls offer natural insulation in the summer and in the winter, thereby guaranteeing a balanced temperature. The resort has a social responsibility toward the local societies around the resort. The majority of the resort staff are from surrounding villages, making the resort]the largest employer in the valley.

4.4 Case Study Four (Aristi Mountain Resort, Greece)

Aristi Mountain Resort offers archeological sites and natural attractions and reflects the architectural aesthetics of the surrounding villages. The resort has a waste heat recovery system that captures the heat released by equipment, which is reused to heat the resort rooms, and LED lighting with sensors is installed throughout the building. The resort uses a high-tech system that cleans wastewater; a device has been installed to reduce water consumption by 30%–40%, and a private sewage treatment plant recycles wastewater for irrigation purposes. According to local customs, the materials used in the buildings are only local materials such as stone and wood. The resort offers various activities, such as taking the guests to mushroom hunting in the forest.

4.5 Case Study Five (Topas Ecolodge, Vietnam)

Topas Ecolodge is integrated with the mountainous topography, and the suites are designed based on the vernacular architecture in Vietnam. The lodge generates energy by using a hydroelectric system. The pool is heated by an air heating system that saves 85% energy compared to a conventional heating system. The lodge has two wells to collect water from a depth of 80 m. The water is then filtered in a filtration basin located in the lodge area. The 33 bungalows were all made out of locally sourced granite quarried from the nearby mountains, and their roofs were built with large palm leaves. The neighboring communities' inhabitants, composed of Vietnamese locals, benefit from the economic engagements with the lodge.

In sum, the analysis of the implementation of sustainable principles based on the four categories reveals that each principle is implemented differently (Table 11.2). Regarding landscape integration, 80% of the case studies applied this principle by studying the topography of the site and integrating it into the design. The best instance of integration with the landscape was demonstrated in Case Study Two (Alila Jabal Akhdar Resort, Oman) because the design team studied the rocks and did not remove any rocks from the site around the resort. They also restored the natural habitat with indigenous plants that were accustomed to the climate and soil conditions, thus effectively integrating the resort into the site's topography. Regarding water and energy efficiency, 60% of the case studies applied the principle in their design and planning. The five case studies have used methods to reduce energy use and efficient recycling systems to recycle water. The best energy efficiency was illustrated in Case Study Five (Topas Ecolodge, Vietnam), which used hydroelectricity to generate energy. Regarding water efficiency, Case Study Four (Aristi Mountain Resort, Greece) created a recycling water system that recycled greywater, which saved up to 40% of the water consumption. Regarding sustainable construction, all the case studies used local building materials and local building methods. However, Case Study Two (Alila Jabal Akhdar Resort, Oman) demonstrated the best use of sustainable construction. The resort has been LEED-certified to maximize local materials used in its construction and minimize its ongoing energy usage footprint. The construction team implemented an ongoing recycling policy through the reuse of local building materials in harmony with the surrounding environment. Regarding social, economic, and cultural engagement to support the local community, 80% of the case studies engaged the local communities either by hiring locals to work at the property or as a supply chain. Regarding this principle, Case Study One (Limalimo Lodge, Ethiopia) demonstrated the best community engagement. For example, the lodge preservation fund was found to

Table 11.2. Matrix of Assessment of Case Studies, by Authors.

Images	Landscape Integration	Water and Energy Efficiency				Sustainable Community		Engagement of Local Community	
	Principle: 1 Adopting Site Topography	Principle1: Energy Abduction	Principle:2 renewable Energy Sources	Principle: 3 Water Sources	Principle: 4 Water Preservation Methods	Principle: 1 Local Building Methods	Principle2 Local Building Methods	Principle: 1 Support Local Economy	Principle:2 Community Engagement
	Very good	Very good	Very good	Excellent	Excellent	Excellent	Excellent	Excellent	Excellent
	Excellent	Excellent	Excellent	Excellent	Excellent	Excellent	Excellent	Very good	Excellent
	Excellent	Very good	Very good	Good	Very good	Excellent	Very good	Excellent	Excellent
	Very good	Excellent	Very good	Good	Very good	Excellent	Very good	Excellent	Excellent
	Excellent	Very good	Very good	Excellent	Very good	Excellent	Good	Excellent	Excellent

Developing a Sustainable Mountain Resort Design

support the renovation of local schools. Moreover, the lodge was also found to play an essential role in developing the area by providing job opportunities to the local community, sourcing food from local farmers, and arranging trips for guests to visit Limalimo village. The lodge also initiated a donation system to the African Wildlife Foundation to support the preservation of the national park. We also noted that the builders who built the lodge and most of the staff were locals and that the lodge involved surrounding villages in guest activities. All five case studies supported the local communities and engaged the local economy in various ways.

5. Results and Discussion of Findings

Aseer has a distinctive mountainous topography that has influenced human settlement throughout history. A sustainable design framework will help preserve the mountainous topography of *Aseer*. Moreover, the *Aseer* region receives an average rainfall of 278 mm, which is adequate for human use and irrigation. Rainwater harvesting could be used successfully to supply the settlements in the *Aseer* region with freshwater and create a reliable source of water for the region. There is high potential to maximize the benefits of solar irradiance and wind in *Aseer* due to the solar radiation in *Aseer*, which is approximately 6,317 kWh/m2, and the constant wind speeds of up to 13 m/s during the summer months (Shawk, 2018). The use of local building materials should take into account traditional local methods, contemporary styles, and the local environmental characteristics of *Aseer*. This framework will create a stable income for the local communities by creating job opportunities for them. Additionally, sustainable mountain resorts have strong potential to be the next local tourist phenomenon. Therefore, the framework will be a useful starting point to guide architects and stakeholders to design sustainable mountain resorts in *Aseer*, especially resorts based on the case study analysis results (Fig. 11.1). The design framework below is divided into four categories: Landscape Integration, Water and Energy Efficiency, Sustainable Construction, and Local Community Engagement. Each category has design principles that are used to offer guidance for the architects. Landscape integration has three design principles: Landscape integration with the site, the design of the resort inspired by the landscape, and the design preserving the mountain topography. Water and energy efficiency have four design principles: energy use reduction methods, renewable energy sources, water sources, and water conservation practices. The third category, Sustainable Construction, has two design principles: local building materials and local building methods. The Local Community Engagement has three principles: supporting the local economy, pride of the culture, and community engagement in resorts.

6. Conclusion

KSA has a wealth of natural and cultural resources, including the Saudi people's incredible hospitality, which international travelers and even many national

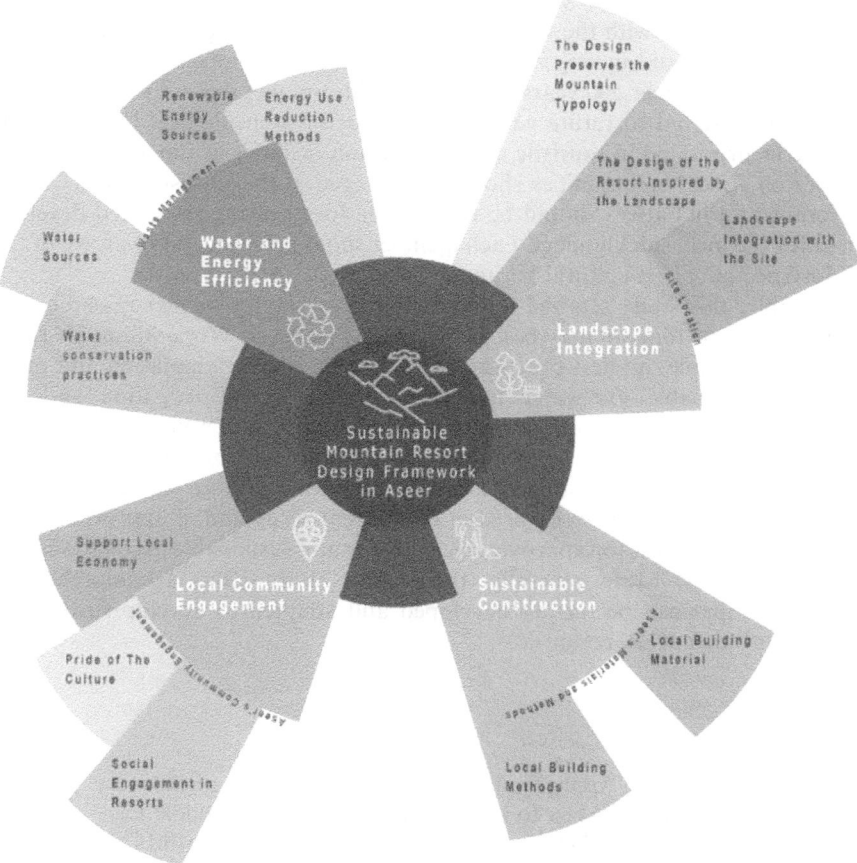

Fig. 11.1. Sustainable Mountain Resorts Design Framework in *Aseer*. *Source:* By Authors.

travelers have yet to discover. The growth of travel and tourism supports the development of state's tourism potential, which will create jobs and a diversified economy while at once unveiling the rich Saudi culture to the world. We have seen how tourism and travel can transform countries, and the WTTC has announced its support for this new chapter of rewriting the history of KSA. *Aseer* has strong potential to establish sustainable mountain resorts integrated with the landscape, given the attractive mountain locations and the mountains' ranges of shapes, colors, and topographies. Seasonal rivers created by rainfall in the valleys of *Aseer* offer a natural source of water. The hot summer sun in the mountains can be used to establish solar panel systems to generate energy in order to achieve the sustainability of alternative energy resources. Local building materials and methods of *Aseeri* construction have proved their durability and are fully integrated with the mountains, in addition to being integrated into the climate of *Aseer* and having a low impact on the environment. The culture of *Aseer* dates back over 500 years and still remains unique; this culture should not only be transferred to future generations as art or archeological buildings but also be incorporated in touristic accommodation facilities as the main theme of the region. Local communities should be engaged in the tourism industry, and governmental initiatives should be responsible for ensuring integrated development for the local stockholders. Each member should respect and be aware of the importance of *Aseeri* cultural heritage.

Notably, this study sets the foundations necessary for further research into how sustainable tourism may best be developed in *Aseer*. Work still needs to be done, for example, on best practices on renewable energy adaptation and practicality, sustainable greywater treatments, and efficient irrigation systems. Additionally, it would also be important to identify the best potential location to construct a resort, considering topography, road access, and passive and active approaches to water harvesting and energy generation. Future studies could also validate the design framework used in the current study and, if approved, use it to develop a checklist for approving licenses for any sustainable accommodation facility in *Aseer*. More generally, the current study offers a comprehensive framework that can be further developed and adapted to develop sustainable tourism in other KSA regions.

References

Aboneama, W. (2018). Applying sustainable development in architecture, planning and infrastructure of Abha to be the first eco-city in the Middle East. *European Journal of Sustainable Development, 7*(4), 289. https://doi.org/10.14207/ejsd.2018.v7n4p289

Abu-Ghazzeh, T. (1997). Vernacular architecture education in the Islamic society of Saudi Arabia: Towards the development of an authentic contemporary built environment. *Habitat International, 21*(3), 229–253.

Al-Bridi, S. (2019). *A family-run "rural" village that attracts visitors in Abha*. Available at: https://shorturl.at/lwxCL. Accessed November 14, 2019

Al-Hababi, H. (2012). The art of women in Asir (Saudi Arabia). *AAS Working Papers in Social Anthropology, 25*, 1–8. https://doi.org/10.1553/wpsa25s1

Al-Yami, A., & Price, A. (2006) 'An overview of sustainability in Saudi Arabia', in *Sustainable development through culture and innovation, Proceedings of 2006 Joint International Conference on Construction Culture, Innovation, and Management*, Dubai, United Arab Emirates, 26–29.

Alharbi, H. (2020). *Framework for designing sustainable mountain resorts in Aseer, Saudi Arabia* Master's Thesis. Dar Al-Hekma University.

Arab News. (2018). *Saudi village of Rijal Alma prepares to join UNESCO World Heritage List'*. Available at: https://www.arabnews.com/node/1351251/saudi-arabia

Arnoult, É. (2020). Residential migration and local employment growth: A study of French employment areas. *Revue Économique, 71*(1).

Booking.com. (n.d.). *Booking.com*. Available at: https://cutt.ly/8jljGGF

Crossley, É. (2020). Ecological grief generates desire for environmental healing in tourism after COVID-19. *Tourism Geographies, 22*(3), 536–546. https://doi.org/10.1080/14616688.2020.1759133

GOV.SA. (n.d.). *Environmental protection in KSA*. Available at: https://www.my.gov.sa/wps/portal/snp/aboutksa/environmentalProtection

Hassan, R. (2019). *Vision 2030: All you need to know about Saudi Arabia's Giga-Projects*. Available at: https://www.arabnews.com/node/1493976/business-economy

Invest Saudi. (n.d.). *Tourism, culture and entertainment - sectors & opportunities*. Available at: https://investsaudi.sa/en/sectors-opportunities/tourism-culture-entertainment/

Jaber, H., & Marzuki, A. (2018). Environmental diversity in Asir region and its impact on tourism development sustainability. *Alexandria Engineering Journal, 24*, 1–6.

Mair, J., & Smith, A. (2021). Events and sustainability: Why making events more sustainable is not enough. *Journal of Sustainable Tourism, 29*(11–12), 1739–1755. https://doi.org/10.1080/09669582.2021.1942480

Mane'a, M. (2015). *[Sustainable tourism: Aseer strategic choice]*. Available at: https://www.alwatan.com.sa/article/255675

Ministry of Tourism. (n.d.). *[Asir, a haven for Saudis from the summer heat]*. Available at: https://pressfile.mt.gov.sa/Home/Details?id=227615

Mohamed, M., Klingmann, A., & Samir, H. (2019). Examining the thermal performance of vernacular houses in Asir region of Saudi Arabia. *Alexandria Engineering Journal, 58*(1), 419–428. https://doi.org/10.1016/j.aej.2019.03.004

National Transformation Program. (2017). *Initiatives for tourism and heritage development*. Available at: https://www.ntp.sa/en/initiatives

National Transformation Program 2020. (2016). *National Transformation Program 2020: Identity and general principles of the National Transformation Program*. Available at: https://www.vision2030.gov.sa/en/explore/programs/national-transformation-program

O'Connor, P., & Assaker, G. (2022). COVID-19's effects on future pro-environmental traveler behavior: An empirical examination using norm activation, economic sacrifices, and risk perception theories. *Journal of Sustainable Tourism, 30*(1), 89–107. https://doi.org/10.1080/09669582.2021.1879821

Oxford Business Group. (2017). *New initiatives set to boost Saudi Arabia's tourist numbers*. Available at: https://oxfordbusinessgroup.com/analysis/helping-hand-new-initiatives-are-set-boost-tourist-numbers

Purandare, J. (2009). Sustainable resort development in sensitive environments: How can tourist developments in popular tourist destinations, such as the Maldives, also be sustainable? *International Journal of Small Economies, 1*(1), 1–14.

Sabbagh, M., Mansour, O., & Banawi, A. (2019). Grease the green wheels: A framework for expediting the green building movement in the Arab world. *Sustainability, 11*(20), 5545. https://doi.org/10.3390/su11205545

Saratu, Y. (2012). *Application of regenerative architectural principles in design of resort hotel; Gurara falls*. Master's Thesis. Ahmadu Bello University. Available at: http://kubanni.abu.edu.ng/jspui/handle/123456789/2173

Saudigazette. (2023). *Saudi tourism's contribution approaching 6%, aiming for 100 million visitors by year end*. Available at: https://www.saudigazette.com.sa/article/637035

Shawk, M. (2018). *Exploring the energy performance of the residential building stock in 3 regions in Saudi Arabia*. Master's Thesis. University of Southampton. Available at: https://www.researchgate.net/publication/331984286. Accessed: date

Som, A. P. M., & Al-Kassem, A. H. (2013). Domestic tourism development in Asir Region, Saudi Arabia. *Journal of Tourism and Hospitality*, 5(S5–001). https://doi.org/10.4172/2167-0269.S5-001

UN-Habitat. (2019). *Saudi cities report 2019*. Available at: https://unhabitat.org/sites/default/files/2020/05/saudi_city_report.english.pdf

UNWTO. (2020). *Impact of COVID-19 on global tourism*. Available at: https://www.unwto.org

World Travel and Tourism Council. (n.d.). *Economic impact reports*. Available at: https://wttc.org/Research/Economic-Impact. Accessed: date

Zawya. (n.d.). *Asir, Saudi Arabia, touristic destination full of natural wonders, heritage*. Available at: https://www.zawya.com

Chapter 12

Rethinking Home: The Influence of the Pandemic on Residential Spaces in Egypt

Yasmin Hesham[a], Hussam Salama[a] and Ibrahim Saleh[b]

[a]German International University, Germany
[b]Effat University, Saudi Arabia

Abstract

The COVID-19 pandemic has altered a number of facets of our daily life, including how we utilize and interact with our dwellings. The epidemic has created new difficulties and opportunities for reconsidering residential space design in Egypt, where a sizable section of the population lives in urban areas with little access to outside public spaces. This chapter explores how the epidemic has affected Egypt's residential areas with the goal of identifying design approaches that might improve inhabitants' quality of life and well-being.

This chapter adopts a quantitative and qualitative approach, a literature review, and an online survey of locals to examine the pandemic's effects. According to this chapter, the pandemic has changed how people use their homes, placing a greater emphasis on leisure time, online learning, and remote work. This chapter also highlights the importance of having access to outdoor spaces, natural light, and ventilation in order to raise the standard of living spaces.

In projecting future trends, this chapter anticipates a paradigm shift toward eco-conscious and technologically integrated architecture. Green roofs, sustainable materials, and energy-efficient designs emerge as essential elements, promoting environmental sustainability and reducing the ecological footprint of residential spaces. Moreover, integrating smart home technologies, augmented reality interfaces, and advanced security systems envisions a futuristic living experience, where architecture seamlessly interfaces with digital innovations to enhance comfort, convenience, and safety.

Based on these findings, this chapter proposes design strategies that can be applied to new and existing residential spaces in Egypt to enhance their functionality and improve residents' quality of life.

Keywords: Home design; immunity through design; post-COVID-19 architecture; impact of the pandemic; apartments design; pandemic architecture

1. Introduction

In February 2020, Egypt announced its very first case of COVID-19. Uncertainty and chaos have spread throughout the atmosphere as the virus spread uncontrollably, and people were still unaware of its consequences. In the second week of March 2020, Egypt declared quarantine. Consequently, people's behavior has been altered, cities are under lockdown, educational facilities are closed, and homes have turned into the fifth place. Home became a place to work, live, and play. It became essential for people to accommodate their spaces (Klaus, 2020).

Citizens of urban areas dedicate 86.9% of their time indoors, which can affect their health positively or negatively (Li, 2017). The pandemic compelled a serious change to our understanding of the city and how we live within it (Li, 2017). Many cities in the world, including Cairo, are on alert. Therefore architects, urban designers, and urban planners are speculating about what solutions need to be proposed to accommodate living with a pandemic, how will our cities and homes react to the new lifestyle, how did it influence our lives, work, and leisure activities, and finally how can we make our cities and homes resilient to future pandemics (Hang, 2021).

With this new development, where people spend most of their time indoors, the environmental quality of homes was exposed. Issues like visibility to natural light, airflow, and exposure to fresh air and green zones have emerged in focus because people aspire to dwell in better standards of hygiene and comfort. This is placing architects and designers in a position to redesign the conventional patterns of organizing residential areas as well as incorporating features that would enhance the degree of living in the residents' homes.

This chapter intends to contribute toward addressing the need to reconsider sustainability requirements for residential buildings. It will also examine how these changes are likely to influence the continuum of future architectural and residential practices in Egypt. Finally, it aims at adding to the existing literature on housing that is resilient and sustainable in the context of Egypt to propose recommendations that can build the Egyptian households' preparedness for future shocks (Klaus, 2020).

2. Literature Review

While medical researchers are urgently getting underway to develop the treatment drugs and vaccines to prevent the coronavirus (Le et al., 2020), reasonable social measures may significantly limit the spread of COVID-19 within the community (West et al., 2020) (Sen-Crowe, 2020). In the context of social distancing, it has been suggested that measurements of personal space are crucial to revisit, along with research on proxemics theories that were clarified in the middle of the 1960s.

The concept of personal space refers to the close, invisible boundaries that enclose an individual's body and are off-limits to outsiders. It can be pictured as a bubble. This particular imagined bubble travels everywhere with people. Hall (Hall, 1966) uses empirical research to determine the relative distances in accordance with personal space, which is likely to be applied to the distances between various individuals based on their interpersonal relationships. This results in the four well-known distance ranges: intimate, approximately 1–46 cm; personal, approximately 46–122 cm; social, approximately 1.2–3.7 m; and finally, public, 3.7–7.6 m. Based on that, Salama (Salama, 2020) debates that "social distancing measures and the minimum allowance of 2 meters personal distance, the relative distance ranges would entirely change."

Throughout history, there have been tremendous debates about the understanding of our perception of home, house, and dwellings. The perception of home is categorized into five aspects. According to Despre, Moore, Blunt, and Dowling, home is a place or site in which we live (Despre's, 1991, Moore, 2000, Blunt & Dowling, 2006). The second aspect, by Mallet, is that home is a spatial dimension; different spatial entities are house, neighborhood, town, state, and country (Mallett, 2004). Gram-Hanssen et al. further explain that home is temporal, a current dwelling in the current time period (Gram-Hanssen & Bech-Danielsen, 2008). Benjamin debates that home is a social relation (Benjamin & Stea, 1995). He considered it from the perspective of the family or the household. From another side, home is a process: the process of homemaking or the process of establishing one's identity in society (Rapoport, 1995).

Architecture is a response to society's needs. Crises, be they man-made or natural, have always had their effect on the form of buildings and cities, albeit with something of a time lag as construction takes time to organize. There have been three worldwide pandemic periods.

The first pandemic period occurred in Eastern Rome, present-day Turkey (541), called the Justinian Plague. In terms of architecture and urban design, many cities and civilizations that could not survive the pandemic have disappeared, such as the Maya civilization. Also, new typologies have emerged, such as tombs and cremation sites, hospital typology, and Valetudinarium typology; a military hospital appeared in Rome, which later became the model for the Lazaretto quarantine hospital in Lisbon (Sehdev, 2002).

The second pandemic period was dominated by the Black Death in Central Asia in the 1330s. In Hungary in 1510, the first municipal quarantine was formed. In addition, the Piazza of the city was considered a place of emergency during outbreaks (Kilwein, 1995, Curl, 1983).

The third pandemic period was mostly the HxNy type of virus. During this pandemic, the hygiene and healthy paradigm emerged as a basic value in policy making as well as preventive and treatment measures, for example, the emerging model of a healthy home for a four-member family by Henry Roberts (De Pierrefeu & Corbusier, 1965). Modernists took a radically different direction, modeling many of their domestic spaces on something reminiscent of a hospital ward. Le Corbusier's famous sink in the hall in Villa Savoye was a response to the Spanish Flu (WELL Building Institute, 2018).

After the outbreak of COVID-19, designing for healthy living has become essential in residential spaces. The WELL Building Standard is a performance-based system that measures, certifies, and monitors built environment features impacting human health and well-being. Its 10 concepts guide architects, designers, and building professionals in prioritizing occupant well-being (Veitch & Galasiu, 2012). Air focuses on indoor air quality through ventilation, filtration, and pollution control (La Rosa et al., 2020). Water ensures access to safe, clean water by addressing filtration, treatment, and quality standards (La Rosa et al., 2020; Mezzoiuso et al., 2017). Nourishment encourages healthy eating by providing nutritious food options and promoting mindful consumption. Light supports circadian rhythms and visual well-being through optimized natural light exposure and lighting systems that mimic natural patterns (La Rosa, 2020; Maas, 2009). Fitness promotes physical activity by integrating exercise spaces and movement-friendly design (Andargie, 2019). Comfort enhances well-being by addressing thermal, acoustic, and ergonomic factors through temperature regulation, noise reduction, and ergonomic furniture (Cohen-Cline et al., 2015; La Rosa, 2020). Mind supports mental health through biophilic design, stress reduction strategies, and spaces for relaxation (Bassi et al., 2019; La Rosa, 2020). Materials minimize environmental and health impacts by selecting low-VOC, responsibly sourced materials with reduced life cycle impact (Akbari, 2021). Community fosters social interaction and engagement by promoting local businesses and strengthening communal ties (Bassi, 2019). Innovation drives advancements in health-focused design by encouraging new ideas and technologies that extend beyond the other WELL concepts (see Fig. 12.1).

With pandemics, the question today is not whether it will happen again. The only question is, when will it happen again? The world community must take steps today to mitigate this threat. The architecture and urban planning fields can play an important role in building healthy environments and shaping cities to make them more disease-resilient (Zarrabi, 2020). This is one of the main driving forces in this chapter since the outbreak of the pandemic resulted in global attention to shared aspects related to the well-being of all individuals without any exceptions or segregations. In a different study by Zarrabi et al. (Tokazhanov, 2020), which examined the population's preferences for healthy home indicators in Tehran following the epidemics, it was discovered that natural light, air quality, visual and acoustic qualities, and open spaces were the most crucial factors, followed by the layout of the home and the workspace. The same study demonstrated the significance of mental well-being criteria by showing that psychological effects on the population outweigh those related to physical health. According to Tokazhanov et al., to ensure resilience and sustainability, future homes should address the phenomenological questions raised by the recent global pandemic—specifically, whether our built environment can

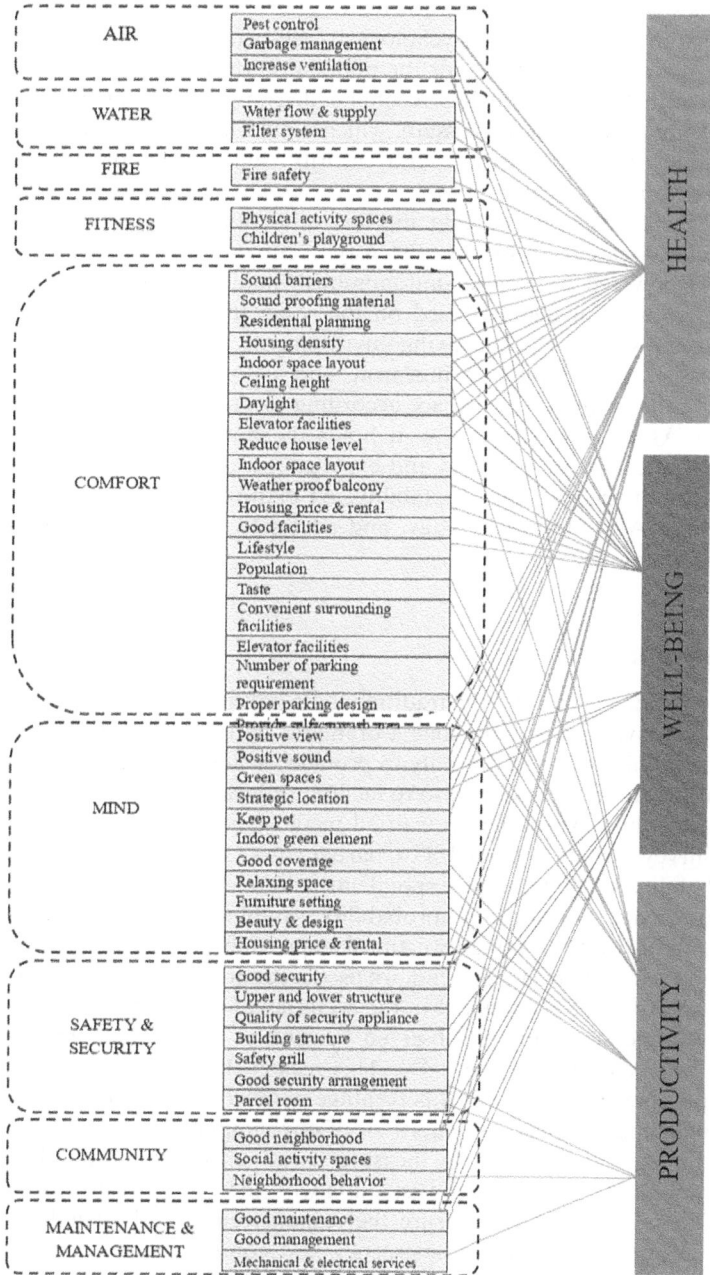

Fig. 12.1. Well Concepts and Elements in Residential Buildings in Developing Countries (By Authors).

reduce the spread of disease, how to create better indoor environments, and how to enhance the physical and psychological well-being of long-term dwellers. In order to make homes suitable for the population during home quarantines, the World Health Organization has recommended improving home environments and reducing psychological pressure, which would help homes perform the role of providing comfort, privacy, and security, all while protecting residents' physical and mental health.

AI is increasingly influencing interior residential architecture, with smart home technologies transforming the way occupants interact with their living spaces. AI-powered systems can autonomously adjust lighting, temperature, and other environmental factors based on the resident's preferences, creating personalized and energy-efficient living environments. In interior design, AI algorithms assist in furniture arrangement and color scheme recommendation, optimizing the aesthetics of a space according to the occupant's taste (Acharya, 2013). As AI continues to evolve, it holds the potential to revolutionize how residential interiors are designed and experienced, offering innovative solutions for comfort, efficiency, and adaptability. AI platforms such as Connix AI, and Finch utilize AI, graph technology, and advanced algorithms to optimize and challenge the design.

3. Methodology

Since the pandemic started, the traditional idea of home as a shelter and a space for family activities has undergone a dramatic shift. It transformed into a multifunctional hub, expected not only to provide shelter and accommodate private and semi-private activities but also to facilitate education and recreation, serve as a workplace, and even offer specialized medical care when required. Thus, an online survey, which included 110 participants, was conducted. It followed nonprobability sampling, and respondents were reached by snowballing. While we acknowledge that this nonprobability sampling approach may limit the generalizability of our findings, we aimed to provide a reasonable estimate of the population parameters. To this end, we used a confidence level of 95%, indicating that we aim to be 95% confident in the accuracy of our sample estimates. Based on our sample size and the observed variability in the data, the confidence interval was calculated to be $\pm 4\%$. This means that we expect the true population parameter to lie within 4 percentage points of our sample estimate, while also recognizing the inherent limitations of our sampling method (Collins, 2006).

The survey was designed to measure users' satisfaction with their home's interior design, as well as their satisfaction with the environment that surrounds them. The survey aims to measure the responsiveness and flexibility of architectural design to respond to emergency and contemporary needs during the COVID-19 pandemic.

However, before sharing the online survey, a pilot test was conducted on 20 people. To facilitate participants, the questions were designed to be short, clear, and easy to read. The online survey is divided into five different sections. The first section assessed the socio-demographic details of the participants, such as age and family size. The second section concentrates on the neighborhood and building description, the characteristics of the building, its walkability, the use of its public space, the journey to the home, the use of elevators, common areas in the building, and whether there are social interactions on roofs and in corridors of the building. The third section concentrates on the house description as a housing prototype, housing level, number of rooms, area, number of bathrooms, and balconies. Section four examines the concept of quarantine and whether the house is used as a quarantine or not. The fifth section covers the concept of staying at home and how staying at home for an extended period affects household needs, such as working from home, the need to connect safely with nature, storage, area, gym, or any other requirements.

4. Results and Discussions

The sample of the study for the survey was 110 respondents, 73.2% females and 26.8% males. The majority of the respondents (53.6%) were graduates and working, with an age range of 24–40 years old. Above 40 years old were 8.2%, while 38.2% were in the range of 18–23 years old. 68.2% of the respondents shared their home with 3–5 family members, 22.5% had 1–2 members, and the smallest group was 9.3% with 6 or more family members. Among the sample studied, 52.1% lived in gated communities. The most critical result of this section was that 75.2% of the respondents encountered either working-from-home situations or an online education. Thus, according to the results, an extra multifunctional space that can serve as an office or study area can be proposed in future plans of residential spaces.

There is general agreement that the lockdown implied a clear shift in the way people use and perceive spaces of their dwellings. Among the sample studied, 52.1% lived in gated communities. When asked about how the frequency of visiting the outdoor common spaces of their neighborhood during COVID-19 changed, 48% showed an increase, 35% no change, and 17% decreased. Although only 46% of the participants confirmed the availability of an elevator, only 18% stopped using the elevator during the pandemic. This section highlights the importance of outdoor spaces in our everyday activities. These spaces can be offered in forms of balconies and terraces or outdoor neighborhood spaces such as courtyards, gardens, green spaces, pathways, walkways, and play areas.

Housing unit descriptions vary between less than 100 m², which was 10%, and the most popular were between 100 and 200 m², with 65%; the other 25% were 200 m² and above. Most of the sampled houses had two bathrooms, with a percentage of 68%, and 24% had more than two bathrooms; the least were 8% with one bathroom. 76% had one balcony, and 24% had more than one balcony.

Eighty-two percent of the participants were affected by COVID-19 and used their home as a quarantine. When asked about the problems during quarantine, the most discussed was the number of bathrooms. Participants with houses including one bathroom (8%) showed interest in an extra bathroom. 65% stated that they prefer not sharing a room and having their own bathroom. Also, 56% approved changes under the name of the *sanitation zone* in areas such as the entrance hallway and kitchen. According to the results, the 1:1 ratio of bathroom to bedroom is the best choice for most of the participants.

When asked about Work-from-home relocation, 52.5% said that the dining room accommodated the work time, while the second room was the bedroom with 20%. When asked about balcony alterations, 37.5% said they bought a seating area and furnished their balcony. However, 15% said they have transformed their balconies into either an interior space or an interior office. When asked about potential changes to follow in future development or when choosing a new home, the respondents indicated that they preferred to add more layers for privacy (35.6%), more interactive spaces (27.3%), more green areas (21.1%), and larger areas (15.8%).

5. Conclusion

The coronavirus pandemic not only produced significant advances in every field of science but also had a notable impact on the field of architectural design. The chapter aimed to show how the COVID-19 pandemic impacted the use of residential spaces in Egypt and what challenges were faced by residents in Egypt in adapting to changes in residential spaces during the pandemic. After reviewing the literature review and the results of the online survey, it was proven that households in Egypt have undergone mild to major changes during the pandemic. Adaptations have ranged from furniture layout changes, converting unused spaces such as the guest room or the guest bathroom into a more functional space such as a home office, assigning a room for quarantine, rethinking the connection to nature by using balconies and roofs, and finally creating new zones such as the sanitation zones in areas such as the entrance hall and kitchen.

The chapter demonstrated that the patterns examined would be better taken into consideration for future home design because adaptations have been made voluntarily by residents. Solutions such as developing outdoor areas that offer both relaxation and recreational activities, such as gardens, patios, roofs, or balconies, are really important to the user. Dedicating workspaces within homes that support productivity and concentration, with ergonomic furniture, adequate lighting, and technology infrastructure, is essential for the new norm adaptation. In addition to this, flexible home layouts and adaptable spaces for multipurpose uses can be a solution, which can be implemented through AI and new technologies in adaptable furniture and in applying lightweight building materials that can be readjusted according to emergency needs.

Several avenues for future research can be identified to further explore and expand upon the implications of residential spaces in response to the pandemic, such as technological advancement, the adoption rates, user acceptance, and the effectiveness of these technologies in diverse housing contexts. Also, investigating the psychological effects of residential design on occupants' mental health, stress levels, and social interactions can be further studied.

References

Acharya, A. S., Prakash, A., Saxena, P., & Nigam, A. (2013). Sampling: why and how of it? *Indian Journal of Medical Specialities, 4*(2), 3–7.

Akbari, P., Yazdanfar, S.-A., Hosseini, S.-B., & Norouzian-Maleki, S. (2021). Housing and mental health during outbreak of COVID-19. *Journal of Building Engineering, 43*, 102919.

Andargie, M. S., Touchie, M., & O'Brien, W. (2019). A review of factors affecting occupant comfort in multi-unit residential buildings. *Building and Environment, 160*, 106182.

As, I., Pal, S., & Basu, P. (2018). Artificial intelligence in architecture: Generating conceptual design via deep learning. *International Journal of Architectural Computing, 16*(4), 306–327.

Bassi, A., Ottone, C., & Dell'Ovo, M. (2019). Minimum environmental criteria in the architectural project. Trade-off between environmental, economic and social sustainability [I Criteri Ambientali Minimi nel progetto di architettura. Trade-off tra sostenibilità ambientale, economica e sociale]. *Valori E Valutazioni, 22*, 35–45.

Benjamin, D. N., & Stea, D. (1995). *The home: Words, interpretations, meanings, and environments*.

Blunt, A., & Dowling, R. (2006). Home. *M/C journal* (Vol. 10, p. 4). Routledge.

Cohen-Cline, H., Turkheimer, E., & Duncan, G. E. (2015). Access to green space, physical activity and mental health: A twin study. *Journal of Epidemiology and Community Health, 69*(6), 523–529.

Collins, K. M. T., Onwuegbuzie, A. J., & Jiao, Q. G. (2006). Prevalence of mixed-methods sampling designs in social science research. *Evaluation & Research in Education, 19*(2), 83–101.

Curl, J. S. (1983). *The life and work of Henry Roberts, 1803–1876: The Evangelical conscience and the campaign for model housing and healthy nations*. Phillimore & Co. Ltd.

De Pierrefeu, F., & Corbusier, L. (1965). *La maison des hommes*.

Despre's, C. (1991). The meaning of home: Literature review and directions for future research and theoretical development. *Journal of Architectural and Planning Research, 8*, 96–115.

Gram-Hanssen, K., & Bech-Danielsen, C. (2008). Home dissolution: What happens after separation? *Housing Studies, 23*(3), 507–522.

Hall, E. T. (1966). *The hidden dimension*. Doubleday.

Hang, M. (2021) *The urban now: Preparing cities for epidemics: Lessons from the COVID19 outbreak. [online]*. IJURR, Available from: https://www.ijurr.org/the-urban-now/preparing-cities-for-epidemics/, last accessed 2021/10/26.

International WELL Building Institute. (2018). *WELL V2 pilot, International WELL Building Institute*. https://v2.wellcertified.com/v/en/overview

Kilwein, J. H. (1995). Some historical comments on quarantine: Part one. *Journal of Clinical Pharmacy and Therapeutics, 20*(4), 185–187.

Klaus, I. (2020) *How the coronavirus could change city planning. [online]*. Available from: https://www.bloomberg.com/news/articles/2020-03-06/how-the-coronavirus-could-change-city-planning, last accessed 2020/03/06.

La Rosa, G., Bonadonna, L., Lucentini, L., Kenmoe, S., & Suffredini, E. (2020). Coronavirus in water environments: Occurrence, persistence and concentration methods - a scoping review. *Water Research, 179*, 115899.

La Rosa, G., et al (2020). First detection of SARS-CoV-2 in untreated wastewaters in Italy. *Science of the Total Environment, 736*, 139652.

Le, T., et al (2020). The COVID-19 vaccine development landscape. *Nature Reviews Drug Discovery, 19*(5), 305–306.

Li, Y. (2017). Urban design and 3 kinds of space-related epidemic diseases. *UIA 2017 Seoul World Architects Congress*, 1–5.

Maas, J., Verheij, R. A., de Vries, S., Spreeuwenberg, P., Schellevis, F. G., & Groenewegen, P. P. (2009). Morbidity is related to a green living environment. *Journal of Epidemiology and Community Health, 63*(12), 967–973.

Mallett, S. (2004). Understanding home: A critical review of the literature. *The Sociological Review, 52*(1), 62–89.

Mezzoiuso, A., et al (2017). Indoors and health: Results of a systematic literature review assessing the potential health effects of living in basements [Ambienti confinati e salute: Revisione sistematica della letteratura sui rischi legati all'utilizzo dei seminterrati a scopo abitativo]. *Acta BioMedica, 88*(3), 375–385.

Moore, J. (2000). Placing home in context. *Journal of Environmental Psychology, 20*, 207–217.

Rapoport, A. (1995). A critical look at the concept home. In *Benjamin and Stea* (pp. 25–53).

Salama, A. (2020). Coronavirus questions that will not go away: Interrogating urban and socio-spatial implications of COVID-19 measures. *Emerald Open Research, 2*, 14.

Sehdev, P. S. (2002). The origin of quarantine. *Clinical Infectious Diseases, 35*(9), 1071–1072.

Sen-Crowe, B., Sutherland, M., McKenney, M., & Elkbuli, A. (2020). A closer look into global hospital beds capacity and resource shortages during the COVID-19 pandemic. *The American Journal of Surgery, 259*(2), 634–636. https://doi.org/10.1016/j.amjsurg.2020.08.015

Tokazhanov, G., Tleuken, A., Güney, M., Türkyılmaz, A., & Karaca, F. (2020). How is COVID-19 experience transforming sustainability requirements of residential buildings? A review. *Sustainability, 12*(20), 8732.

Veitch, J. A., & Galasiu, A. D. (2012). *The physiological and psychological effects of windows, daylight, and view at home: Review and research agenda*. National Research Council Canada.

West, R., Michie, S., Rubin, G., & Amlôt, R. (2020). Applying principles of behaviour change to reduce SARS-CoV-2 transmission. *Nature Human Behaviour, 4*(5), 451–459.

Zarrabi, M., Yazdanfar, S.-A., & Hosseini, S.-B. (2020). COVID-19 and healthy home preferences: The case of apartment residents in Tehran. *Journal of Building Engineering, 35*, 102021.

Chapter 13

Indoor Air Quality, Mitigating CO_2 Concentration in Classrooms Using Adjacent Corridors and Atriums

Feras Balkhi, Mostafa Sabbagh and Mohannad Bayoumi

King Abdulaziz University, Saudi Arabia

Abstract

This chapter studies the classroom's indoor air quality (IAQ) during the preparatory (freshmen) year at Jeddah. An existing and active building was used as a case study. The variables affecting IAQ were measured and analyzed by installing sensors to measure and record these variables in this classroom. After that, research was done to determine the optimal range of these variables and compare them to check whether these results were within the acceptable range of each variable. The results show that it is important to propose improvement measures to reduce CO_2 concentration and ensure thermal comfort. Occupants need to realize that the quality of the indoor environment is important for their health, comfort, and efficiency.

Keywords: Indoor air quality; air quality in schools; CO_2 concentration; classroom ventilation; atrium

1. Introduction

Spaces greatly impact the lives of occupants. Indoor air quality (IAQ) is an essential factor that decides occupants' level of satisfaction and performance. Classroom is critical due to high density; the overcrowding of classrooms is a serious and quite common issue, where educational institutions are commonly overlooked or ignored as the retrofitting of these spaces has limited or no budget for quick solutions. The larger the classroom, the greater the dilution of levels of carbon dioxide (CO_2) and pollutants, and the longer good air quality can be maintained. In an average-sized classroom with a volume of 181 cubic meters, 30 students, and no ventilation, the air quality becomes poor in just 30 minutes (Al-Hemoud et al., 2017). Investigations are needed to provide more information about the IAQ in Saudi Arabian classrooms and its effect on the space efficiency and educational system. Exchanging air between classrooms and common spaces can serve as a quick solution to improve overall CO_2 concentration levels in overcrowded educational buildings.

2. Literature Review

Indoor Air Quality (IAQ): Refers to the air quality within and around buildings and structures, especially as it relates to the health and comfort of building occupants (Alaidroos and Mosly, 2022; Anonymous, 2023).

The most important factor that affects the IAQ is the ventilation; as the air is confined to a closed space without renewal, it can be contaminated by several pollutants, including radon, carbon monoxide, carbon dioxide, bacteria, and other volatile chemical particles (ArchDaily, 2018; Bakó-Biró et al., 2012).

Humans, by their nature, are the main indoor source of carbon dioxide in most buildings. Carbon dioxide (CO_2) is easy to measure as a surrogate for indoor pollutants. Indoor CO_2 levels are a good indicator of ventilation efficiency, which directly indicates the quality of the indoor air (Anonymous, 2023). The most measured parameter of occupants' presence and densities in the space is CO2, which also indicates ventilation adequacy indoors to monitor IAQ (Bauhaus et al., 2012). CO_2 is mainly increased and affected by the low volume of classrooms, high-density occupancies, and insufficient ventilation (EPA, 2019). Moreover, carbon dioxide is considered a critical factor affecting students' attendance, health, or performance (Feith, 2022).

In an epidemiological cross-sectional study that included 1,053 school children aged 13–17 years. Studied the following measurements: room temperature, CO_2 level, and relative humidity; building characteristics, including mold infestation, were assessed, and dust was collected from floors, air, and ventilation ducts during a working day. The authors reported that they did not find a positive association between building-related symptoms and the extent of moisture and mold growth in the school buildings. Also, they found that five of eight building-related symptoms were significantly and positively associated with the concentration of colony-forming units of molds in floor dust: eye irritation, throat irritation, headache, concentration problems, and dizziness (Hassan Abdallah, 2017).

In Oklahoma City, a study was conducted on third-grade classrooms of 12 elementary schools that were recently renovated to various degrees or were newly constructed under different seasonal conditions. Continuous monitoring of CO_2 data, occupancy data, and space characteristics were used to model the ventilation system's effective fresh air supply using the Transient Mass Balance Method.

The author found that schools have generally adequate temperature control, extremely low nonoccupant-related pollutants and little outdoor vehicle-related pollutants. But there was a lack of adequate fresh air ventilation in many cases, perhaps to the detriment of academic performance. The author added a model of a ventilation system with effective fresh air supply using a transient mass balance method, and effective fresh air ventilation rates for people-related pollutants corresponded well with good CO_2 control in the classrooms (jbadmin, 2023).

In a parallel study of a university in Saudi Arabia, the analysis is based on two classrooms' physical environmental measurement data. Participant votes on standard subjective thermal rating scales were collected from 499 adult female students, which were correlated with relevant environmental parameters such as humidity, radiant temperature, air velocity, and self-reported clothing levels. CO_2 concentrations and temperatures are important variables within buildings; they affect the occupant's performance and particularly cognitive performance regarding all mental activities such as thinking, reasoning, and remembering.

The authors concluded that decreasing classrooms' temperature from 25°C to 23°C and also increasing the temperature from 20°C to 23°C while decreasing CO_2 levels from 1800 ppm and/or 1000 ppm–600 ppm significantly improved the performance of adult female students in memory and attention tasks. Also, the cold, hot, and warm sensations can negatively affect mental performance for memory and attention tasks, while a mild cooling sensation can improve mental alertness.

This chapter simulates the same environmental conditions as the research sample (Kilpatrick, 2014).

The effects of classroom ventilation on pupils' performance were investigated in eight primary schools in England. In each school, the concentrations of CO_2 and other parameters were monitored for three weeks in two selected classrooms.

The author made interventions in 16 classrooms, maintaining the temperature and improving the ventilation rate within an acceptable range using a purpose-built portable mechanical ventilation system. As a result, the provision of outdoor air to the classrooms was improved from the prevailing levels of about $1^1/_5$ per person to about $8^1/_5$ per person.

The author found that low rates of ventilation in classrooms significantly reduce pupils' attention and vigilance and negatively affect memory and concentration. The physical environment therefore affects teaching and learning (Mendell et al., 2004).

In Egypt, a study of thermal comfort and indoor CO_2 concentration of children's classrooms in two governmental schools. The examination of the CO_2 concentration observed that the CO_2 level in most of the classrooms was found to be within the acceptable level of ASHRAE, with an average of 497 ppm. But some other classrooms have higher levels above 1000 ppm. The author found that the reason for this problem was that teachers closed the doors and depended on mechanical fans and single-sided ventilation from windows for ventilation without continuous airflow and fresh air. Also found CO_2 level decreases during the school break in 30 minutes due to the opening door without student occupation (Meyer et al., 2004).

3. Methodology

This chapter shall investigate a prototype classroom building in Jeddah as a case study. The classrooms involved in the study were selected as case samples to examine thermal comfort and CO_2 concentration (Tekin & Arikan, 2023). In a set of different types of ventilation (hybrid ventilation and air conditioned), the case window condition is not designed with natural ventilation systems (no opening windows). Also, one should not ignore the overcrowding issue of classrooms by reconsidering the number of occupants, which causes a high level of CO_2 concentration.

First will be to select and study one classroom as a case sample. Using the field measurement devices, we will set up the device in the middle of the classroom with a height of 1.1 m for the level of the occupants' breath, to evaluate the IAQ of the space. Also, the measuring device will evaluate the relative humidity and temperature of the study sample to calculate the thermal comfort effect. Validate using the collected data. Field observations such as space dimensions and the occupants' number of the space to get the full current condition of the case sample. Then, simulating the variables using software (IDA ICE). Finally, apply the results to all classrooms of one floor of the building to see what the influences of any change may cause by one classroom to reach a better method of ventilation and space efficiency with the lowest potential losses of changing the space. Aiming to upgrade the IAQ of classrooms in Saudi Arabia to confirm the findings and scale the problem size, which may lead to new policies and the refurbishment of schools.

There are two more types of variables affecting the case study: (1) Management variables. (2) Design variables. Using these variables, we are going to suggest discussion and solutions depending on the results and observations.

At last, this chapter will be based on the findings and recommend them as points.

Measurement devices were installed in one of the buildings of the current preparatory year in an educational classroom to measure the quality determinants of these enclosed spaces.

The variables were monitored in more than one period, depending on the space condition in terms of use. Install accurate measuring devices that detect and record environmental quality variables in indoor spaces where they measure temperature and relative humidity within the case sample.

- *Physical measurement* (HOBO onset data logger U10-003) specifically for measuring CO_2 concentration in air, temperature, and relative humidity.
- *Simulation* (IDA ICE) IDA Indoor Climate and Energy is a building performance simulation (BPS) software. IDA ICE is a simulation application for the multi-zonal and dynamic study of indoor climate phenomena as well as energy use. The implemented models are state-of-the art; many studies show that simulation results and measured data compare well.

Indoor Air Quality   173

The two most important variables affecting the thermal comfort in the classroom are temperature and relative humidity. The data average readings were shown on the psychrometric chart to determine whether the results were within the range of the thermal comfort zone or not. Fig. 13.1A. As shown in the diagram, the data average is placed in the comfort zone.

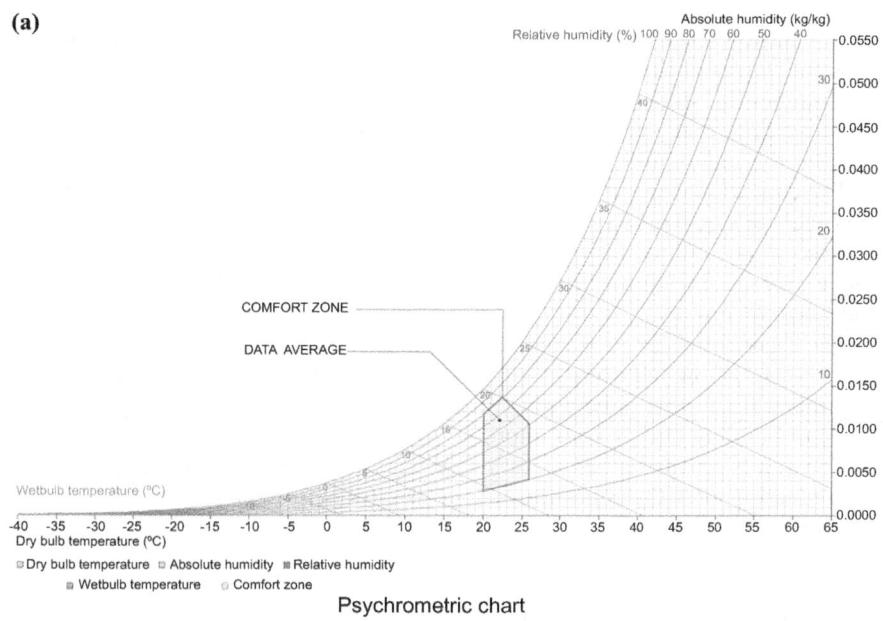

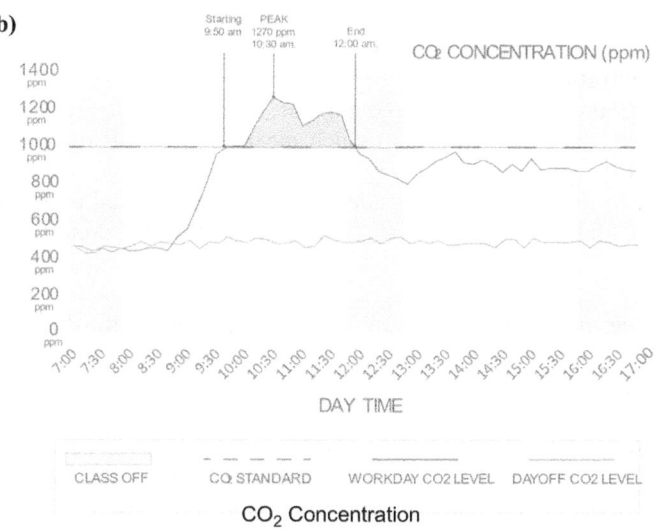

Fig. 13.1.   Environmental Measures. *Source:* By authors.

Data average: Temperature: 22.25 C—Relative humidity: 66.5%
Data taken: October 13, 2019

Field measurement (CO_2 concentration): The charts show a high increase in CO_2 concentrations on working days due to the classroom being full of students. Consequently, the carbon dioxide emissions due to student's congestion increase to a concentration level of 1270 ppm, which causes complaints of drowsiness and poor air Fig. 13.1B.

Validation: After taking the physical measurements and comparing them with the simulation result measurements from the simulation program while entering the same values of the variables (the timing and duration of the break times and the number of students), we notice a slight difference in the results of the measurements that does not exceed -2.75% or $+2.75\%$ as a margin of error between the reality and the simulations.

The educational space was studied on two different days, one on a day off and the other on due workday when students were in the classroom.

According to data analysis, there is an increase in the concentration of CO_2 above average during the workday, causing students' complaints of drowsiness and poor air quality.

The classroom is in good condition with an average humidity of 66.75% and a temperature below the average by 21.87°C in the thermal comfort zone, but the best thermal comfort is between 23° and 25°C. This causes increased cost and waste in building energy consumption.

The aim is to answer this question: What is the quick solution approach for the reduction of CO_2 concentration in classrooms, without affecting thermal comfort?

3.1 Modeling: Occupants Number (Management Related)

CO_2 concentration can be reduced by reducing the number of students in the classroom; the large number of occupants in the indoor spaces increases the rates of CO_2 concentration.

Standard: Classroom square or rectangular, 65 m^2 with furniture in rows and freely arranged, fits 30–36 students (which means 1.8–2.0 m^2 for each student) (Toyinbo, 2019).

According to the standard, the student number was reduced to 30 students in the classroom, and we can notice a slight decrease in the CO_2 concentration level by 12.5%.

  i. *Simplifying the study case:* Using the IDA-ICE program, three spaces are allocated (classroom space, allocated from the corridors for each classroom, and allocated space from the atrium for each classroom).

The classroom space was filled with the same number of occupants of this space under the real circumstances, and then I opened all three spaces to each other. The results are shown as shown in the diagram below.

We observe a decrease in the concentration of CO_2; it reaches 946.23 ppm at its highest concentration point.

   ii. *Occupied timeline schedule:* Taking advantage of the cold air in low-density interior spaces. Since there are low occupant densities in some of the internal spaces, such as the corridors and atriums, the problem can be avoided by using the air switch between the spaces that are usually occupied only for short times (breaktime period) and spaces with high intensity of use (such as the classrooms).

This will achieve the goal of reducing CO_2 pollution without increasing electrical energy consumption by conditioning outdoor air.

   iii. *HVAC system design:* Since there are low occupant densities in some of the internal spaces, such as the corridors and atriums, the problem can be avoided by using the air switch between the spaces that are usually occupied only for short times (breaktime period) and spaces with high intensity of use (such as the classrooms).

Applying the proposed solution idea by using the simulation programs. Using the simulation software, all the spaces on one of the building floors will be opened to each other to verify the effectiveness of the proposed solution (Fig. 13.2).

   Current condition: When entering the variables into the simulation program for an entire floor of the building based on the following data (the maximum capacity of the educational spaces and the timing and duration of the break times is equal to 15 minutes between every two sessions), the results appear as follows (Fig. 13.3A).

We notice the highest value of CO_2 concentration levels in educational spaces, reaching 2008 ppm. When applying the idea in the simulation program to an entire floor of the building and opening the spaces to each other according to the following variables data (the maximum capacity of the educational spaces and the timing and duration of break times equal to 15 minutes between each two sessions), after that, if we add some mechanical solutions (as an example CO_2 sensors & VAV HVAC systems), the results are shown as follows (Fig. 13.3B):

We notice a decrease in the highest value of the CO_2 concentration in educational spaces from 2008 **PPM** to 880.8 ppm, and this is a very good improvement. Looking at the average values of CO_2 concentration levels in educational spaces, we find that it's generally decreased by 49.3%, as we can notice a slight increase in CO_2 concentration levels in the corridor's spaces (the highest reaches 1088 ppm), which is acceptable.

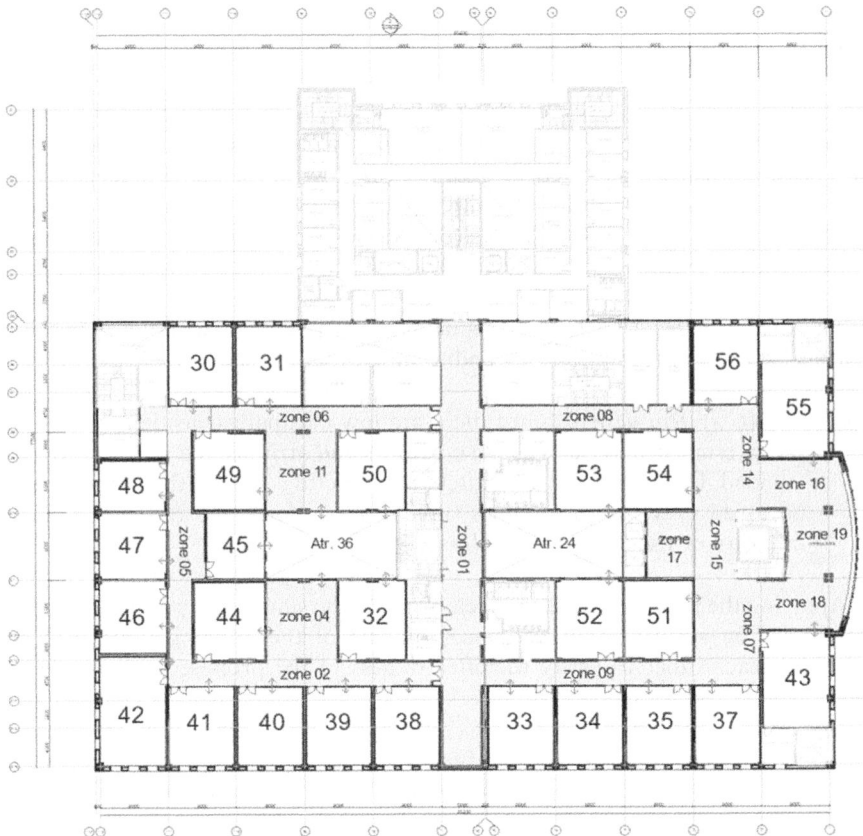

Fig. 13.2. Mitigating Classrooms With Corridors. *Source:* By authors.

4. Conclusion

The research study on IAQ in classrooms is very important, as classroom overcrowding constitutes a significant increase in CO_2 levels, as the analysis showed, which seriously affects occupants, which calls for the importance of research and reconsideration. This chapter will be a quick solution for the design of the existing school buildings in the short term, as the long-term solutions for the development of the existing buildings require modification of the design of the classrooms related to the IAQ (Tekin & Arikan, 2023). The results showed that reducing the concentrations of air in the classrooms by taking advantage of the adjacent areas (i.e., the corridors and atrium) is due to the low density of occupants most of the time in them. So, the problem can be avoided by allowing

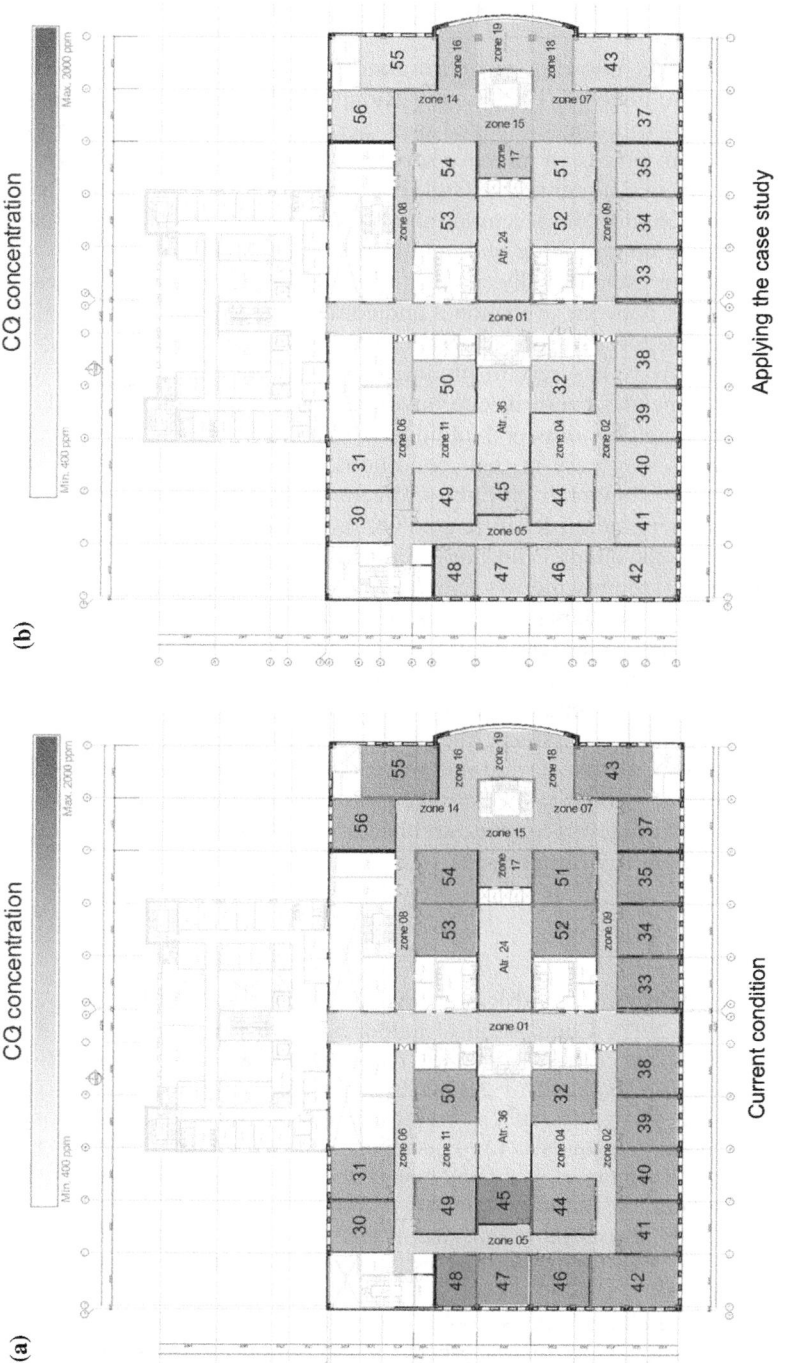

Fig. 13.3. Measurements of CO_2. *Source*: By authors.

the exchange of air entering the classrooms to purify it and reduce the concentrations of CO_2.

In conclusion, the following recommendations are presented based on the research, study, and analysis. First, spaces should be designed with dimensions and sizes that align with their intended uses. Second, adjusting student session schedules and break times can improve space utilization and air quality. Third, reducing the number of students in a single educational space in proportion to its size can enhance comfort and ventilation. Fourth, improving the mechanical systems of building conditioning and ventilation will allow more fresh air into the air conditioning cycle. Finally, adding windows between interior spaces to enable air exchange between educational and common spaces can help maintain IAQ while reducing energy waste when external windows are opened.

However, this study has certain limitations. The study in this chapter was restricted to a single classroom in one building, limiting the generalizability of the results to other classrooms or buildings, where adjacent areas such as corridors and atriums may vary in their conditions. Additionally, the study only measured a limited number of variables affecting IAQ, excluding factors like ventilation rates or pollutant levels (e.g., VOCs), which may also play a crucial role. Furthermore, the chapter did not examine the impact of outdoor fresh air on IAQ, as the classroom windows remained closed during the study.

To build upon this chapter, future studies should expand their scope to include multiple classrooms across different buildings in Jeddah or other cities, allowing for more comprehensive insights into IAQ challenges in educational spaces. Further research could also explore additional factors, such as the effectiveness of ventilation systems, the impact of VOCs, and how outdoor air influences the Age of Air (AoA) and thermal comfort when windows are opened. Additionally, future studies could examine classroom design, space geometries, and optimal occupancy levels to refine architectural and environmental strategies for healthier learning environments.

References

Al-Hemoud, A., Al-Awadi, L., Al-Rashidi, M., Rahman, K. A., Al-Khayat, A., & Behbehani, W. (2017). Comparison of indoor air quality in schools: Urban vs. Industrial 'oil & gas' zones in Kuwait. *Building and Environment, 122*, 50–60. https://doi.org/10.1016/j.buildenv.2017.06.001

Alaidroos, A., & Mosly, I. (2022). Preventing mold growth and maintaining acceptable indoor air quality for educational buildings operating with high mechanical ventilation rates in hot and humid climates. *Air Quality, Atmosphere & Health*. https://doi.org/10.1007/s11869-022-01277-x

Anonymous (2023). Thermogenics acquires plains mechanical services. *Engineered Systems, 40*(5), 7. https://www.proquest.com/docview/2811286851?sourcetype=Trade%20Journals

ArchDaily. (2018). Building better schools: 6 ways to help our children learn. https://www.archdaily.com/903061/building-better-schools-6-ways-to-help-our-children-learn

Bakó-Biró, Zs, Clements-Croome, D. J., Kochhar, N., Awbi, H. B., & Williams, M. J. (2012). Ventilation rates in schools and pupils' performance. *Building and Environment*, *48*(48), 215–223. https://doi.org/10.1016/j.buildenv.2011.08.018

Bauhaus, D., Brockhaus, M., Lohmann, D., Merkel, D., & Sturge, J. (2012). *Ernst and Peter Neufert Illiii I Fourth Edition*. https://byarchlens.com/wp-content/uploads/2020/11/Neufert-4th-edition.pdf

EPA. (2019). *Indoor air quality (IAQ)*. US EPA. https://www.epa.gov/indoor-air-quality-iaq

Feith, J. (2022). How's the air quality in Quebec schools? Here's what we found. *Montreal Gazette*. https://www.montrealgazette.com/news/article92629.html

Hassan Abdallah, A. S. (2017). Thermal monitoring and evaluation of indoor CO_2 concentration in classrooms of two primary governmental schools in new Assiut city, Egypt. *Procedia Engineering*, *205*, 1093–1099. https://doi.org/10.1016/j.proeng.2017.10.176

jbadmin. (2023). Thermogenics acquires plains mechanical services. *Thermogenics*. https://thermogenicsboilers.com/news/thermogenics-acquires-plains-mechanical-services-sioux-city-ia/

Kilpatrick, K. (2014). Sick classrooms caused by rising CO2 levels. *The EAG of North America*. https://energyalliancegroup.org/sick-classrooms-require-energy-efficient-solutions-2/

Mendell, M., Lei, Q., Tsai, F., Cozen, M., Macher, J., & Shendell, D. (2004). Association of airborne moisture-indicating microorganisms with building-related symptoms in 100 U.S. office buildings. *Epidemiology*, *15*(4), S165–S166. https://doi.org/10.1097/00001648-200407000-00438

Meyer, H. W., Würtz, H., Suadicani, P. V., Valbjørn, O., Sigsgaard, T., Gyntelberg, F. (2004). Molds in floor dust and building-related symptoms in adolescent school children. *Indoor Air*, *14*(1), 65–72. https://pure.au.dk/portal/en/publications/molds-in-floor-dust-and-building-related-symptoms-in-adolescent-s

Tekin, Ö.F., & Arikan, İ. (2023). Evaluation of the relationship between sick building syndrome prevalence and indoor air quality in schools. *Eskişehir Türk Dünyası Uygulama ve Araştırma Merkezi Halk Sağlığı Dergisi*, *8*(1). https://doi.org/10.35232/estudamhsd.1222791

Toyinbo, O. (2019). Chapter 4 - Indoor environmental quality. *ScienceDirect*. https://www.sciencedirect.com/science/article/abs/pii/B9780128117491000031

Chapter 14

Adapting Placemaking to Climate Change: Redefining the Placemaking Diagram

Tarek Saad Ragab, Ghadeer Alawi and Mady Mohamed

Effat University, Saudi Arabia

Abstract

Successful public spaces necessitate ongoing adaptations to address the evolving challenges posed by contemporary urban systems. There exists a probability of further effects related to climate change, including heightened temperatures, intensified Urban Heat Islands, and increased frequency of temperature disparity waves. These modifications have the potential to impact the range of human thermal comfort in public spaces, so directly affecting their levels of viability. The primary objective of this chapter is to establish a set of design guidelines that can effectively mitigate the impact of changes in human thermal comfort on urban environments. This chapter integrates this result into a universal instrument known as "The Place Diagram." The instrument in question has been developed by the Project for Public Spaces (PPS) to assess both present and future developments in public spaces, as well as to quantify the criteria for determining their success. The methodology employed in this chapter involves a desktop analysis of data obtained from a comprehensive review of both classical and contemporary literature pertaining to the philosophy of public space. It is anticipated that the results will serve as a catalyst for the advancement of the extensively utilized public space diagram.

Keywords: Public spaces; placemaking; thermal comfort; climate adaptation; climate change

1. Introduction

The concept of *"placemaking"* was drawn upon by early researchers such as Whyte (1980) and Jacobs (1961). Their research merges different professional spheres. Their concept of placemaking and successful public space has been associated with the urban realm's physical, social, cultural, and spiritual qualities. However, the concept of successful public spaces requires constant adjustment to adapt to contemporary cities' rising challenges. This research emphasizes the global phenomenon of temperature rise/decreased thermal comfort due to possible climate change. New spheres, such as climatology and microclimate, shall be integrated to address the concerns of outdoor comfort.

This chapter reconsiders the "place diagram" to ensure climate adaptability. The structure of this chapter is divided into three parts: discussing the existing place diagram, an analysis of the concept of thermal comfort, and finally, restructuring the diagram based on the integration of the new essential measures. The chapter concludes with a developed generic tool to ensure the concept of not only placemaking but also place-keeping in a century that may be threatened with increased intensities of heat waves and urban heat islands as a result of potential climate change.

The main aim of this work is to propose an integrated generic assessment tool for successful public spaces. This tool is to be used at local and international levels to evaluate current and future development of public spaces. To achieve this aim, three objectives were fulfilled: first, to analyze the concept of placemaking and its diagram; second, to study the concept of outdoor human thermal comfort; and third, to formulate a final set of guidelines and a generic assessment tool for successful public spaces. Such a tool would be used to evaluate various examples of public spaces such as plazas, courtyards, green parks, community parks, and public waterfronts.

The theoretical framework illustrates the revision of the literature to establish the criteria adopted in the work. The work scope deals with environmental comfort (thermal, visual, and acoustic) and physical comfort (edge, landscape, and urban furniture). This chapter is further concerned with the environmental part of thermal comfort.

2. Literature Review

Understanding the multidimensional aspects that define the public space is critically essential. According to the Oxford English Dictionary (1993), a public space is defined as "Developments that are freely accessible to the public and are intended for social interaction, relaxation, or outdoors." Public space is typically defined as a physical urban setting that is accessible for all citizens, regardless of age, race, gender, ethnicity, or socioeconomic status. Public spaces are an integral part of the public realm, a series of urban settings that facilitate formal and informal public life (Cho et al., 2015). They accommodate interactive social opportunities through daily interactions, communication paths, vibrant trade, or event venues. They also facilitate physical activities such as walking, sitting, and relaxing. Furthermore, they are considered as symbols of local traditions, meaning, and identity.

The "Project for Public Spaces" (PPS) organization, founded in 1975, developed the most recent model for evaluating successful places. PPS poses a question of "What makes a Great Place?" To answer this question, they have applied methods such as observation, surveys, and interviews. After evaluating thousands of international public spaces, they developed the placemaking diagram, which refers to four principles of successful urban design: (1) Sociability; (2) Uses and Activities; (3) Access and Linkages; and lastly, (4) Comfort and Image. These key attributes were derived from both qualitative (intangible) and quantitative (tangible) criteria of livable public spaces. PPS has completed projects in more than 3000 communities in 43 countries and is considered the premier center for best practice, information, and resources.

The sociability attribute involves creating opportunities for social interactions with family, friends, and strangers, which, in return, creates a stronger sense of attachment to their society as well as the space that nurtures such kinds of social undertakings. Sociability level is measured by the number of women, children, and elderly within the space; the presence of social networks; the livability of street life; and the possibility of evening use. The dimension extends also to include the cultural and social exchange through commercial undertaking markets, physiological activities, and cultural events.

Uses and activities refer to the types of activities available and the space's ability to attract users in for different seasons. The activities provided in the city public spaces strengthen the sense of belonging and reflect chances of urban justice. As a core of societies, public spaces draw individuals for recreational activities such as sitting, walking, biking, cycling, playing, and exercising. Days of the week and special vacations influence the usage of these spaces. The type of activities is associated with multiple factors, including users' age, culturally revealed behavior and preference, and users' income level, among others.

Access and linkage include the ease of accessibility, the connectivity to adjacent areas, the circulation within the space, the availability of public transit, the degree of walkability, and the ability to read directions within the space. Generally, accessibility relates to ease of entrance and use of the space. It involves allowing entrance and use for all people within the society, including different ages, races, ethnicities, nationalities, genders, or disabilities. It can be measured by the availability of parking, pedestrian activities, circulation routes, transit usage, and the availability of trails.

The last attribute is comfort and image. Comfort in the current place diagram comprises perceptions about safety, walkability, and the availability of sitting options. The image includes the built environment characteristics of the space and its surroundings. It involves the perception of cleanliness, attractiveness, and spirituality. This chapter critiques this last attribute and argues for further development.

Public spaces play a significant role in the alleviation of the extreme climate resulting from climate change (EPA). Thus, a discussion must be made upon the ability of the public spaces to incorporate mitigation and adaptive means to climate change implications. This, in return, contributes to enhancing human comfort within these spaces.

This chapter questions the criteria of comfort and image as highlighted in Fig. 14.1. In the current place diagram shown, the criteria of image and comfort should be separated. The only principles in the diagram that relate to users' comfort are walkable and suitable (in the intangible sphere) and environmental data (in the tangible sphere), which relates to protection against unpleasant sensory experiences such as sun and wind. Also, safety is currently considered a subcategory of comfort. However, safety is an essential attribute and should be categorized as the main criterion with its own weight. Safety measures include safety from hazards, crimes, and accidents (intangible elements). According to the Planning Institute of Australia, safety measures of public spaces should

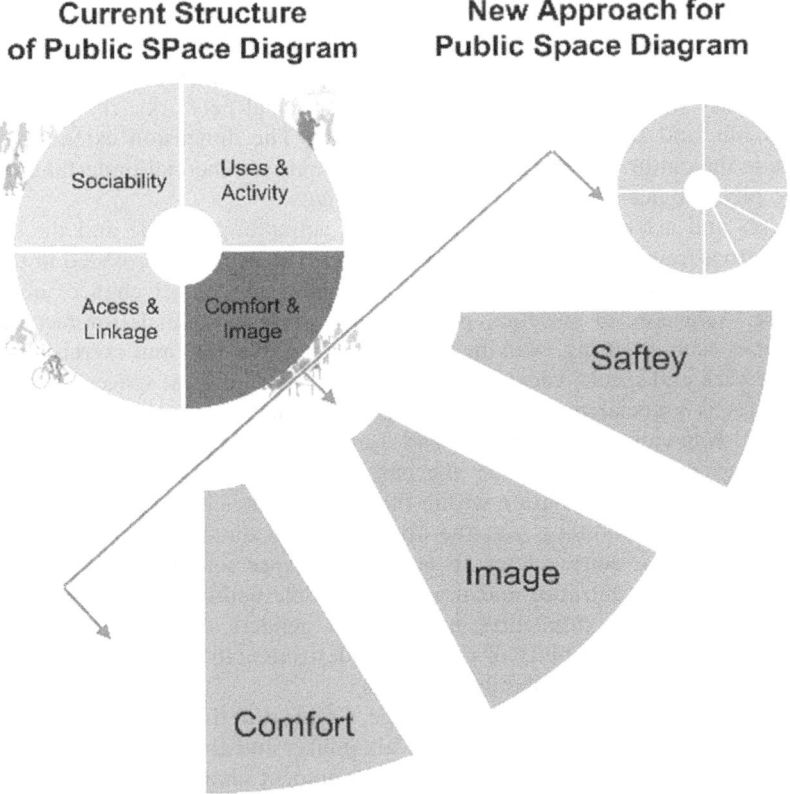

Fig. 14.1. New Approach to the Place Diagram to Incorporate Measures of Climate Change. *Source:* Author.

include having clear entrances and exits; safe street crossings, clear hazard signs, street buffers between pedestrians and roads, and visible areas within the space (tangible elements) (Healthy Spaces & Places, 2009).

Fig. 14.1 illustrates how the current structure of the place diagram can incorporate possible impacts of climate change. Considering the implications of increased temperature, and thermal comfort should gain its own criteria in the evaluation of public spaces. To approach the new integrated place diagram, this chapter focuses on reviewing existing theoretical and empirical research related to outdoor thermal comfort. First, the concept of thermal comfort is analyzed. Then, the chapter proceeds with establishing quantitative criteria that directly influence the qualitative attributes of outdoor human comfort.

Public spaces are characterized by the presence of people who have chosen to use them. Users' activities in open spaces are divided into necessary activities, which occur regardless of the space quality, and optional activities, which only occur by choice (Carmona, 2010). Comfort is an indicator of the length of time people use the place.

Human comfort is defined as a condition of mind reflecting a satisfaction with the surrounding environment (ASHRAE, 2017; Hassan Abdallah et al., 2020). The term is used to describe a sense of relaxation or a state of the individual's physical and mental well-being in their environment.

Perception of comfort is a result of the total perception of the surrounding environment, which is known as the microclimate. The perceived space is a reduction of the real space where a few elements are perceived, and only some of them are memorized. Thus, people keep a subjective and simplified image of the space reality. Thermal comfort in this chapter relies on the microclimatic conditions, which can limit, increase, or direct people's behavior.

When considering qualitative criteria, the (intangible) dimensions of a sense of comfort include environmental factors, physical factors, and social/physiological comfort (Varna, 2014). Environmental comfort relates to the surrounding environment within a space, including thermal, visual, and acoustic aspects. Physical comfort is influenced by urban elements that affect posture and movement, such as sitting, walking, and standing. Social/physiological comfort is linked to the character and ambiance of a space. This chapter focuses on environmental and physical factors under human comfort, as shown in Fig. 14.2, while the third factor (social/physiological) is excluded in this section because it is sufficiently covered under the main attribute of sociability in the PPS diagram (Fig. 14.1). By fulfilling sociability criteria, social/physiological comfort is inherently achieved. Furthermore, this chapter emphasizes the environmental attribute of thermal comfort and its relationship to climate change, as previously discussed.

When establishing quantitative criteria, the measures of these factors should be analyzed. Physical comfort is measured by design-related elements such as edge, floorscape, and urban furniture. Edges are the linear components that

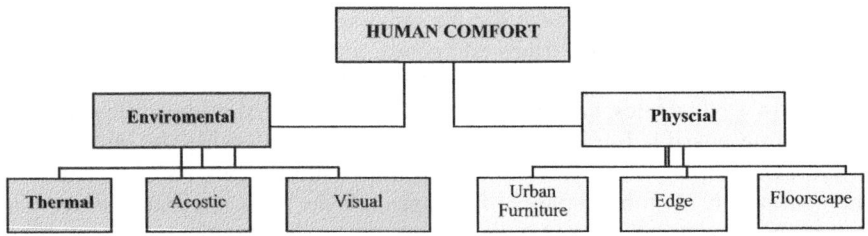

Fig. 14.2. Outdoor Human Comfort Factors. *Source:* Authors; Adopted from Lynch, 1960; Carmona, 2010.

define the space, which include screen walls, building facades, changes in floor level, and shorelines (Carmona et al., 2010).

The floorscape consists of the ground surface that covers hard pavement as well as the landscape. Urban furniture is any three-dimensional element that enhances the space, such as seating and lighting fixtures (Verna, 2014).

Environmental comfort is measured differently. Visual comfort is related to the quality of lighting, clarity, and views of the space. Acoustic comfort is associated with the level of noise reached in the space. Thermal comfort is the main concern of this chapter and will be discussed in the following section.

Thermal Comfort: With the increasing concerns of rapid urbanization and global warming, the issue of outdoor thermal comfort has gained considerable attention. According to the International Standards of ASHRAE and CIBSE, thermal comfort is a condition of mind that reflects the occupants' satisfaction with the surrounding thermal condition.

Thermal comfort is based on the balance between the human body and its surrounding environment. The internal body needs to maintain a stable temperature of 37°C to stay comfortable. This balance is maintained by a continuous exchange of the heat of the human body and its surrounding environment. This may occur by radiation, conduction, convection, and evaporation (ASHRAE).

When metabolized food releases energy, a healthy human body attempts to lose heat to the ambient environment. Under moderate environmental conditions, the human body absorbed the environment for at least one hour and thrived to achieve this thermal balance. The steady-state heat flow equation is expressed by Fanger (1970) as follows:

$$H - \text{Ed} - \text{Esw} - \text{Ere} - L = K = R + C$$

where H = internal heat production in the human body by the level of activity. The higher the activity rate, the more the heat loss has to be for thermal balance. Ed = heat loss by water vapor diffusion through the skin. Esw = heat loss by sweat evaporation. Ere = sensible heat loss by evaporation. L = latent heat loss by respiration. K = conduction from the outer surface of the clothed body. R = radiation loss from the outer surface of the clothed body. C = convection heat loss from outer surface.

If the heat leaving the human body is greater than the heat entering it, the thermal perception is cold. In contrast, if the heat entering the human body is greater than the heat leaving it, the thermal perception is warm or hot. The process of heat exchange between the human body and the surrounding environment is influenced by many factors, as discussed in the following section.

Factors influencing outdoor thermal comfort in this chapter include climatic factors, human factors, and the built environment (Erell et al., 2011). The climatic environment encompasses components such as air temperature, humidity, wind speed, and solar radiation. The human environment refers to people's behavior in achieving thermal preference, including clothing selection and activity levels. The built environment relates to urban design and building methods, including material selection, the amount of shading, vegetation, water features, and building orientation.

Climatic Environment: Outdoor Thermal comfort is influenced by environmental components such as air temperature, humidity, wind speed, and solar radiation (ASHRAE 55). Since these components can be measured by weather measurement tools such as the parameters, they would be included as quantitative (tangible) measures of thermal comfort.

Air Temperature: Air temperature is the average temperature of the air surrounding the occupants, measured by a weather parameter known as the dry bulb (ASHRAE 55). The design of outdoor spaces has little impact on mitigating air temperature. Yet some urban strategies can reduce their effect and will be discussed later in this chapter.

Mean Radiant Temperature: The average temperature of the surfaces surrounding a point will exchange thermal radiation with the human body (CIBSE). This means that the amount of heat transferred into the environment is related to the surface's/material's ability to absorb or emit heat. Solar radiation of materials would be discussed later in this chapter.

Wind Speed: According to ASHRAE 55 Standards, wind speed is defined as the rate of air movement at a point. Wind speed influences the use of outdoor spaces directly by its mechanical force or indirectly by manipulating thermal conditions. Generally, air speed slower than 100 feet per minute is considered pleasant or unnoticed. Higher than that, it may lead to discomfort (CIBSE).

Humidity: Humidity refers to the water vapor in a given volume of air. High levels of relative humidity may cause discomfort by acting against the evaporation cooling effect of sweating. Humans are sensitive to slight temperature changes but they don't perceive differences in the relative humidity range between 25% and 60% (ASHRAE 55). Higher than this range, humidity can cause discomfort due to the high moisture on the skin. Lower than 25% can lead to skin, eye, and noise dryness.

Human Environment: The second factor influencing outdoor thermal comfort is the Human Environment. This factor is more related to human-chosen action, including level of activities (metabolic rate) as well as clothing insulation.

Metabolic Rate: Metabolic rate is the level of transformation of chemical energy into heat and mechanical work by metabolic activities within an organism. The scale of the metabolic rate depends strongly on the level of effort, which is expressed by Mets (ASHRAE 55). Each Met is the metabolic rate of a seated adult, which equals 58 W/m2 BSE.

Basically, the more physical activity occurs, the more heat is produced. The lowest value occurs when an adult is sleeping (70 W) and is about 100 W when awake and comfortably rested. In intense physical activities, it can be as high as 800 W.

Clothing Insulation: Clothing influences human thermal comfort by offering thermal insulation suitable for the environment. It is expressed by CLO units (CIBSE). In hot climates, clothes protect the body from solar radiation, but they might prevent heat loss, leading to overheating. It is important for clothing to allow the cooling effect of air movement.

Built Environment: In addition to the environmental and human environments, the built environment is the third factor influencing outdoor thermal comfort. It is controlled by factors related to urban settings and configurations that could mitigate the heat effect by controlling the urban microclimate. It is an important element to consider during the planning and designing process.

As mentioned previously in this chapter, environmental parameters such as air temperature, mean radiant temperature, relative humidity, and wind speed are the most influential factors to thermal comfort. These parameters can be controlled or modified using urban intervention methods such as the use of cool materials, shading, vegetation, water features, and building configuration. Each element will be discussed next.

Cool Materials: Materials used in urban components such as pavement, building's façades and roofs contribute to the external thermal environment. Their thermal properties determine how the sun's energy is reflected, emitted, and absorbed. Materials classified as "Cool Materials" have two properties: (1) high solar reflectance and (2) high infrared emittance.

High solar reflectance, or albedo, is the percentage of solar energy reflected by a surface. Materials with higher solar reflectance (measured between 0 and 1) reflect more sunlight and thus have cooler surface temperatures.

Infrared emittance determines the ability of a material surface to absorb heat. It specifies how well a surface radiates energy away from itself compared to a black body operating at the same temperature. Light colored and coated surfaces absorb less heat than dark ones. Commonly applied materials such as steel, stone, concrete, and asphalt, have higher heat capacities than dry soil or sand, for example. The higher the albedo, the better the effect on mitigating the environment's heat.

Shading: Shading elements such as trees and devices are preferred in urban design in hot areas. These elements provide shading by blocking the incident solar radiation, which influences the outdoor thermal atmosphere. Studies have found a significant difference between thermal comfort sensation on sunny days and in shaded areas.

3. Case Study Analysis

A milestone project in the use of shading devices to increase thermal comfort is the Hajj Terminal at King Abdulaziz International Airport, Saudi Arabia. The whole structure covers more than 42 hectares, composed of 210 tents. Published data shows it reflects about 76% of the solar radiation. The structure can maintain a notable 27°C temperature under the tent even with temperatures reaching up to 54°C outside.

However, shading options should be balanced in public spaces and not overused. Otherwise, it can block views and cause other types of discomfort.

Vegetation: In addition to shading benefits, vegetation contributes to the improvement of the microclimate by evaporation. A large amount of radiation imposed upon vegetation is retained to be used for transpiration; only about 1–25% is used to heat the air. Such a method can allow for the moderation of the heat gained from the sun to the environment. However, high evaporation in high-humidity areas may lead to discomfort. Thus, the comfier range of humidity mentioned earlier in this chapter (between 25% and 60%) should be considered.

Water Features: Water features are also an effective heat sink technique that contributes to improving the human thermal comfort level, especially in dry areas. Water features such as fountains, water streams, water ponds, and shallow water, as well as water spray in public spaces, can dissolve part of the extreme urban heat through the evaporative cooling system. However, similar to vegetation, the amount of water vapor provided in the air must be balanced within the range of acceptable humidity; otherwise, it would lead to discomfort.

Building Orientation: Building Orientation surrounding the public space influences thermal comfort through controlling the solar radiation and wind flow. Studies focus on building aspects known as the urban canyon ratio or Height-to-width ratio (H/W).

H/W: It represents the ratio between the average height of the adjacent building and the average height of the open space. The difference between the ratios is the quantifiable exposure to the sky known as sky view factor (SVF). The more amount of sky is seen in a given surface, the higher the exposure to solar radiation, leading to decreased thermal comfort.

In terms of wind flow, air movement relies on basic principles of fluid dynamics, with canyon geometry playing a significant role. The channelization effect occurs when wind moves parallel to the canyon's orientation, which helps flush out pollutants but may cause pedestrian discomfort at high wind speeds. The Venturi effect increases wind speed as it flows through narrow openings, which can be beneficial in hot climates by enhancing air movement and improving pedestrian comfort. The bar effect occurs when air moves at a 45-degree angle over a street canyon, influencing airflow patterns within the space.

4. Results and Discussion of Findings

When evaluating the long-term success of public spaces, attributes of comfort shall provide generic guidance in public spaces, considering obstacles and challenges. Addressing human comfort, especially thermal comfort, can ensure space sustainability. The objective of restructuring the place diagram is to provide generic guidance in providing long-term successful public spaces in a century that may be threatened with intense temperature rise.

5. Conclusion

This chapter argues for restructuring the place diagram to consider the importance of human comfort in cities facing the challenge of temperature rise. The approach to improve the microclimate and adaptation to climate change has been analyzed and then integrated with the successful public spaces criteria. New comfort criteria include Environmental Comfort: Thermal, acoustic, and Visual; and Physical comfort criteria include: Urban furniture, edge, and floorscape. These aspects were integrated into the existing PPS diagram. The new generic tool was introduced with consideration of climate and thermal comfort. The new model ensures the success, resiliency, and sustainability of public spaces by incorporating elements of thermal comfort and its urban measures of climatic and built environments.

References

ASHRAE. (2017). *ANSI/ASHRAE Standard 55-2017: Thermal environmental conditions for human occupancy*. ASHRAE.

Carmona, M., Heath, T., Oc, T., & Tiesdell, S. (2010). *Public places, urban spaces: The dimensions of urban design* (2nd edn.). Architectural Press/Routledge.

Carmona, M. (2010). Contemporary public space: Critique and classification, Part One: Critique. *Journal of Urban Design*, 15(1), 123–148. https://doi.org/10.1080/13574800903435651

Cho, I. S., Heng, C.-K., & Trivic, Z. (2015). *Re-Framing urban space: Urban design for emerging hybrid and high-density conditions*. Routledge.

Erell, E., Pearlmutter, D., & Williamson, T. (2011). *Urban microclimate: Designing the spaces between buildings*. Earthscan.

Fanger, P. O. (1970). *Thermal comfort: Analysis and applications in environmental engineering*. Danish Technical Press.

Hassan Abdallah, A. S., Hussein, S. W., & Nayel, M. (2020). The impact of outdoor shading strategies on student thermal comfort in open spaces between education buildings. *Sustainable Cities and Society*. https://doi.org/10.1016/j.scs.2020.102124

Healthy Spaces & Places. (2009). *A national guide to designing places for healthy living*. Planning Institute of Australia/National Heart Foundation/Australian Local Government Association.

Jacobs, J. (1961). *The death and life of great American cities*. Random House.

Lynch, K. (1960). *The image of the city*. MIT Press.

Varna, G. (2014). *Measuring public space: The Star Model*. Ashgate.

Whyte, W. H. (1980). *The social life of small urban spaces*. Project for Public Spaces.

Printed and bound by CPI Group (UK) Ltd, Croydon, CR0 4YY
16/02/2026